TEACHING STUDENTS

STUDENTS

— ABOUT —

DEATH

TEACHING STUDENTS

— ABOUT —

DEATH

A Comprehensive Resource for Educators and Parents

Edited by

Robert G. Stevenson, EdD
Eileen P. Stevenson, RN, MA

The Charles Press, Publishers
Philadelphia

The Charles Press, Publishers
Post Office Box 15715
Philadelphia, PA 19103
(215) 545-8933

Library of Congress Cataloging-in-Publication Data

Teaching students about death: a comprehensive resource for educators
   edited by Robert G. Stevenson & Eileen P. Stephenson with 32 contributors.
      p. cm.
  ISBN 0-914783-50-5
  Includes bibliographical references and index.
  1. Thanatology. 2. Death. I. Stevenson, Robert G.
II. Stevenson, Eileen P.
HQ1073.T4 1995
306.9'07—dc20
                                           95-20266
                                         CIP

Printed in the United States of America

ISBN 0-914783-50-5

Dedication

This book is dedicated to the students of River Dell High School and in particular to Grant Danzer, Keith Erb and Yoshitaka Huriuchi who are missed by all who had the good fortune to know them.

The students of River Dell provided invaluable assistance in the production of this work, in particular: Kristina Becker, Michelle Guilbert, Karen Horstman, John Huang, Laura Hurm, Rachael Levine, April Millian, James Parisi, Benjamin Poon, Jeanne Schott and Terry Vo.

Editors

Robert G. Stevenson, EdD
Founder, Death Education Programs
River Dell High School
Professional Grief Counselor
Oradell, New Jersey

Eileen P. Stevenson, RN, CSN, MA
School Nurse/Health Educator
Joyce Kilmer School
Professional Death Educator
Mahwah, New Jersey

Contributors

Ronald Keith Barrett, PhD
Department of Psychology
Loyola Marymount University
Los Angeles, California

Michael K. Bartalos, MD
Assistant Professor of Clinical Pediatrics
College of Physicians and Surgeons
Columbia University
New York, New York

Joseph Cafaro, MA
School Psychologist
River Dell High School
Oradell, New Jersey

Janice I. Cohn, DSW
Director, Helping Children in Crisis
New York Center for Crisis Services
New York, New York

Laura S. Ellis, PhD
Professor of Early Childhood Studies
Graduate School of the College of New Rochelle
New Rochelle, New York

Richard R. Ellis, PhD
Professor of Counselor Education
New York University
New York, New York

Ed Gallagher
Writer and Producer
White Plains Cable Access Commission
White Plains, New York

Joyce Garvin, MS
Formerly, Director of Gifted and Talented Program
and the Fine Arts/Writing Foundation
River Dell High School
Oradell, New Jersey

Steven Geschwer, MA
School Psychologist
Board of Education of the City of New York
Doctoral Candidate
Ferkauf School of Psychology
Yeshiva University
New York, New York

Ellen Greenfield
Patient/Guest Relations Coordinator
West Hudson Hospital
Kearny, New Jersey

Richard Hansen, MD
Formerly, Department of Psychiatry
Queens Hospital Center
Jamaica, New York

Mary Kachoyeanos, RN, PhD
Associate Professor of Nursing
University of Wisconsin
Milwaukee, Wisconsin

Jack Kamins, PhD
Formerly, Clinical Psychologist
Region IV Division of Special Education
Board of Education of the City of New York
Brooklyn, New York

John Kiernan, MBA
International Center for the Disabled
Formerly, Administrator/Coordinator
Organ Recovery Program
The Presbyterian Hospital
New York, New York

Myra Lipman, PhD
President, Parents League of New York
New York, New York

Henry Lipton, PhD
Supervisor of Psychology
Region IV Division of Special Education
Board of Education of the City of New York
Brooklyn, New York

Claire Marino, MA
Counselor, River Dell High School
Oradell, New Jersey

Mary Ann Morgan, MEd
Death Education Consultant
London, Ontario, Canada

Maria J. Paluszny, MD
Professor of Psychiatry
Medical College of Ohio
Toledo, Ohio

Harry L. Powers, EdD
Former Principal
River Dell High School
Oradell, New Jersey

Fred Rosner, MD
Director, Department of Medicine
Mt. Sinai Services at Queens Hospital Center
Jamaica, New York
Professor of Medicine
Mt. Sinai School of Medicine
New York, New York

William A. Rowane, MD
Fellow in Child Psychiatry
Medical College of Ohio
Toledo, Ohio

Judith S. Rubenstein, EdD
Educational Consultant
Winchester, Massachusetts

Stanley Shapiro, MD
Formerly, Department of Psychiatry
Queens Hospital Center
Jamaica, New York

Arlene Shneur
Parent and Widow
New York, New York

Ozzie Siegel, PhD
Formerly, Department of Psychiatry
Queens Hospital Center
Jamaica, New York

Eileen P. Stevenson, RN, CSN, MA
Certified School Nurse/Health Educator
Joyce Kilmer School
Professional Death Educator
Mahwah, New Jersey

Robert G. Stevenson, EdD
Founder, Death Education Programs
River Dell High School
Professional Grief Counselor
Oradell, New Jersey

Edward Stroh, PhD
Former Director of Guidance
River Dell High School
Oradell, New Jersey

Judy Sussman
Former President
Parent-Teacher Organization
River Dell High School
Oradell, New Jersey

Terrence Tivnan, EdD
Assistant Professor of Education
Harvard Graduate School of Education
Cambridge, Massachusetts

Christine VanDerVelde, MA
Art Teacher
River Dell High School
Oradell, New Jersey

Kit Wallace
Assistant Head
The Cathedral School of St. John the Divine
New York, New York

David Willcock
Office of Religious Programming
BBC-TV Center
London, England

Contents

Introduction

Truly a pioneering effort, *Teaching Students about Death* is a collection of experiences and ideas gathered from an impressive group of professionals. Designed as a resource for school educators, guidance staff and parents, this book provides an enormous amount of information on the subject of death education. At the center of death education lies the goal of incorporating the subject of death into the school curriculum. This is particularly necessary because for many parents, the topic of death is often too complicated and overwhelming to discuss even at home with children, and as a result, children are often ill-prepared to deal with death when it occurs. Even though this closed-lipped approach to the subject of death is usually well-meant, it does nothing to help young people. In fact, it only makes matters worse. When the death of a loved one occurs before a child has ever considered the implications of death and the pain of loss, it stands to reason that the child will have a more difficult time coping than he would if he had been given *beforehand* the tools necessary to cope with the loss. It makes sense that the less mysterious the topic is for young people, the easier it will be for them to deal with the loss and trauma that accompanies death.

While it is true that the classroom is not supposed to be a psychological clinic where anxiety is lowered and behavior is modified, if we are going to teach the "whole" child (which we must if we are going to be responsible educators), we need to address the major issues that adversely affect his life. In light of the fact that death is something that today's young people are faced with on almost a daily basis — whether in the news or in their personal lives — it is of the utmost importance that children are helped to learn something about it.

Not surprisingly, helping young people deal with the confusion and grief that accompanies death is a task that many educators and parents find particularly daunting. Most adults have a hard time dealing with death themselves and they certainly are not born with the ability to help others cope with something as painful, complicated and personal as death and dying. It is not the school's goal to take the place of parents; the idea is for both of them to work together. And, in the schools that offer death education programs, we have witnessed improved communication between children and parents, and between families and schools. This book has been designed specifically to help the teachers, counselors and parents who are the first adults young people turn to for support in times of major loss. These adults need to develop a solid understanding of the dynamics of childhood bereavement in order to give useful answers to young people's questions and concerns. As well, teachers and parents must learn the skills needed to fortify and comfort the children in their care. Before they can do this effectively, they must learn how to come to grips with their own attitudes toward death and dying. This book discusses these issues thoroughly, and provides many practical methods and plans of action.

Most young people will admit to a sense of confusion and fear about the subject of death. It is common knowledge that if losses are not worked through, they often present long-term repercussions. With the careful assistance provided in this book, youngsters can be helped to confront their losses in a healthy way. The record will show that in those schools where even one course on death education exists, the students who participate not only receive immediate help, but they obtain long-range benefits as well. The knowledge provided by death education programs is unique; by obtaining a perspective on dying, one's outlook on living is greatly enhanced. So too are one's relationships with others.

The principal aim of this book is to serve as a one-volume reference tool to assist educators in launching or expanding their death education capabilities, whether in public or private, primary or secondary school settings. Readers will find many references to the death education program at River Dell High School in Oradell, New Jersey. This program provides many good examples of theory put into practice. The students who have been part of this program over the past 25 years, as well as their parents, are as much authors of this book as are the contributors listed by name. The River Dell experience has been reviewed and described in televised reports and in many articles in newspapers, magazines and journals, both in the United States and abroad.

The centerpiece of the River Dell program is the course called "Contemporary Issues of Life and Death." It has been a fine model for death education programs throughout North America. In the broadest sense, the course shows how all parts of a school community — students, parents, teachers and neighbors — can join together to find positive solutions to the difficult problems that young people experience when faced with death and loss.

Teaching Students about Death addresses the theory and practice of death education from many perspectives and vantage points. The changing character of children's views of death and the different way they experience and demonstrate bereavement at different ages (Kindergarten through 12th grade) is given close and detailed attention. The phenomenon of the death of a classmate is examined from the viewpoint of parents and teachers, but most importantly, from the responses and reactions of the young people themselves. The nature of the death — sudden, violent, expected, unexpected, or the result of murder, illness or suicide — affects the way survivors respond. This book addresses these differences in several separate chapters. The preparation of teachers for their role as death educators is the subject of two chapters. The thorny issue of how a child's religious training (or simply his parents' religious denomination) affects his concept of death, and hence the nature of his bereavement, is sensitively discussed.

Also discussed in detail is the actual application of death education programs and the specific roles different people play: parents, the school nurse, the school psychologist, homeroom teachers, guidance counselors, health and physical education instructors, members of crisis intervention teams and parent-teacher organizations, and outside observers such as reporters and TV documentary crews who can influence public opinion with their impressions. Several chapters look at the interdisciplinary aspects of teaching about death. English teachers, creative writing teachers, art teachers and librarians can make a significant contribution to the effectiveness of a death education program and this book discusses specific ways and different projects in which they can use their expertise to teach about death. Another issue, never before considered in this context, is included here: the relevance of classroom instruction about organ and tissue donation to the topic of death education.

While still in its developmental stage, great strides have already been made in death education. The contributions contained in *Teaching Students about Death* will be of enormous practical value to educators and parents who wish to participate in the evolution of this much-needed subject as it becomes a more accepted part of the overall process of education.

TEACHING STUDENTS

STUDENTS

— ABOUT —

DEATH

1

What is Grief?

Robert G. Stevenson, EdD

We use the words "grief" and "grieve" all the time, but do we understand what they really mean? The dictionary contains the following descriptions of these words:

Grief (gref) n. 1. intense mental anguish. 2. a source of remorse or acute sorrow. *grieve (grev) v.* 1. to cause to be sorrowful. 2. to experience anguish or sorrow.

These words are also often used in a variety of contexts, such as:

- Don't give me any grief!
- He's alone in his grief.
- She's been grieving for over a year.
- The bargaining unit is grieved by the action of...

It is useful to think of the grief process as medicine. When the proper amount is taken, medicine can heal, but too much can be injurious and sometimes even fatal. Consider some of the emotions experienced by those who are bereaved after losing someone to death. Many feel lonely, empty, scared and confused. For some, it feels as if everything they believed in has suddenly been pulled out from beneath them. Many find it hard to know what to do about these feelings and don't know how to resolve their pain. As a result, they do nothing. They just exist the best they can without doing anything to improve their situation. Because a deceased loved one will never return, survivors often feel as if the terrible pain they feel will never end.

Interestingly, many of these feelings are precisely the same emotions felt by some people who attempt suicide. In other words, the emotions felt by the bereaved are so strong that they are often the same emotions that cause people to want to kill themselves. Clearly, grief is a very potent feeling.

Grief can cause both physical and emotional distress. Some researchers say that typical *acute* grief reactions may come in waves that can last for 30 minutes or more. Physical complaints may include headache, indigestion, nausea, vomiting, diarrhea or constipation, shortness of breath (accompanied by the feeling that a heavy weight is pressing down on the chest), fatigue, acute lack of or increased appetite, restlessness, muscular weakness (especially in the legs or hands), insomnia or nightmares. Other feelings may range from general sadness to specific agonizing pain to profound feelings of guilt or anger.

Bereaved people may become depressed and plagued by fears that are both real and imagined. Due to the intensity of experiencing the death of a significant other, some survivors feel as if they are losing their minds, or that they may die from the physical and mental assault.

Try to recall a time when you yourself went through an experience that was so painful that made you feel as if your legs couldn't support you, as if your arms and hands could not find the strength to open a bottle of soda or pick up a cup of coffee, as if you had just been kicked in the stomach. Certainly this is not the kind of memory that any of us like to recall. These are the same types of reactions that are sometimes brought on by survivors' emotional reactions to thoughts of the deceased.

Memories of the deceased are triggered in a variety of ways. A conversation, a familiar place, a familiar phrase, a smell, a piece of music, or a particular time of year makes us recall an incident. Most people try to block and avoid those things that trigger painful memories. In particular, many try to avoid speaking or even thinking about the deceased. They no longer go to certain places or call upon friends who may stir up memories of the deceased. To exacerbate a survivor's already difficult situation, other people often do not know how to act around those who are bereaved and grieving. Should they discuss the deceased? Should they act as if nothing happened in case discussing it will make the survivor sad? And if they don't speak to the bereaved about the loss, will that person be offended? Is it appropriate to send a card on the anniversary of the death of a friend's child? Indeed, it is a difficult situation for both survivors as well as their friends and families.

The more the bereaved impose any of the above-mentioned limits on themselves, the more they tend to retreat from life. Often, the harder they try to push thoughts of the deceased away, the more preoccupied they seem to become with them.

The way this process works is illustrated well by Asian philosophers who try to reach "truth" by first totally clearing their minds until they obtain a state that is entirely free of thought. This requires such complete concentration, discipline and practice that when novices try it, they usually find that their minds are constantly active and that the harder they try not to think of something, the more their minds center in on the very thing that they are trying to elude. In the same way, the more one tries to get rid of painful memories, the more these memories will intrude. This pattern can persist until one is almost constantly plagued by distressing thoughts. Sometimes, the bereaved reach a point where they actually "see" the deceased and they may begin to question their sanity. Despite the best and most valiant efforts, the pain of loss is extremely hard to deal with and the resulting reactions are often so painful that they are unbearable.

As an escape and sometimes as a subconscious way of denying reality, some bereaved people begin to engage in a whirl of constant activity, for example, throwing themselves headlong into work. One bereaved woman, while complaining of having no time for herself and no time to relax since her father's death, only minutes later spoke of possibly getting a second job to "fill in her free time." This attitude is not unusual. Often, filling one's time with an activity such as work can effectively block painful thoughts, but only temporarily. It is important to point out that denial is not always a bad thing; in fact, especially during the early stages of a loss, as I will discuss below, denial can be very useful for certain people because it allows them to come to comprehend their loss gradually.

As if the problems encountered during the normal grief process are not complicated and painful enough, there are other behaviors that cause self-destructive activity. It may be easier for others to be around the bereaved person who holds back her emotions, but there is very little else that can be considered beneficial about this sort of emotional self-control; in fact, being silent is a dangerous way of behaving when one is experiencing pain. It is normal and healthy to seek emotional release at some point in the grief process. Without intending to do so, when others compliment and encourage emotional containment, they are really thinking more about themselves and only hindering the recovery of their bereaved friend or relative.

Some people turn to the use of alcohol or drugs to dull the pain of loss. Most of us remember hearing the line (in old movies if not our own experience), "Here, take this. It'll help." But painkillers are only a temporary way to alleviate the pain of loss. Then, at a later time when friends and relatives are not available for support, and the drugs no longer do the trick, reality hits home. It may take years to recover from a loved one's death, but the longer the interruption or delay of the grief process, the more serious the possible later complications will be. Carrying a 20-pound pack on your back is not too hard at first, but, be assured, that same weight becomes harder to carry as time passes.

SELF-INJURY AND GUILT

Some people feel guilty about being alive after a loved one has died and they inflict injury to themselves to express this feeling. Some become excessively generous and give away treasured or needed possessions or money. They may use grief as self-punishment, using the feelings of the pain of loss to replace the feelings of guilt. Some bereaved people may withdraw from life and become apathetic about everything: "If my loved one can't enjoy life, then I won't either." In some cases, the thought of suicide may accompany grief and sometimes thought is turned into action: "If my loved one can't return to be with me, then I will go to be with him."

AVOIDANCE AND DENIAL

When grief is so painful that it becomes overwhelming, sometimes people feel so disoriented that they become entirely dysfunctional, making it easy for a bad situation to become worse. It is important to note that in some cases, especially early on in the grief process, denial, whether consciously or subconsciously achieved, can play a useful role. Denial can give bereaved people a little time to come to grips with their loss. When one encounters a disaster such as the death of a dearly loved person—a loss that is so disorienting and frightening—it tends to overwhelm to a point that very little in the way of recovery can be accomplished. Denial can help one compartmentalize the overwhelming nature of loss; by not allowing the flood gates to open all at once, denial can help one face a loss *gradually*, thereby paving a smoother road to recovery and possibly facilitating the understanding of a loss.

However, when that same denial is continued for too long, it can interfere with emotional recovery, blocking the avenues that need to be opened so that one can return to any semblance of normal life after a terrible loss. Often, denial only postpones the suffering that inevitably occurs after a bad loss. In other words, denial may be helpful in the short term, but it does nothing to ease the pain of loss in the long run.

Some people try to hold onto memories of the deceased by keeping their belongings. However, it is a sign of potentially destructive grief if a bereaved person takes this too far by preserving *all* of the possessions of the deceased, creating a mini-museum, or holding onto belongings for an extended period of time. People can soon become trapped by the things they try to hold on to. However, they can soon become trapped by this behavior. Not only will their attempt to stop time, so to speak, not bring back those who have died, but it can block their ability to work through their grief and may even obstruct the return to a manageable life and normal responsibilities.

TIME AND GRIEF

Another complication in the grief process is time. What is the "normal" time rate at which the bereaved should move through the grief process? Medical professionals tell us many different things. In one poll, Rabbi Earl Grollman found that the average person estimates that grief following death lasts for about 2 weeks. However, for most persons, this is probably something they would like to be true rather than an honest assessment of how long grief actually lasts. On the other hand, other professionals have not offered a much clearer picture. In 1973, Thomas Hackett stated that a "normal" grief reaction runs its course in 4 to 12 weeks, during which time the bereaved move through three stages: denial (which should last only a few days), acceptance, and reorganization. Grief that lasts longer than 3 months is seen as a possible indication of an "abnormal" grief reaction. In 1980, Robert Kavanaugh listed the following seven stages of grief: shock, disorganization, floods of emotions, relief, guilt, loss/loneliness, and reestablishment. He also believed that it was "normal" for grief to last for one year or longer. Despite growing evidence to the contrary, a review of employee contracts will show that there are still employers who feel that 3 days to 1 week should be long enough for employees to "attend to the necessary details" of saying goodbye to a loved one.

Everyone in a family experiences grief when family member dies, but no one ever feels exactly the same way at the same time. In fact, friction may result if the timing of respective family member's feelings of grief are out of sync, making them unable to relate to each other's feelings at the "right" time, or relate to them at all, for that matter. For example, one couple suffered the death of their 3-year-old child. The mother, who was often alone at home with her sorrow, was faced by daily reminders of her loss. It was a hard year of tears and pain for her, but she was able to move steadily through her grief and was finally able to attain a modicum of acceptance of the loss of their child. By facing her loss—regardless of whether or not she deliberately chose to do this—and remaining dormant in the rut of her misery, she was able to reestablish a new life without her beloved dead child. In contrast, after the death of their child, her husband entered a long period of denial. After all, he was not used to seeing his daughter much during the week because he was always away at work. Following her death, he found reasons to stay longer at the office and he began to work on weekends as well. Finally, after a year, his defenses broke down and he began to acknowledge his grief. Once he started facing his loss, he was finally able to acknowledge his grief and understand why he had thought that his wife was relatively unaffected by the loss. Because he had withdrawn and isolated himself—to a point that he was not even aware of where his wife was with her grief—and because he had denied his true feelings for so long, he didn't realize that his wife had made progress in recovering. She, in turn, could not face the possibility of being dragged back by her husband into the pain of a loss that she felt she had put behind her. The couple differed chiefly in the length of time it took them to begin moving through the grief process, and this difference in pace caused a real crisis in their relationship.

After months of anticipatory grief, a widow who was her dying husband's primary caregiver seemed to have grieved for only a short time compared to other family members who had the luxury of being able to deny the reality of her husband's illness because they were only peripherally involved. Lists of stages or time schedules used by professionals to evaluate grief do have some value, but they must always be considered secondary to the individual.

Quite a few people are now attacking Elisabeth Kübler-Ross's five "stages" of grief. (Dr. Kübler-Ross herself has recently rethought her theory regarding the stages of grief. She now believes that it is not necessary to grieve a death at all if one believes in life after death, in other words, because death can be seen as the beginning of a new life, there is no reason to mourn death.) Much of the criticism of Kübler-Ross is made by professionals who try to make people fit into the five stages, rather than using her research to broaden their understanding of what people who are grieving may be experiencing. A similar difficulty confronts the layperson who sees behavior models as rigid standards to which they must conform. We need to keep our priorities in perspective; it is the *individual* who must be considered first.

CHILDREN AND GRIEF

Children face very special problems in working through grief and have special needs because of the great diversity of their reactions. Listed below are just some of the many variables that impact on their grief:

- The age of the child is important to consider because children view death differently as they mature.
- How well are their caregivers coping? Children get the cues for their behavior from the way their parent(s) or other caregivers react to the loss.
- The facts of what actually happened need to be explained to the child. If not, children tend to "fill in the blanks" themselves, often with distortions that are so frightful that reality pales by comparison. Children often feel that a wish or thought they may have had caused the death. Also, do not assume that shipping the children to a relative's house on the day of the death or funeral will prevent them

from realizing that something very serious has occurred and that someone they are used to seeing is suddenly no longer around. Young children usually comprehend more than they are given credit for; when a death occurs, they will know that something has happened and for that reason, they should be told of the death. After all, the people that exist in a child's life do not simply disappear with no reason, and it would be cruel to allow children to think that sudden, unexplained disappearance is normal and therefore could happen to them. It is essential therefore that children be given careful attention.

- There are three basic issues that must be conveyed to children about death: they must be helped to understand that death happens to everyone and everything that is alive; that the body no longer "works" after death, that it is completely non-functional; and finally, that the physical aspects of death are permanent, in other words, that death is an irreversible condition. These points need to be repeated and reinforced, a responsibility that parents share with teachers.
- If there was a ritual (a wake or funeral), were the children allowed to attend? Children who have a role to play in death rituals can benefit by the activity because it can help them offset the feeling that death (especially sudden or senseless death) makes life seem to be out of control. As with other things, children have a short attention span when dealing with sorrow. If children do choose to attend a funeral or wake, it is important for them to have the support of adults whose primary concern is the child's best interests and not their own personal grief. A child who wants to leave the ceremony must have that option, even if it's in the middle when others may feel that it is inappropriate.
- Children need someone to listen to them. All too often, survivors are too deeply affected to be attentive to the needs of the child—needs that are not always easy for others to realize, understand and fulfill.
- Is the child's school involved in meeting the needs of grieving children? Bereaved children often experience a drop in academic performance and they may exhibit changes in mood or behavior. The way in which teachers and counselors react, if they react at all, can have a strong impact on a child. Parents need to know what is happening to their children while they are in school if they are going to be able to work with educators in a way that will help their children cope with loss due to death.

SUMMARY

What can we do to help young people deal with the grief that we all must face when a significant other dies? How can we help them cope with other inevitable losses? This brief overview shows what grief is, what it may become, and some of the main issues that should be considered when trying to help children who are in this situation. Children suffer from many of the same feelings of pain from a loss due to death as do people of all other ages, but they also have an entirely unique set of reactions and problems. At this difficult time, children can benefit from quality care and support from the important people in their lives. Parents, relatives, teachers and peers all have a role to play in a child's grief process. The school is one place in which they can work together to help bereaved young people.

2

Childhood Bereavement: A Conspiracy of Silence

Steven Geschwer, MA

He that lacks time to mourn, lacks time to mend.
Eternity mourns that. Tis an ill cure
For life's worst ills to have no time to feel them.
—Sir Henry Taylor, *Philip Artevelde*

Research has shown that when a child or adolescent experiences the death of a significant other, the consequences can be extensive and complicated. One reason that it is so hard for children to cope with death is that traditionally they have been left out of the mourning process and, because of their age, are generally deemed not competent enough to handle a situation as difficult to comprehend and as painful as death. Children are often denied attendance at funerals and visits to cemeteries, left out of discussions concerning the deceased, and on the whole are considered to be better off not knowing anything about death. This is based on the premise that the less a child knows, the better off they will be. Edna St. Vincent Millay characterized childhood as "the kingdom where nobody dies." This is a secure feeling, even though is it not true, and adults often want to hold on to this idea (Feifel 1974).

There is, however, a growing realization that there may be serious consequences for children later on in their lives if, as children, they are led to believe certain things about death that are not true or accurate. "We must not shut out children from the realities of death. A child is not protected by attempts to shield him from death. Rather, his emotional growth is hindered" (Feifel 1974).

Sometimes a parent's attitude toward death poses more of a problem for a child than the child's own difficulties in coping with death. Negative effects can result when parents (or other caregivers) ignore children's feelings and thoughts. As Feifel says: "In actuality, we find that proscription of death matters in the child's world displays more of the anxiety and concerns of the parent and adult than of the child's genuine capacity to manage knowledge of the existence of death."

When a loss occurs, the family unit and its chemistry will almost always change permanently and each surviving member must try to come to terms with the new situation. For the child, this struggle is not just a matter of coping with the pain of death itself. After a death, the quality and number of problems children will have depend in large part on the preexisting role that the deceased person played in the family system. Because a parent plays such a pivotal role in a family, this is especially true for children who lose a parent. Children in this situation must also face the difficulties of dealing with the surviving parent's grief, expectations that the parent may have of them (many of which may be unreasonable), being excluded from the mourning process, and also the fear of losing the remaining parent.

Some people believe that age is a major cause of the difficulties children have dealing with loss. A child's concept of death is very different from an adult's. It was formerly believed because children's cognitive processes are undeveloped, they cannot complete the mourning process and, therefore, taking any part in the process would affect them adversely.

Others do not agree; they believe that there is no significant difference in the effect of death on people of different ages (Bowlby 1980; Elizur and Kaffman 1983). Recently, developmental psychologists have found that children can understand death at a much younger age than was previously believed. There are three concepts that are thought to determine a child's perception of death: irreversibility—once something dies, it cannot come back to life; nonfunctionality—when something dies, it cannot perform living acts; and universality—all living things will eventually die, including oneself (Speece and Brent 1984). In her seminal study on children's concepts of death in 1948, Maria Nagy found that by 9 or 10 years of age, children can grasp these concepts. However, in a review of 36 studies, Speece and Brent (1984) determined that even younger children—between the ages of 5 and 7—were able to understand death. Adah Maurer (1974) believes that children can understand death very early in childhood and even when they are infants. Maurer observed that by the age of 3 months, almost all children play the game "peek-a-boo," and she questioned what it is about the game that seems to bring joy to children. Maurer believes that one of the most important feelings in life is being appreciated and noticed by others. "This feeling of selfhood, this being recognized as a person who is welcome, is sometimes called self-esteem or ego cognition or just the feeling of being alive! And that is what a baby gets from [peek-a-boo]."

Maurer feels that because children are so close (in time) to when they were conceived, their particular concern about their existence is very important. She writes, "It is difficult to imagine a world where we are not.... So the child who asks where the baby was before he was born is not asking about adult sexuality. He is asking a deeply philosophical question, if you will. He is asking about nonexistence" (1974).

Various studies have demonstrated this same point—that for children, issues other than age appear to be more important in determining their emotional adjustment to the death of a loved one. Elizur and Kaffman (1982) compared the responses of children who seemed significantly impaired by their fathers' death with those who seemed to have less difficulty. The authors claimed that the children who had a difficult time with the death of their fathers demonstrated severe emotional problems and the children who handled the trauma more easily had significantly fewer problems. In the comparison, they found similar variables present in the more successfully adjusted children that seemed to account for the differences.

The children's overall responses to the loss of their fathers were found to be divided into two categories: short-term and long-term effects. The short-term effects of the loss seemed to be affected by the relationship between the members of the family before the father's death, while the long-term effects were influenced by the relationships and environmental atmosphere that developed between surviving family members following the loss.

The study showed that during the early months directly following the initiation of mourning, the child's response and adjustment seemed to depend on pre-death conditions. These included: whether family conflicts existed prior to the loss and what the child's psychological state was prior to the death. However, after the initial period following the loss, conditions such as how the surviving parent and child get along, the availability of a surrogate parent, and the ability of the surviving parent to deal with feelings of grief seem to affect the child's long-term recovery and prognosis (Elizur and Kaffman 1983).

Children at high risk for short-term negative effects tend to come from families where there was marital disharmony and frequent fighting between the deceased parent and the child. In addition, the high-risk child also tends to have problems handling frustration and shows poor impulse control. Children displaying long-term negative effects were primarily found in families in which the surviving mother did not allow her children free and open expression of their grief, thereby creating an atmosphere of emotional constriction. Surviving parents who restrict their children's open expression of sadness can cause them to react in a way opposite to that which is desired and the children seem to suffer significantly more. As well, their problems are further exacerbated when their mothers hold back their true feelings of grief from the child.

This finding confirms the observation that emotional restraint of grief displayed by the surviving parent makes it difficult for children to express their own feelings, intensifies children's loneliness, and increases anxiety and confusion regarding the meaning of a sudden death (Elizur and Kaffman 1983).

At low risk are children who come from a well-adjusted family and tend to be independent and well-adjusted for their respective age groups. Parents from these types of families allow their children the opportunity to convey their thoughts and feelings of grief. Children at low risk also tend to be able to handle stressful and anxiety-producing situations with relative ease. Although they may display some anger or frustration, these are normal emotions that do not have adverse ramifications. In addition, low-risk youngsters tend to adjust well to new situations and are able to make independent decisions.

Elizur and Kaffman's study also found that the mother who was most helpful to her children who had recently lost their father allowed them to honestly express their real emotional needs. The children who had this opportunity were significantly more well-adjusted than the children who did not. These mothers encourage their children to communicate freely and openly about any feelings they may have about themselves, as well as those that pertain to the family. They also encourage their children to ask questions concerning death and their deceased father, and they attempt to answer their children's questions clearly and honestly.

Elizur and Kaffman (1983) concluded that although the stress of the loss created difficulties in adjustment and caused sadness and pain, the effects of that loss on the short and long term were determined by factors that did not pertain to age, sex, or even the death itself, but rather by whether the children were allowed to express their grief openly with the support of the surviving parent.

In another study designed to determine the family structure most conducive to a child's recovery from the loss of a parent, Vess and his co-workers (1985) found that there were two kinds of families whose roles varied significantly enough to cause different adjustments—a "person-oriented" and a "position-oriented" family. According to Vess' team, each member of a family has a role to fulfill. When one of those members dies, how that deceased person's role is filled will determine the future emotional success or failure of the child and the rest of the family.

In a *person-oriented* family, members have an opportunity to assume their roles according to merit. In addition, lines of communication are open among family members, allowing each member to express personal thoughts and feelings. On the other hand, in a *position-oriented* family, the roles are fixed; each member is only allowed to fulfill a specific and limited responsibility. There is very little or no discussion or communication between family members so that each person is locked into a role without ever establishing what is actually the best role for that individual or that family. This situation apparently places family members under undue stress.

When contrasting these two family types, Vess agreed with Elizur and Kaffman, finding that families who allowed free expression of sadness and grief tended to adjust far better to a loss that those who did not. In fact, Vess' team found that communication between family members is the single most important element in reorganizing the family structure following a death of one of its members. When there is freedom to openly express anger, guilt, sadness and other feelings, the family is significantly more open and adaptable to any necessary change of roles that the surviving family members must assume. This environment offers the family the opportunity to select the most qualified family member to assume the responsibilities of the deceased, in other words, the family member "[who] best fits the capacities of the remaining members."

In a family where there are strict roles and no communication, the likelihood of added problems for surviving members is significantly greater. When children cannot express themselves, problems can often multiply. "In contrast, a closed communication structure restricts the grieving process. A 'conspiracy of silence' may develop in the family, in which everyone is aware that the others have feelings, but no one knows how to talk about them and, in fact, prefer that they keep their grief to themselves" (Vess et al. 1985). As a result, roles may be filled by those who are least likely to fill them well, or who are less deserving, and this, in turn, can ruin any chance the family may have to recover because the unit has been weakened twice—once by the death, and again by experiencing potentially damaging role changes. In some families in which a death has occurred, roles may never change. The family's overall ability to function in the future will be reduced and the environment for surviving family members will be forever stressful (Vess et al. 1985).

Research reveals that many adults tend to ignore their children's grief and that they isolate them from significant others at a time when their need for communication is usually at its greatest. Kastenbaum (1974) discovered that more than 75 percent of those adults who were part of his research study believed that children very rarely, if ever, think about death and that they are better off when they don't think of death. This study also revealed that, as parents, 75 percent felt obligated to "protect" their children from the topic of death (in other words, to skirt the whole issue completely).

Finally, a study by Helen Rosen (1985) found that most of the adults she questioned who had experienced the death of a sibling when they were children had not been able to discuss or share their feelings of grief with anyone at the time of the death. Rosen's findings point out that when children experience the loss of a sibling, they face obstacles that will inhibit their ability to discuss their feelings and this prevents them from being able to work through their loss. The tendency to keep feelings inside usually emanate first from within, perhaps as an instinctual attempt to avoid and deny painful feelings. This behavior can also be reinforced by families who lack the willingness or ability to communicate with their children about the topic of death.

Why should we be so concerned about what children may think if they are left alone with their own thoughts—thoughts that they may have arrived at on their own? Why is silence or a lack of communication a potential factor in determining the severity of the response to loss? The death of a loved one is most always a memory that stays with a person forever and the thoughts, feelings and visions that a child has *at the time of the loss* are often the memories that will they will recall later. Several studies show that the earliest and most vivid memory that many adults have were incidents that involved death and one can assume that the death of someone close will surely leave a lasting impression on a child. Also, the way parents approach the issue of death with their children at the time it occurs is of critical importance.

Children's thoughts are often not based on reality, but on magical ideas or on the assumption that to *think* something is to *do* it. "For the child, reality exists within his thoughts and feelings" (Mitchell and Schulman 1983). This belief is acquired at birth, when just a scream or cry can bring everything the child needs, be it food or warmth or the appearance of a parent. This creates within the child a distorted thought process that confuses cause-and-effect relationships. In essence, children believe that they are all-powerful. Becker (1973) writes:

> [The child] has magical powers, real omnipotence. If he experiences pain, hunger, or discomfort, all he has to do is to scream and he is relieved and lulled by gentle loving sounds. He is a magician and telepath who has only to mumble and to imagine and the world turns to his desires.

At a very early age, children believe in these powers and only with time and through cognitive development do they learn differently. Solnit (1983) describes this process in the child:

> ...the child experiences wishes and thoughts as magically potent. To wish or want strongly carries with it the risk and probability that the thought is father to the act. The child is not yet aware, as the older individual painfully learns, that there are many intermediate steps between a wish or thought, and a thought-directed act.

With power comes a sense of responsibility and the potential for arriving at false conclusions. If something that a child thinks does occur, then that child may be convinced that he caused it to happen, whether or not in reality he had anything to do with it at all. The penalty for this type of thinking can be great. If a child's thoughts and wishes come true, then he believes that it is his responsibility when a negative event occurs to someone that he had a bad thought about. A child may be led to think, "If my thoughts can lead to another's death, then I am at the mercy of others' thoughts and wishes." Understandably, this type of thinking makes the world a very scary place for children to live in.

In a world where children come to expect their wishes and thoughts to be answered immediately, parents are sure to fail—some more than others. When parents fail, children may see them as all bad and direct feelings of hate toward them. Many a parent has been hurt or even killed in a child's fantasy world.

Becker (1973) explains: "When the child experiences inevitable and real frustrations from his parents, he directs hate and destructive feelings toward them and has no way of knowing that malevolent feelings cannot be fulfilled by the same magic as were his other wishes." How many children have not, in anger, wished a parent or a sibling dead? And if a parent does happen to die, the children who had these thoughts may consider the death a fulfillment of their wish. Terrible feelings of guilt and fear may overwhelm them. It can also imply that they will die if someone wishes them dead. Without discussion of these feelings, a child can easily come to erroneous conclusions about reality from these magical and distorted views. Such erroneous conclusions can predispose or direct the child in a direction that may lead toward pathology. Therefore, as Ordal (1983) stated, "[Children] should be allowed to express this [type of thinking], and be made to know that they were in no way responsible for the death, and to express any other 'negative emotions.'"

Some adults are not aware that their children have these magical thoughts and that they can arrive at distorted conclusions. Perhaps they are so intent on their child not being included in the death effect that they fail to look for and recognize a child's unique plight. In addition, feelings of guilt and rage can be so overwhelming to children that they repress these thoughts and only in later life might they emerge as a personality determinant. To make matters worse, apparently this "repression is so immediate and effective that we rarely see this process in its pristine form" (Mitchell and Schulman 1983).

As children get older, their magical thinking decreases and their thoughts and feelings become more reality-oriented. They become better able to understand causation and effect, and to draw more realistic conclusions about the world around them. Once they go to school, most children no longer see the world as all-magical. By this time they have experienced many more situations and their current developmental stage allows for more realistic thinking. By the time they are in school, most children have at least begun to understand that the *thought* does not necessarily cause the *act*. "This allows the child to comprehend the distinctions between death and absence, between dying and going away, and to have an effective awareness of the difference between memory and fantasy" (Solnit 1983).

When a child is at the age when his language skills are not developed enough to understand the subtleties of adult language, he may misunderstand adult explanations. If a child is left alone with no one to talk to, he can take an innocent adult explanation and distort it in a way that may be very evil and negative. When children listen to adults, they tend to take everything literally (Brent 1978). As a result, they may not understand irony, for example, or sarcasm, or certain kinds of humor. Brent used the example of his own child who would wake up screaming in the night asking for a bottle containing "warm water and sugar." His child was afraid of running out of fuel because he had heard that while they were on vacation, their car had died for that very reason. To run out of fuel, therefore, meant death to this child.

Another example of children's misconceptions because of language was reported by Koocher (1974), who told a story about a boy who refused to go to bed because he overheard his mother's conversation about a man "who got a heart attack, fell out of bed and died." The boy "had no idea what a heart attack was or where it came from. He certainly knew what falling out of bed was, though, and if doing that could...maybe 'get you' a heart attack and die, then no one was going to get him in a bed."

Misconceptions such as these indicate why it is so important to include children in the discussion of death. They hear the words, but by taking things literally, they may not pick up on the intent. When children are not included, adults will not be aware of what they think and will have no opportunity to identify or correct their misconceptions. When children are allowed to participate in conversations regarding death, they hear directly, and can ask questions and be questioned.

As mentioned earlier, there are some people who believe that children can be sheltered from the pain of death; that if the subject is not discussed with them, then they can be prevented from learning about something that is legitimately scary—that life does end, that all people (and animals) will at some time die. Some parents do not want to ruin their child's innocent existence in which events as dreadful as death do not occur. Death is a hard thing for adults to comprehend, let alone a small child who doesn't possess half the knowledge of an adult. However, the reality is that children are exposed to death every day and there is no way to hide it from them.

Kastenbaum (1974) believes that there is no evidence to support the idea that children do not come in contact with death or that they can be sheltered from it during their childhood years. He further points to the input that television—a major source of information—has on children regarding the topic of death.

> How long can a child sit in front of the glowing tube without witnessing death or death talk in some form? Cartoon characters flirt with annihilation, often returning to life after being crushed, burned, devoured, dropped off a cliff, drowned, turned inside out, and so on. On the "grown up" programs, there may be a freshly slain corpse every five minutes or so. News reports on television and radio present very curious and indirect death messages.

In addition, because of our social structure there is no way to limit one child's interaction with another; a child who knows nothing about death will inevitably come into contact with a child who has had an experience with death. A friend's father dies, an animal gets hit by a car, a teacher's illness becomes fatal, a student develops a terminal disease and passes away—these are just a few examples of what any child may experience. It is, therefore, quite clear that to "protect" or silence a child does not serve the purposes intended by adults. Kastenbaum (1974) says: "It is difficult to defend the proposition that children are unacquainted with death. More tenable is the proposition that often we are not sufficiently acquainted with our child's thoughts and experiences."

Despite of this awareness and understanding by adults and parents that silence and closed communication regarding death can adversely affect children and predispose them to future problems, the practice continues. Fifty years ago in America, when death occurred more frequently, society at least discussed death and dealt with it directly. A religious society and a close-knit, extended family existed to offer support and to provide answers to disturbing questions. Today, with people's better health and increased life span, as well as the fact that more families are separated, and with the current societal compulsion to "stay young," the discussion of the topic of death is looked upon with distaste and denial by many. To be reminded of our own mortality by others is something most people do not want to hear or discuss. As a result, and often with the best of intentions, this practice continues.

Crase and Crase (1976) suggest that if we want to be more helpful to children, we should share with them our own thoughts and feelings concerning death. This is not easy and can be very uncomfortable for adults. However, part of the growing-up process is to discover life's pitfalls as well as its good points. Children cannot learn and grow if they are kept from reality. "No one can have this adventure for him, nor can death be locked in another room until a child comes of age" (Crase and Crase 1976).

Why, then, does our society continue to leave children out of the arena of death? Nature endows us with an instinct to survive; perhaps the denial of death is one component of this instinct. Any reminder of our mortality seems to make many of us shrink back and children only seem to intensify, if not cause, this reaction. Perhaps because of their youth, children remind adults that they are getting older and their own deaths are approaching. Those who have not accepted the undeniable fact of death find the mere *thought* of it frightening. Through silence, perhaps people feel that they will be able to avoid acknowledgment of their eventual demise, even if it is only a short-lived thought.

In an attempt to distance themselves from death, adults create a fantasy in which children are put in a world that is different from the one in which they live. As Kastenbaum (1974) points out: "The vision of childhood as a world apart seems primarily to be an adult invention for adult purposes." The intent of this illusion seems designed to be a form of protection for adults who are vulnerable. The fear of death is so prevalent in present-day American society that perhaps adults need this delusion to prevent themselves from having any thoughts that pertain to death.

Maslow (1968) also feels that our society's fear of death is designed for adults' protection. Many people have difficulty facing truths that demonstrate their weaknesses and that challenge their ego. "This fear is defensive.... It is protection of our self-esteem, of our love and respect for ourselves. We tend to be afraid of any knowledge that could cause us to despise ourselves or to make us feel inferior, weak, worthless, evil, shameful" (Becker 1973).

Although this fear of mortality may always be present, lurking in the back of our minds, we cannot think about it all the time or we would have a great deal of difficulty being able to function. Therefore, many people try to repress this fear. However, at various times and for various reasons, this fear comes to the surface. For example, because of their lack of understanding of death, their misconceptions and their questions, children can bring out this fear. As a result, adults are forced to confront a topic that they really do not want to face. Many adults cannot bring themselves to discuss death with children. They deal with the situation by trying to avoid it and justify their actions by deciding that children are better off not knowing about death. Reasons for this vary, but there seem to be several themes that account for this suppression.

It seems "natural" for us to bury our parents when they die, just as it was natural for our parents to bury their parents, and, following this natural order, our children will bury us. As Maurer (1974) so eloquently puts it:

> Our children are our immortality. The river of life flows through us and on to the next ripple and the next, each generation shaped by the one before. Changes wrought by the contour of the times are less definitive than the flux of the inveterate pressure to proceed. The sorrow and joy with which each generation contemplates the next lies in the knowledge that the next will bury

the last. While the spark from our torch ignites the next, we ourselves are gutted to ashes. Our children will outlive us.

This idea may seem frightening and may interfere with our willingness to discuss death with our children. When there is a loss and an adult must face a child who wants to discuss the event, that adult is reminded of his own fate and his own vulnerability. Apparently, adults have great difficulty dealing with this.

Kastenbaum (1974) believes that there are four "vulnerable points" that prevent adults from being able to be open with their children about death:

1. They wish that their children could somehow be immortal. The occurrence of a death reminds them that their children will eventually die too, and this thought may be too difficult for them to accept. If parents see their own immortality through their children, this narcissistic view creates a wish that their children would never die, and conversations with their children concerning death remind them of these unrealistic wishes.

2. Through children, parents cannot help but become aware of the aging process, and this makes them confront the fact that they are getting older. Facing the reality of life's passage may be too difficult for some adults to bear and the likely response is avoidance. This realization that their place is being taken over by the "moving-up" generation frightens adults and creates discomfort for them.

3. Death reminds parents that they will be survived by their children who, in turn, will be survived by their children. Kastenbaum refers to man's deep-seated desire to be immortal. When this unconscious wish is jostled by events beyond their control (such as a death) and by children (who want answers or have questions that must be addressed), some adults clearly will have a hard time admitting that they are in fact mortal. This "passing the torch dynamics" again is moving parents along the continuum of the increasing recognition of the undeniable fact that they are not immortal.

4. Death is final, a thought that is quite difficult even for adults to accept. Therefore, avoidance of all thoughts and experiences relating to this reality is often undertaken regardless of cost. It is easy for adults to rationalize that they are doing this for the child, but in reality they are doing it to protect themselves from experiencing overwhelming anxiety. In essence, as Hagin and Corwin (1974) point out, adults are so reluctant to admit that death is final and that it will eventually claim *them*, that they are unable to give their children the help that they need to cope with the topic of death.

Clearly, Kastenbaum feels that most adults have great difficulty coming to terms with their anxieties concerning their own death. It is also discomforting for parents to think that their children might also have to face these same feelings. This thought apparently brings out feelings of protectiveness; their silence may be an attempt to keep their children from experiencing these same fears and anxieties. In addition, adults may feel incapable of explaining or answering their children's direct questions about death. Apparently, adults seem to feel that avoidance and omission solve this dilemma.

Humankind has devoted its medical and technological past, present and future to the prevention of death—or at least the prolongation of life. Its success over the last 30 to 40 years has made death less commonplace and perhaps easier to avoid talking about than it used to be. Therefore, when a loss occurs, we are reminded of our fears and weaknesses of being mortal, and this realization brings attempts to deny these thoughts. Children interfere with this denial. Unlike adults, they are not yet aware of death's finality. Their probing and disconcerting questions force adults to face many realities that they have spent a lifetime trying to escape. Therefore, to continue avoiding children's questions, adults employ distancing techniques and rationalizations designed to reduce their guilt.

Essentially, this reaction may take place because man tries to forget that he is part of nature, subject to the same laws and codes that animals are. In reality, man lives a certain period of time and when his time is up and bodily functions cease, he dies. To many, the thought of actually being dead and no longer existing is so perplexing and distressful that it causes total suppression of the idea. How can humans, who are endowed with lofty qualities (compared to animals), be subject to the same fate as all other living creatures? As Becker (1973) writes: "This is the paradox. [Man] is out of nature and helplessly in it. He is dual, up in the stars and yet housed in a heart-pumping, breath-grasping body that once belonged to a fish and still carries the gill marks to prove it." Being aware of our duality is most problematic and the questions it provokes seem to cause adults great trouble. For some, denying this fact becomes an obsession. However, because death is a very obvious fact of life, it is pretty hard for anyone to "forget" completely. Becker says, "The irony of man's condition is that the deepest need is to be free of the anxiety of death and annihilation, but it is life itself which awakened it and so we must shrink from being fully alive."

At certain times, this paradox of existence becomes impossible to put aside. When a loved one dies, all of these repressed thoughts may rise to consciousness and overwhelm the survivors. In an attempt to deal with these thoughts, man struggles, using all of his energy to avoid facing the inevitability of living.

However, children are different and will persist with their questions and discussions—especially if they are allowed to. Therefore, some people believe that somehow children must be taught about the fear and dread of death so that they, too, can learn to avoid the topic. Silence seems to accomplish this goal and, if possible, some parents want to make sure that the idea that life can and will end never intrudes upon the magical, if distorted, thoughts of a child's vivid imagination. Being silent about the topic quickly teaches children to avoid and repress any thoughts and ideas involved with death and dying, just like their parents have done. If we are to help our children and ourselves come to terms with death, it is this silence which must be overcome.

REFERENCES

Becker, Ernest. *The Denial of Death.* New York: The Free Press, 1973.

Bowlby, John. *Loss, Sadness and Depression: Attachment and Loss,* Vol. III. New York: Basic Books, 1980.

Brent, S. Puns, metaphors, and misunderstandings in a two-year-old's conception of death. *Omega* 8(4):285-293, 1978.

Crase, D.R. and D. Crase. Attitudes toward death education for young children. *Death Education* 8:31-40, 1979.

Crase, D.R. and D. Crase. Parental attitudes toward death education for young children. *Death Education* 6:61-73, 1976.

Elizur, E. and M. Kaffman. Children's bereavement reactions following death of a father: II. *Child Psychiatry* 21(5):474-480, 1982.

Elizur, E. and M. Kaffman. Factors influencing the severity of childhood bereavement reactions. *American Journal of Orthopsychiatry* 53(4):668-676, 1983.

Feifel, H. Psychology and the death awareness movement. *Journal of Clinical Child Psychology,* Summer 1974, pp. 6-7.

Feifel, H. and V.T. Nagy. Another look at fear of death. *Counseling Clinical Psychology* 49(2):278-286, 1981.

Hagin, R. and C. Corwin. Bereaved children. *Clinical Child Psychology,* Summer 1974, pp. 39-40.

Kastenbaum, Robert. Childhood: the kingdom where creatures die. *Journal of Clinical Child Psychology,* Summer 1974, pp. 11-14.

Koocher, Gerald P. Conversations with children about death—ethical considerations in research. *Journal of Clinical Child Psychology,* Summer 1974, pp. 19-21.

Maurer, Adah. Imitations of mortality. *Journal of Clinical Child Psychology,* Summer 1974, pp. 14-17.

Maurer, Adah. Maturation of concepts of death. *British Journal of Medical Psychology* 39:35-41, 1966.

Mazlow, Abraham. *Toward a Psychology of Being.* New York: Van Nostrand, 1968.

Mitchell, N. and A. Schulman. In J.E. Schowalter et al., eds., *The Child and Death.* New York: Columbia University Press, 1983.

Nagy, M. The child's theories concerning death. *Journal of Genetic Psychology* 73:3-27, 1948.

Ordal, Carol C. Death seen in books suitable for young children. *Omega* 14(3):249-277, 1983-84.

Rosen, Helen. Prohibitions against mourning in childhood sibling loss. *Omega* 15(4):307-316, 1984-85.

Solnit, A. Changing Perspectives: Preparing for Life of Child. In J.E. Schowalter, et al., eds., *The Child and Death*. New York: Columbia University Press, 1983.

Speece, M.W. and S.B. Brent. Children's understanding of death: a review of three components of a death concept. *Child Development* 55(5):1670-1686, 1984.

Vess, J., J. Moveland and A. Schwebel. Understanding family role reallocation following a death: a theoretical framework. *Omega* 16(2):115-128, 1985-86.

3

Death and the School-Aged Child

Michael K. Bartalos, MD

The knowledge and insight that can be found in books have always had a magnetic effect on me. Therefore, it was no surprise that while walking down a Manhattan street recently, I couldn't help myself from stopping to look at a sidewalk display of books. Being especially interested in unusual books, I began looking through a volume entitled *Tarot des Grands Inities d'Egypte* when I noticed that all 22 tarot cards pictured in the book were given names except for one card—number 13. My curiosity sufficiently roused, I bought the book and took it home for further scrutiny. I soon discovered the reason for the peculiar omission of card number 13, which is "La Mort," or Death. It is a word, the author informs us, "qui n'existe pas dans l'esoterisme symbolique" (Victor 1979). In other words, there is a symbol but no word for death. The existence of death is indeed acknowledged, but it is not described or discussed. This brief example of a very old practice still holds true; today in American society, many still feel that the mention of death is taboo.

It has long been acknowledged that, as children grow, they go through formative periods, each one of which is critical to their future characters. Because most children attend school during these formative years—in the United States, for almost 9 months of the year, which is more time than they spend at home—school has a great deal of influence on children, especially young children who are still in their formative years. In his book *Utopia*, Sir Thomas More wrote: "To the priest is entrusted the education of children and youths....They take the greatest pains from the first to instill into children's minds, while still tender and pliable, good opinions, which are also useful for the preservation of their commonwealth" (Sturtz 1964). Much earlier, in *The Republic*, Plato suggested that children should receive an education until the age of 17 or 18 (Cornford 1966). Regarding his views on education, Plato wrote: "...shall we simply allow our children to listen to any stories that anyone happens to make up, and so receive into their minds ideas often the very opposite of those we shall think they ought to have when they are grown up? No, certainly not. It seems our first business will be to supervise the making of fables and legends, rejecting all which are unsatisfactory; and those which we have approve...molding their souls with these stories...." The recurrent theme expressed by both Thomas More and Plato is influencing children's minds.

Indeed, our schools have a very important function in society. A teacher's job is not limited merely to teaching the typical subjects listed in the curricula, but also to instill in their pupils appropriate behaviors and ethical standards. Because teachers are among the mind-molders of today's youth, they have a tremendous amount of responsibility to the people who will be living in the world of the future—and these are today's youth. And there is no reason why part of this influence cannot include frank discussions about death. After all, if it is a teacher's job to teach a student about life, how can the subject of death—an integral part of life—be neglected?

WHY TEACH DEATH EDUCATION IN SCHOOL?

I contend that a person's understanding of life as it really is—and this clearly includes the acknowledgment of death, especially if this understanding begins during childhood—is essential to the development of a healthy psychosocial perspective on the world. Births and deaths are as much a part of everyday life as are marriages, divorces and anniversaries. If we truncate children's orderly acquisition of life experiences by closing our eyes (and therefore theirs) to the existence of death, its impact will be more traumatic and confusing at the time when they suddenly are confronted with it. In today's world, with the enormous amount of violence (death inflicted by shootings—both intentional and unintentional—has skyrocketed in recent years), and illness (in particular, AIDS), among many other causes of death, children will most likely encounter death before reaching adulthood.

In other words, I feel that it is simply unrealistic and irresponsible not to provide some form of death education to the young people in our schools. This chapter outlines, with brief discussions, a sample curriculum that I feel could be beneficial to children and, therefore, to the rest of society.

Suggestions for a General School Curriculum

First of all, the curriculum must offer a balanced presentation. The topic of death can, and usually does, generate controversy. While the subject of death should not be shunned, neither should it be overemphasized. A fine balance must be reached in which death is discussed at an appropriate time, in an appropriate context and in a nonemotional manner. Second, teachers must be emotionally and intellectually prepared to teach students about death. It is unlikely that any curriculum or course will be better than the person who teaches it. Before embarking on the difficult task of teaching a course on death, teachers must first resolve any personal issues or conflicts they themselves may have regarding the subject. Because teachers' preparation along with their ongoing professional development is too large a topic to be addressed here, this chapter will assume that the teachers selected to offer death education courses are adequately trained to teach about death and are psychologically well-balanced in terms of their own attitudes toward death. Third, death education, or as it increasingly called "life education," should be age-appropriate. In the late 1920s, children's attitudes toward death began to be explored (Chadwick 1927; Stern 1927). The first developmentally oriented book on the subject, *The Child's Discovery of Death*, was published in 1940 in the United States by S. Anthony. It is now generally accepted that death means different things to children at different ages (Nagy 1965).

An age-appropriate curriculum should address carefully and completely the following concepts:

- Life has a beginning and an end (every child understands that babies and kittens grow bigger as time passes and most children have seen a dead animal or death on television and in the movies).
- Death means the entire cessation of life. While memories can remain forever, when people die, no other part of them continues to exist. Some believe that a person's "soul" remains, but it should be made very clear to children that death is the opposite of life.
- Death can happen instantly or it can be a prolonged process (which may include pain, loss of bodily functions or the loss of mental function, and in some cases, both).
- Death can be (a) the result of an *external* event, such as an automobile accident or (b) the result of a process that takes place *inside* the body, such as an illness or (c) the result of a willful act that is inflicted either by oneself (suicide) or by someone else (murder), which can be willful or accidental.
- The subject of suicide must be handled carefully so as not to make it too "intriguing" or "romantic." This is especially true for teenagers who, because adolescence is an inherently difficult stage of life for most people, are often unhappy and confused. When these emotions are brought to a head, the idea of ending it all by committing suicide is sometimes attractive. (Of course, this feeling is true for people of all ages, but for adolescents, who often do not know "who they are" yet,

the chances of rash and unrealistic thinking are more pronounced than in older people (whose decision to commit suicide is often carefully thought out and determined as preferable after many years of living). In light of this, clear guidelines regarding suicide and how to approach the topic with different age groups must be provided to all educators who teach about suicide—as well as those who just *discuss* suicide with students—by experts in the field.

- Every living thing will eventually die. Even though we know that life has to end someday, it often hurts to think about leaving the world and that loved ones who survive the deceased will feel the pain of loss.

- In light of the above, children should be reminded of the real value of life. We should try to fill life with activities that will contribute to everyone's welfare, not just our own, and we should strive for satisfaction. Because life is finite, every moment should be valued. Each life is unique and every person's contribution to society is unique. This is true for all people and therefore, every life should be considered sacred.

- Life is a perpetual process—a thought that may provide some consolation to those who cannot fathom the idea of dying. While each individual life will eventually come to an end (and sometimes when we least expect it), new lives are constantly begun, each carrying a new promise for the future. In other words, life is a cycle that is repeated again and again; this is the universal law of nature. While animals share the same mortal fate as humans, we differ from animals in a critical way—we are aware that our existence on earth is finite and this is knowledge that we all have an obligation to use.

Special Curriculum Needs

Carl G. Jung said about the young that their "Youthful longing for the world and for life, for the attainment of high hopes and distant goals, is life's obvious teleological urge" (Feifel 1965). Statistically speaking, many young people can look forward to the realization of their hopes and goals. Unfortunately, some will inevitably be denied the same opportunities.

Teaching about death, like teaching about any other subject, must be based on the recognition and understanding of the heterogeneity that exists among students and in schools. When teaching about death and dying, it is important for teachers and students to contemplate the psychological differences between past death experiences and possible future death experiences. It is also important for teachers to be aware that there are some groups of young people who may be in need of special attention when discussing death. These groups include:

1. Young people who are suffering from an illness that is expected to cause their death in the near future. Examples that come to mind immediately are incurable malignant tumors and AIDS. It is essential that all teachers are aware of which, if any, of their students are terminally ill and that they exercise the greatest amount of tact and sensitivity when discussing death and death-related issues when terminally ill students are present.

2. Young people who are suffering from an illness that will cause death, but not necessarily in the near future. There are genetic diseases that threaten life in the early postnatal period, and another group of illnesses that mostly affect school-age children, such as Duchenne muscular dystrophy and cystic fibrosis. Children with these illnesses suffer gradually and their capacity to live normal lives slowly decreases with the passage of time until they finally succumb to the disease and die. Most terminally ill children are aware of their limitations and know that their lives will be drastically shortened. They are likely to experience difficulties in their struggle with the complex concept of leaving the world—of losing life. Therefore, they will need special attention and help. Religion, or any kind of spiritual assistance, can help and be of great comfort in this situation. A teacher must remember, however, that each student's personal beliefs and coping styles must be respected, regardless of the educator's personal views.

3. Young people who experience temporary alteration of psychological processes. Altered psychological processes can increase the likelihood of suicide and even murder. It is important for teachers, other school personnel, schoolmates and parents to pay attention to sudden or slowly developing psychological changes. If noticed in time, it may be possible to prevent unnecessary tragedies. Illicit drug use is a known cause of some behavioral changes. Depressive states, whether genetically or environmentally induced, can cause suicidal tendencies or violence toward others. As well, although they often go unnoticed, the deaf represent a uniquely threatened group and have a high frequency of depression. Because of communication difficulties, any significant depression they may be experiencing often goes unrecognized. Understandably, it is important for teachers, parents, friends and relatives of the deaf to be aware of the special problems they may experience.

4. Young people who, because of a unique element in their lives, have a greater chance of experiencing death. There are groups of people who are more likely than others to confront death. Children in this group include those who have a classmate, friend or relative who has a terminal illness or other fatal ailment. A special case of this sort is represented by members of families in which a deadly genetic dis-

ease—such as Huntington's chorea—is perpetuated from generation to generation. Since this disease manifests itself in midlife, children who are at risk can grow up constantly fearing that they might be carrying the dreaded gene. These individuals live under the sword of Damocles, so to speak, and this is a terrible burden.

5. Another group of children who are especially likely to encounter death are those who live in high-crime areas. From personal childhood experience, I can attest to the fact that living in a war zone also places a child in this category. In a war-torn environment there is a substantially increased likelihood of experiencing the deaths of soldiers, strangers, or family members and even of being killed yourself. Sadly, there are presently large numbers of children who currently live in these conditions and every day they witness death due to violence, famine and illness.

6. Yet another socially induced condition that currently increases children's chances of witnessing brutality and the disappearance or death of loved ones exists in many countries that are under authoritarian rule. It has not yet been discovered what particular effects this has on young people.

Unexpected Death

When unexpected death occurs, reactions are sometimes more extreme than they might be in circumstances in which death and violence are daily occurrences. For this reason heightened sensitivity and immediate action are often required for those in contact with children who experience a sudden loss. Examples of unanticipated deaths are: a sudden heart attack, death from an airplane crash, an unintentional drug overdose, a suicide, or a fatal injury.

SHOULD TEACHERS BE PROFESSIONALLY TRAINED TO TEACH STUDENTS ABOUT DEATH?

Every teacher must be familiar with psychological principles and the developmental aspects of teaching young people. It does not seem unreasonable to extend this knowledge of psychology to include thorough training in thanatology, especially as it applies to children. Teachers of children in grade school have different needs than teachers who deal with high-schoolers. I feel strongly that there is a need for teachers of students of all ages to acquire, feel comfortable with, and have an increased awareness of all issues connected with the teaching of death.

In addition to classroom teachers, there are several other school personnel who have critical roles to play in connection with teaching students about death. For example, the school nurse must be included in every program of death education; often the school nurse is a figure that students feel comfortable with. In addition, because they have an understanding of the child's psyche, school psychologists are particularly well-suited to receiving a more in-depth training in the psychosocial aspects of death and its effect on school-age children. Both the school psychologist and school nurse should have specific roles to play when a school community responds to an emergency situation. Because of their knowledge in this area, psychologists are the logical people to coordinate the efforts of counselors and teachers within the school and to summon additional help from outside sources, if the need arises.

CONCLUSION

Some educators and parents express confusion about the place of death education in the overall scheme of school curricula. Family-life curricula, including, for example, the subject formerly called "sex education," have become commonplace in our schools and a course on family life would be incomplete if it excluded the topic of death. Indeed, the two subjects (really, it's only one—you cannot discuss life without discussing death) can logically be combined. Every course on human development must include discussion of the life-creating process—how life starts—and this provides a perfect opening for a teacher to begin a discussion about death. For example, if a teacher is discussing pregnancy with students and the wonderful promise of the new life that can come with it, how can the fact that this promise of a new life can be halted at any time *not* be discussed; the fertilized egg can be expelled, the fetus can be miscarried or be stillborn or the newborn may have physical defects that will shorten or end his life. In a family-life curriculum, death *has* to be mentioned as a possible course of events or else teachers will only mislead their students. It makes sense that a discussion centered on the cessation of life can logically follow. The transition from one topic—living—to the next—dying—is a smooth one, and in my opinion, it is a discussion that can hardly be *avoided*.

There are "teachable moments" that may lend themselves well to a smooth transition into death-related discussion in other courses. For example, news reports on current catastrophes, family occurrences that a child might relate aloud to the class, the death of a pet, a dream that a child chooses to discuss or a child's drawing that suggests death or dying are a few of these opportunities. The possibilities are endless and they will occur. If the teacher is including a discussion of death, it is necessary that the teacher is comfortable with the subject. Perhaps even more important, however, is that the teacher be especially sensitive to the way the students react to the discussion and if they notice that a student seems particularly uncomfortable, that perhaps there is a reason; perhaps that child needs to be talked to by himself instead of in front of the rest of the class. As discussed earlier in this chapter, unbeknownst to a teacher, one student may have just experienced a death and a class discussion of the topic might be uncomfortable and painful for him. Also, it is important that a teacher never insist that a child discuss a topic such as death if he does not want to.

Death is a fact of life…every life. By not shying away from discussing *all* the facts of life, we can make our schools better places of learning and growing. It may help to point out to students—especially very young students—that the only way we can prevent death is by not being born in the first place. To live means to face death, and to die means to have been alive. Teachers who want to be realistic will give their students the full picture, and it is these students who at an early age will be able to learn to accept the sometimes frightening fact that life and death are inseparable.

REFERENCES

Anthony, S. *The Child's Discovery of Death.* New York: Harcourt Brace, 1940.

Chadwick, M. Die Gott-Phantasie bei Kindern. *Imago* 13:383-394, 1927.

Cornford, F.M. (trans.) *The Republic of Plato.* New York: Oxford University Press, 1966.

Grollman, E.A. *Talking about Death: A Dialogue Between Parent and Child.* Boston: Beacon Press, 1990.

Jung, C.G. The Soul and Death. In H. Feifel, ed., *The Meaning of Death.* New York: McGraw-Hill, 1965.

Morgan, J.D., ed., *The Dying and the Bereaved Teenager.* Philadelphia: The Charles Press, 1990.

Nagy, M. The Child's View of Death. In H. Feifel, ed., *The Meaning of Death.* New York: McGraw-Hill, 1965.

Schowalter, J.E., et al., eds., *Children and Death: Perspectives from Birth through Adolescence.* New York: Praeger, 1987.

Stern, W. Zur Psychologie den reifenden Jugend. *Zeitschrift für Pedagogische Psychologie* 28:1-20, 1927.

Sturtz, E., ed., *St. Thomas More's Utopia.* New Haven: Yale University Press, 1964.

Victor, J.L. *Tarot des Grands Inities d'Egypte.* Boucherville, Quebec: Editions de Mortagne, 1979.

4

Children's Responses to a Friend's Death (as Told by Their Parents)

Janice Cohn, DSW

The last quarter of the twentieth century has seen our society become increasingly violent. In 1970 there was an average of 363.3 violent crimes per 100,000 people in the United States. Since then, the number has risen steadily. By 1982, this figure had risen to 538 and by 1992, it had climbed again to 758 (FBI Crime in the United States Annual quoted in Statistical Abstracts of the United States 1994). Between 1970 and 1991 there was over 100 percent increase in the number of violent crimes. In 1995 it was estimated that one out of 20 American households is victimized by violent crime each year (U.S. Bureau of Justice Statistics 1995).

Children and adults must cope with the consequences of violence, both as a general environmental factor and as it personally affects them, their families and the communities in which they live. Studies on domestic violence and children's reactions to violence as it is portrayed in the media have been conducted (Goranson 1969; Williams and Crane 1974; Lester 1991). However, there have been few studies on children's responses to the violent death of a friend. The crime statistics for 1990 reported that there were 373.7 homicides per 100,000 people. Throughout the 1970s and 1980s, it was widely accepted that approximately 5000 children were murdered each year, many by their parents or guardians (U.S. National Center for Health Statistics cited in Statistical Abstracts of the United States 1994). And, we must add onto this tragic figure the increasing number of children who are killed by other children.

As the incidence of violence increases, more and more children will experience the violent death of a peer, either as a result of random violence or of accidental death or domestic child abuse. What are the emotional consequences for children confronted with such tragedies? How can parents, mental health professionals and educators most effectively help the children in these situations to deal with their emotions and anxieties? The following case study may provide concerned adults with helpful insights.

One day in early winter, a seriously depressed young mother threw herself and her 5½-year-old son, Joshua, out of a window. The child died and the mother survived. In this chapter, we will explore the emotional and behavioral reactions to this event experienced by youngsters who knew Joshua and who were told about the circumstances of his death.

The children examined in this study were perhaps typical of many solidly middle-class, urban children in the United States. They did not live in a high-risk, high-crime environment, and yet, during the 4 weeks before Joshua's death, two doormen in their neighborhood had been shot and killed during robbery attempts. Also, at approximately the same time, John Lennon, much admired by many of these children's parents, was senselessly murdered in the city in which they lived. These acts occurred against a backdrop of mounting publicity and alarm about the then unsolved murders of young, black children in Atlanta.

Information for this study was obtained through extensive, open-ended interviews with the parents of children who knew Joshua. These interviews offer a unique opportunity to examine young children's behavior and affective reactions, as observed and reported by their parents, to a particular kind of violent act—the murder of a friend. They help us to understand more fully how children react to such tragedies. What is the dominant type of response experienced by children under these circumstances? Do children tend to display anxieties focused on fear of death, fear of punishment or mutilation, fear of separation, or fear of loss of love of the object? How do children attempt to protect themselves from experiencing such anxieties?

Attempting to study children's reactions to a totally unexpected, traumatic event presented a number of dilemmas. First, because this particular situation had never been investigated before, there were no preexisting, pretested research methods that could be used. It seemed important to interview the parents as quickly as possible after the death, when specific memories and emotions were still fresh. It was felt that if we had to wait weeks or months for an interviewing instrument to be developed and tested for validity and reliability, the parents would not be able to correctly recall their children's responses in as much detail or with as vivid emotion as they would if they were interviewed promptly. Therefore, an open-ended interview format was used in all instances.

It was also decided not to interview any children directly. This decision was made because of concern that it might be psychologically harmful to some children to have their feelings and memories of Joshua's death probed by a stranger. It was also felt that during one scheduled interview with an unknown researcher, many of the children would not be able to fully express their complex emotions related to this event. Additionally, it was anticipated that parents would understandably be reluctant to allow a researcher to discuss such a painful and upsetting subject with their children. The fact that all information about children's reactions to Joshua's death was obtained from their parents and therefore subject to the respondents' individual perceptions must be considered a major though unavoidable limitation of this study.

The other limitation is that our studied population was a relatively small, homogeneous group of parents who shared similar educational and socioeconomic backgrounds. The families were urban, well-educated, middle-class and almost exclusively white. We do not know whether these children's reported reactions are representative of children from other backgrounds. The limitations of the study are balanced, however, by the opportunity it provided to examine, for the first time, children's responses to the violent death of a peer who, in this case, was killed by a parent.

THE SAMPLE

Of the 26 families interviewed, 19 were two-parent families, three were single-parent families in which the mother was the custodial parent, and three were single-parent families in which the parents were divorced, but shared child custody equally. In one family, the parents had separated only recently and had not yet made child custody arrangements.

A total of 38 parents from the 26 families were interviewed, including 26 mothers and 12 fathers. The parents' ages ranged from 29 to 49 years old. Twenty-seven parents (71.1 percent) were between the ages of 30 and 36, and 10 (26.3 percent) were between 40 and 49 years old. All of the parents were well-educated: four parents had attended college, but had not obtained degrees; 14 parents (36.8 percent) had bachelor's degrees; and more than half of these had either a master's degree or a doctoral degree. Twenty-two parents (57.9 percent) reported that they had no religious affiliation, 10 parents (26.3 percent) described themselves as Jewish, and six parents (15.8 percent) identified themselves as Christian. All families resided in the borough of Manhattan in New York City.

Of the 29 children whose reactions to Joshua's death were examined, there were 16 boys and 13 girls whose ages ranged from 4 to 10 years, although the majority of children were under the age of 7. Thirteen children—almost one half of the sample—were the oldest in their respective families. Eight children, less than one-third of the sample, were the youngest child, with the exception of one child who was a middle child. The other seven children had no siblings.

ANALYSIS OF THE DATA

A content analysis of the data determined that the responses most frequently shown by the children were requests for information regarding Joshua's death, intellectualization, anxiety and curiosity about death in general. They also exhibited general anxiety reactions, sadness and empathy. These responses, as well as others experienced by the children—disorders of affect, propitiation, somatic symptoms, phobic and counterphobic reactions and anger—will be discussed in detail later in this chapter. The discussion here relates only to the 8 weeks following Joshua's death. Finally, the children's responses as reported by their parents at a 6-month follow-up will be discussed separately.

Requests for Information About Joshua's Death

Twenty-five of the 29 children indicated a clear need to obtain specific information about Joshua's death and parents repeatedly emphasized how relentless their children were in their attempts to obtain this information. This appeared to be an extremely important part of the children's struggle to integrate and understand what had happened. It was as though they were consciously and repeatedly trying to use their cognitive skills to put together the pieces of a confusing and frightening puzzle.

It is important to note that none of the parents reported trying to stop or discourage their children's constant stream of questions about the death. They said that they answered each question as best they could, although they soon discovered that the same questions tended to be asked over and over again even after the question had already been answered, sometimes more than once. Particularly frequent were questions about Joshua's mother's motivations for killing her son, as well as inquiries concerning what had happened—where did Joshua land, what did they do with the body, and other questions regarding the logistics of his death.

- Steven, age 6, kept asking, "Was Joshua's mother really sick? She didn't *look* sick. Did anyone know she was sick?"
- Heather, age 6½, asked over and over again, "How did it happen? Didn't anyone tell him to stay away from the window? Why wasn't he asleep?"
- Martin, also 6½, wanted to know: "How was Joshua's mother sick? How can you be sick in the head? Was Joshua's father sick too?"
- Patricia, age 8, spent much time speculating about Joshua's death, and asked her mother: "Why did Joshua's mother do it? Had he been bad? Why didn't his mother die too?" She finally concluded by herself that

Joshua's mother was bigger and that Joshua's bones were more easily crushed.

- Paul, age 9, kept asking his parents: "Why would a mother throw her son out the window?"
- Jane, age 5, wanted to know: "Which ledge of the building did Joshua land on? Where was Joshua? Where was Joshua's father? Where was Joshua's mother? Where was the window?"
- Craig, age 6½, asked, "What had Joshua looked like after he went out the window? Was there blood? What happened to Joshua's body? How did they get the body away from there?"
- Peter, age 8½, asked his mother several times, "How do you think he felt? Did he suffer? Was he in pain? Did he cry? Did it hurt? How long did it take him to land on the ground? Was there blood?"

Intellectualization and Rationalization

Twenty of the children used the techniques of intellectualization and rationalization to cope with Joshua's death. This defense tended to be used most frequently and felt most intensely during the first day or two after the children were told that Joshua had died.

It is interesting that to begin the process of coping with the essentially unacceptable fact of a friend being killed by a parent, all of the children (except those in the very youngest age group) utilized the higher-level defenses of intellectualization and rationalization rather than the more primitive defenses of denial, projection or displacement. This is a positive prognostic indicator of the degree of the strength of these children's egos.

Several children's reasoning about why Joshua's mother had thrown him out the window was varied and sometimes strikingly insightful:

- Jane, age 5, thought that "maybe Joshua's mother was so unhappy that she didn't want to live any more and didn't want to be without her son."
- Sarah, 6½, reported to her mother, "I was talking to my friend Elizabeth, and we decided that Joshua's mommy was picking up newspapers and throwing them out the window, and made a mistake and threw Joshua out instead."
- Elizabeth, also 6½, was speculating with her parents about Joshua's mother and said, "Maybe she was so sick that no one believed her, and she did this so they would believe her."
- Patricia, age 8, while telling her mother what had happened, explained, "Joshua's mother did what she did because she was very sick and had a lot of problems."

- Larry, an 8-year-old, pondered about Joshua's mother and finally came to the conclusion that "if she wanted to die herself, maybe she wanted Joshua to die, too, so he wouldn't be alone."
- Joseph, age 8½, said, "Maybe Joshua did something very, very bad."
- Paul, age 9, decided that Joshua's mother must have been sleepwalking and didn't know what she was doing.

Curiosity and Anxiety Regarding the Concept of Death

Maurer (1966) has postulated that curiosity about death is often a major defense that children use to counteract anxiety provoked by the concept of death. Menig-Peterson and McCabe (1977-1978) have also noted the strong curiosity that children over the age of 5 exhibit about death, although they emphasized that young children frequently suppress or deny their true, affective reactions to the concept of death.

In this study, the children were faced not with the abstract idea of death, but with the actual, violent death of Joshua, their friend and contemporary. This might explain the fact that no parents reported a noticeable lack of emotion when children showed curiosity about the death after learning that Joshua had died. Eighteen of the children were judged to have displayed curiosity or anxiety about the concept of death.

Perhaps because of the relatively large number of parents in the sample group who described themselves as having no religious affiliation, few children, no matter what their sex or age, focused on the question of the existence of God and heaven. Questions tended to center on the concrete, biological implications of the concept of death:

- Marjorie, age 5, upon hearing of Joshua's death, asked her parents: "Will Joshua still grow?" "Where is he now?" and "Is he still a little boy?" When she spoke to her parents about the fact that Joshua had died, she said that "he was like a flower that wilted."
- Martin, age 6, asked his mother to explain what death meant.
- Helene, almost 7 years old, talked with her mother about death and decay and likened the concept of death to "when oranges rot."
- Patricia, age 8, asked "What happens to people after they die?" and "What happens to their bodies?" She also spoke about her interest in reincarnation, a subject that seemed to comfort her. "You're always somebody," she said, "you're never nobody."
- Philip, age 8, focused most of his questions on the general concept of death, particularly the inevitability of death. He asked, "Why do people have to die? Will I have to die? What will happen when I die?" He kept emphasizing that he strongly resented the fact that life did not last "forever."

Sixteen of the children were judged to have experienced noticeable anxiety in response to Joshua's death. The particular type of anxiety children manifest often serves as a diagnostic clue to the particular developmental tasks with which they are grappling (Blanck and Blanck 1974; Freud 1970; Mahler 1968). However, it can be postulated that the kind of anxiety children experience in response to as dramatic and frightening an event as a child being killed by his mother will probably be directly related to that specific event.

On the basis of the data analysis, it was determined that 11 of the children's reactions could be clearly differentiated and categorized as fear of harm, fear of separation from their parent, or fear of loss of love. Some children directly articulated their fear of being harmed, whereas others seemed to communicate this fear by their actions.

- Several days after Joshua's death, Andrew's mother became angry with him. In response, Andrew, age 5, plaintively asked her, "Will you throw me out the window?"
- The day after Steven, age 6, found out about Joshua's death he asked his mother with seeming casualness, "Would you throw me out the window? Are you sick, too?"
- Shortly after learning of Joshua's death, Heather, age 6½, suddenly insisted that her mother stay with her at night. Her mother felt that she was frightened of being abandoned. When her mother would try to leave the room, Heather would say, "If you loved me, you'd stay with me. How will I know what you'll do when I'm sleeping? How do I know you won't leave?" Appearing very upset, she asked tremulously, "Would you ever throw me out the window?"
- Several days after Joshua's death, Elizabeth, age 6½, went to her mother and solemnly said, "I have a question to ask. Would you ever do that to me?" Her mother reassured her that she would not, but days later, when her father asked Elizabeth, "Do you really think your mommy or I would throw you out the window?" she responded by saying, "Well, sometimes you can feel one way and act another."
- For several weeks after Joshua's death, whenever Sarah, aged 6½, did something that angered her mother and for which she knew she would be punished, she suddenly suggested specific punishments that she felt might be appropriate. Since she had never done this before, her mother felt that it was a response to her fear, albeit unarticulated, that she, too, might be thrown out the window.
- Immediately after Peter, age 8, heard about Joshua's death, he went to his mother and said he had heard that Joshua's mother had thrown him out the window because she was crazy. Anxious and upset, he said to her, as if confiding a horrible and confusing secret, "I didn't

say anything, Mom, but I know she *wasn't* crazy. I used to see her all the time and she looked like all the other mothers!" The implications of this seemed to be especially unnerving to him.

Disorders of Affect

Deutsch (1937), Rochlin (1953), Shambaugh (1961) and others have commented on the striking lack of affect displayed by young children when confronted with the death of an important loved one. In their content analyses of children's narratives about death, Menig-Peterson and McCabe (1977-1978) also noted children's lack of affective reactions to the death of strangers, pets or relatives. This has been attributed to the inability of a child's ego that is not yet developed to a point where children are able to deal with the task of mourning (Deutsch 1937). In their study, all disorders of affect were judged to reflect omission of affect rather than reversal of affect. It is noteworthy that there was no significant correlation between age and children's use of this response. This finding does not support the postulation that very young children's egos are less equipped than those of older children to deal with the emotional implications of death and, therefore, tend to display a higher incidence of omission of affect.

Thirteen of the children studied were judged to have experienced this response. Omission of affect, when it was observed, tended to occur almost immediately after a child was told that Joshua had died. By the time a week had elapsed, some children's lack of noticeable affect decreased sharply, suggesting that they needed time to absorb and integrate the fact of Joshua's death before they could respond affectively. It should be noted, however, that even during the period when children first learned of Joshua's death, when this response was most prevalent, feelings of sadness were more frequent than omission of affect for the aggregate and for three of the five age groups.

Feelings of Sadness

Sixteen children (or more than half of the sample) were judged to have shown sadness. Interestingly, there were no significant differences regarding the frequency and intensity of their display of sadness between the children who had siblings and the children who did not. It was anticipated that children who had a sibling with whom they had a meaningful emotional bond or who they resented or had "bad thoughts" about—thoughts that could later trigger guilt if anything happened to that sibling—would experience feelings of sadness more frequently and intensely than those without siblings. However, this was not the case. Children's feelings of sadness were expressed in various ways:

- Patrick, age 5½, frequently and with great sadness told people that he had lost his best friend, Joshua, and that now he had no best friend. Joshua died during the Christmas season, and one morning Patrick spoke with his mother about the tree they would have. He said he wanted to make a special tree ornament for Joshua—"a red shiny ball"—and spoke again about how sad it was that Joshua would miss Christmas.
- Steven, age 6, explained to his mother that "When Florence [his pet hamster] died, I was half sad—she was just a pet. When Joshua died, I felt *really* sad, because he was a person."
- Elizabeth, 6½, declared to her parents, "I'll be sad my whole life! I will never forget it."
- Paul, age 9, spoke with his mother about how sad he felt after he found out about Joshua's death. He repeated over and over, "I can't believe he's dead—here one day and gone the next. It's so sad." Some children did not articulate their sadness overtly or specifically, but this was only inferred by the child's parent or by the child's mood or actions.

Empathy

In a 10-year study of 300 children, Yarrow and Wexler (1981) found that "as early as 12 months of age a child exhibits some helping behavior such as touching, patting or some other sympathetic gesture toward an adult or child who appears to be in distress." Fifteen of the children in our study indicated empathy for Joshua and his father upon learning of Joshua's death.

- Andrew, age 5, expressed sympathy for Joshua to his mother, and remarked that "Joshua didn't have a very long life. He was only 5, and you really don't remember the first couple of years very well."
- David, age 6, confided to his therapist: "When I'm not doing anything I think a lot about Joshua. I wonder how he felt when he fell—was he scared, did he feel it? It must have been pretty awful for him."
- Elizabeth, 6½, upon hearing of Joshua's death almost immediately asked her parents, "When is the funeral?" She insisted that she had to go because "Joshua was a child and he would want a child to be there." She later reflected sympathetically, "He never even had his 6th birthday."
- Patrick, 5½, was Joshua's best friend. After Joshua's death, it was initially hard for Joshua's father to see Patrick. Patrick knew this and seemed to understand. He said, "It's because I was a good friend of Joshua's. I make him remember Joshua, and Joshua is no more."

- Ginny, age 5½, often commented on how Joshua's father must miss him, and how sad it must be for him.
- Donna, age 6, said to her mother, "You know, Mommy, I feel bad for that daddy. Now he has no mommy and no little boy."
- Two girls, age 5 and 6, drew pictures for Joshua's father, so that "he would feel better."

Propitiation

Piaget (1951) described young children's need to please or mollify their parents, whom they perceive as omniscient, powerful and capable of protecting them from harm. Maurer (1966) has postulated that this defense mechanism is frequently used by young children in their attempts to understand, accept and cope with the concept of death. This defense takes on even greater significance when children must cope with the death of a peer who literally was killed by his parent.

It is interesting that although the children in the sample had to cope with the traumatic fact that a mother was capable of fatally harming her child, a relatively small percentage of the sample was judged to have shown any sign of propitiation. However, it must be remembered that the information on which these figures were based was provided by the children's parents who were also shaken by the event and who, for the most part, had anticipated that their children would naturally require greater affection and reassurance because of it.

Only six of the children were found to have used propitiation as a way of coping with Joshua's death. It is noteworthy, however, that there was a significantly positive relationship (p<.05) between a child's age and the use of this response. Piaget (1951) linked the use of propitiation to children's developmental period, usually around the age of 5, when they begin to form a conscience. Thus, it is not surprising that in this study, children at the lower end of the age spectrum, who presumably were just beginning to experience the emergence of a conscience, showed a lower incidence of this response. The children displayed various uses of propitiation:

- Leslie, age 6, suddenly began to clean her room conscientiously shortly after Joshua's death.
- According to her mother, Elizabeth, age 6½, had been going through an "Oedipal thing" before Joshua's death. She had told her mother, "I used to love you better, but now I like Daddy better." She took pains to say that she *liked*, but didn't *love* Mommy, and sometimes even hated Mommy. Immediately following Joshua's death, however, she kept repeating to her mother that "I think that I really love you better now," and she suddenly became extremely affectionate toward her.

- Peter, age 8½, suddenly became "super well-behaved and coopera-tive." One Saturday, shortly after Joshua's death, he said to his mother, "You know what? I think I should help you with the chores." He had never done this before.
- Joseph, 8½, suddenly started giving his mother extravagant compli-ments on almost everything she did. This was strikingly un-characteristic behavior for him.
- Larry, age 8, began taking better care of his younger sibling and doing a better job of cleaning his room during the weeks succeeding Joshua's death.

Several parents described their children as being generally more affec-tionate and accommodating after they heard of their friend's death.

Somatic Symptoms

Anna Freud (1970) and other theorists have established the connection between children's somatic symptoms and stress. Therefore, it was antici-pated that a significant number of the children in our study would have experienced physical disorders such as stomach pains, sleep difficulties and so forth. Interestingly, the incidence of somatic symptoms reported was relatively small, especially in relation to the high level of anxiety the children experienced. The somatic symptoms that were reported were almost exclusively limited to sleep difficulties. One exception was a 5-year-old girl who, upon hearing about Joshua's death, seemed to have experi-enced a case of temporary paralysis in her legs. This reaction, however, lasted only briefly.

Phobic and Counterphobic Reactions

The results of this study did not support Maurer's (1966) theory that young children frequently use counterphobic reactions to "taunt death." Only four of the 29 children studied were judged to have shown this response. When children did display counterphobic reactions, they tended to do so by displaying very provocative behavior toward a parent—usually the mother—such as playing too near an open window or by daring others to harm them.

- Almost immediately after hearing of Joshua's death, Patrick, 5½, began repeatedly swaying and falling down near the living room window. He would fall again and again and cry out, "Look Mommy, I'm falling like Joshua!"
- One day shortly after Joshua's death, Sarah, age 6½, did something naughty. Her mother told her, "You make me angry when you do

that." Sarah replied heatedly, "If you're so angry, why don't you just throw me [out the window]!"

- Several weeks after Joshua's death, Steven, age 6½, was being held by his mother in front of a partially open window so that he could see an especially pretty cloud formation. Suddenly he yelled out, half jokingly, "Push me, push me!"
- Elizabeth, also 6½, argued with a friend several days after Joshua's death. When various tactics did not elicit the desired response from her friend, she finally declared that she would throw her friend "out the window."

Anger

Six children were judged to have experienced feelings of anger in response to Joshua's death. There is no clearly discernible reason why so few children were reported to have experienced this feeling. It may be that any anger or distrust they were feeling toward parents in general inhibited them from articulating this particular feeling to their own parents. It is also possible that allowing themselves to feel anger toward Joshua's mother would require that they accept the premise that she killed Joshua "on purpose" and the thought that a mother could do such a thing was too overwhelming an idea for their egos to integrate. Thus, the oldest children whose egos presumably were more fully developed, would have been more capable of confronting this fact than younger children. It is also possible that this finding is more reflective of parental perceptions than the actual incidence of anger the children experienced. When the children did show anger, it tended to be directed toward Joshua's mother or toward "the powers that be."

- During the days immediately after Joshua's death, his best friend refused to speak to his own mother about various aspects of his life, specifically the things he used to talk about with Joshua. When his mother asked him about this, he said angrily, "I could tell my friend Joshua, but she killed him, and now I don't have a best friend."
- Steven, age 6½, declared angrily, "Joshua was too young to die. He's not supposed to die that young!"
- Heather, 6½, stated with considerable anger, "I don't believe in God any more. If He existed, He wouldn't let this happen."
- Joshua's death had occurred during a period when Joseph, age 8½, was coping with a number of other problems. Shortly after he heard of Joshua's death, he burst out to his mother, "I hate God! Damn God! So many bad things have happened to me!"

FOLLOW-UP

Approximately 6 months after Joshua's death, the children's families were interviewed again, this time by telephone. One family could not be reached. In almost every case, the mother of the family was questioned.

Although it is impossible to gauge the effect that Joshua's death will have on these children in later years, a large majority of the mothers reported the cessation of any unusual behavior patterns that their children had displayed during the first weeks after Joshua's death. They stated that with the passing of time the children did not appear to be experiencing any overt reactions to the event. Among those children reported to be still experiencing some reactions to the event, the most common feelings were anxiety reactions (n = 5), anger (n = 5), sadness (n = 5), phobic or counterphobic behavior (n = 4), requests for information (n = 3) and propitiation (n = 2).

CHILDREN'S PERCEPTIONS OF THE FINALITY OF DEATH

As noted earlier, there is disagreement among researchers about when children attain sufficient ego development to understand the concept of death. To briefly recapitulate, Anthony (1940), Nagy (1948), and Childers and Wimmer (1971) concluded that only after the age of 8 or 9 are children able to understand the biological components of death. In a later study, Formanek (1974) found that only 6 percent of children under the age of 7 had an "adequate understanding" of the concept of death, and that only 20 percent of children between the ages of 7 and 9 showed awareness that death is universal and final.

In contrast, Anna Freud and Burlingham (1943) and Furman (1964) concluded that it is possible for children between 2 and 3 years of age to have some awareness of the finality of death. Steiner (1965) and Swain (1979) reported that children usually must reach the age of 5 years before they display any real understanding of death's biological implications. Kane (1979) identified the age of 6 as the time when children frequently begin to articulate "adult" ideas about death.

The parental interviews used in this study were reviewed to determine the level of children's understanding of the finality of death. The criterion for concluding that a child did understand this concept was a direct statement made by the child that indicated awareness that Joshua was irrevocably gone. Such remarks as "Joshua is no more" and "Joshua will never be able to have a birthday again," were viewed as reflecting this awareness.

Using these guidelines, 80 percent of the 25 children for whom a judgment could be made did appear to understand that death is final and irrevocable. Interestingly, although the sample of children under 5 was too small to yield any conclusive data, the vast majority of children between the ages of 5 and 7 were judged to have shown a clear understanding of the irreversibility of death. These findings most closely concur with those of Steiner (1967), Swain (1979) and Kane (1979).

CONCLUSION

Three of the six most common responses that children experienced—requests for specific information regarding Joshua's death, curiosity or anxiety regarding the concept of death and intellectualization or rationalization—were motivated by the children's need to know and understand more about death. Thus, their cognitive skills were important in helping them work through and—at least partially—resolve their needs.

It was found that the older children showed a significantly higher incidence (p<.05) of requests for information, anxiety reactions, phobic and counterphobic reactions, propitiation and anger than did the younger children. Thus, even though the existing developmental literature does not necessarily lead to this conclusion, it can be theorized that children's ability to experience and *communicate* these responses may well be related to their attainment of a certain level of ego development. Analysis of the data did not reveal any subgroups that appeared to have particular emotional vulnerability to this kind of event. However, this question bears further examination.

What do these findings indicate? They might be interpreted as suggesting that the children studied experienced relatively mild and transitory responses to Joshua's death. One could speculate that if this were the case, it may well have been related to the fact that all children were told the truth about Joshua's death by their parents; they were encouraged to talk about their feelings; their questions about the event were answered honestly and repeatedly. Moreover, parents did not attempt to minimize the scariness of the event or try to distract their children's attention from what had happened. In essence, according to the respondents' reporting, parents on the whole seemed well aware of the psychological implications of Joshua's death and tried to provide their children with comfort, support and an opportunity to communicate their feelings. No one reported discouraging their children from asking questions about even the goriest aspects of the death.

It is important to note that the parents who were part of this study were in some ways not typical. They were particularly careful with their reactions and responses to their children's reactions to the death of a friend and as a result their children received unusual support and help with their grief. It would have been of particular interest to compare this group of children's responses with a control group of children who were discouraged from talking about their feelings. However, no such control group was available.

It is noteworthy that responses such as denial, regression, behavior problems and eating disorders, which traditionally have been seen as indications that a child is experiencing psychic distress, were reported to have occurred only infrequently among the children in this study. Based on analysis of the parental interviews, many of the children studied were judged to have above average cognitive and verbal abilities. Therefore, this study's findings can also be interpreted as suggesting that the children tended to use higher-level and more intellectually oriented defenses to cope with Joshua's death than other children of the same ages might have done. These children's excellent ability to use language to communicate their fears and concerns may have lessened the frequency with which those feelings were translated into nonverbal behavioral responses, for example, regression and somatic symptoms.

It must also be considered that the parents' perceptions of their own children's responses to Joshua's death may not have been accurate. Some researchers who have studied children's responses to terminal illness (Spinetta et al. 1973) and to violence in the environment (Sigal 1968) have concluded after interviewing both children and their parents that children frequently are more aware of and distressed by the implications of death and violence than their parents tend to realize. This may have been reflected in the data obtained in this study.

IMPLICATIONS FOR CLINICAL PRACTICE AND EDUCATION

According to the findings, the children in this study coped relatively well—both intellectually and emotionally—with a traumatic event that presented some of the most frightening possibilities that young children can confront: that a child much like themselves had died a violent death, that he had been killed by his own mother and that his father had been powerless to protect him.

It would have been understandable and perhaps even probable for these children's parents to have tried to protect their children from these distressing facts by hiding or altering the truth, by trying to distract their children from the event and its implications, or by asserting that Joshua was happier after his death than he had been in life. However, all of the parents interviewed presented Joshua's death to their children in an honest way and all parents took the position that it was indeed a horrible, frightening and unfair thing that had happened. Thus, the children received strong, clear messages from their parents that it was perfectly acceptable to be upset, angry, sad and frightened and that there was no aspect of the death that their children could not ask them about, even if it meant answering the same questions over and over again. It should also be noted that no parents reported encouraging children to "be brave." When children cried, instead of discouraging tears, many parents wept along with their children. Almost all of the children had the opportunity to express and to begin to work through their feelings in an attempt to gain some mastery over their confrontation with death and they were able to share this process with their parents.

This information strongly implies that it can be therapeutic for parents and teachers to tell children the truth about death, even one as horrific as Joshua's. It is possible that when a peer has met a violent death, children's fantasies and fears can be more frightening and upsetting than the actual facts, especially if they suspect that adults are not being honest with them. It must be considered that withholding the truth may actually have far-reaching *negative* effects on children's ability to trust their parents, however protective a parent's motive for doing so may be. It should be emphasized, however, that parents must take cues from their children regarding how much information they should share about such events. When children indicate that they are not ready to deal with the truth, either by seeming uninterested or by displaying defenses such as denial or fantasy, then parents must respect these signals and refrain from further information that could be more damaging than helpful.

Further study of children's responses to the death of a friend is clearly needed. It is to be hoped that additional research will be done on different demographic groups of children to add to our knowledge of this compelling area.

REFERENCES

Anthony, S. *The Child's Discovery of Death*. New York: Harcourt Brace, 1940.

Blanck, G. and R. Blanck. *Ego Psychology*. New York: Columbia University Press, 1974.

Childers, P. and M. Wimmer. The concept of death in early childhood. *Child Development* 42:1299-1301, 1971.

Deutsch, H. The absence of grief. *Psychoanalytic Quarterly* 6:12-22, 1937.

FBI Uniform Crime Report. Washington, DC: U.S. Government Printing Office, 1979.

Formanek, R. When children ask about death. *Elementary School Journal* 75:92-97, 1974.

Freud, A. The symptomatology of childhood: a preliminary attempt at classification. *Psychoanalytic Study of the Child* 25:19-41, 1970.

Freud, A. and D. Burlingham. *War and Children*. New York: International Universities Press, 1943.

Furman, R. Death and the young child: some preliminary considerations. *Psychoanalytic Study of the Child* 19:321-332, 1964.

Gelles, R. *The Violent Home*. Beverly Hills, CA: Sage Publications, 1972.

Goranson, R.E. A Review of Recent Literature on Psychological Effects of Media Portrayal of Violence. In R.K. Baker, ed., *Report to the National Commission on the Causes and Prevention of Violence, IX. Mass Media and Violence.* Washington, DC: U.S. Government Printing Office, 1989.

Kane, B. Children's concepts of death. *Journal of Genetic Psychology* 134:141-153, 1979.

Lester, D. The climate of urban areas in the United States and their rates of personal violence, suicide and homicide. *Death Studies* 15:611-615, 1991.

Mahler, M. *On Human Symbiosis and the Vicissitudes of Individuation.* New York: International Universities Press, 1968.

Maurer, A. Maturation of concepts of death. *British Journal of Medicine* 39:35-41, 1966.

Menig-Peterson, C. and A. McCabe. Children talk about death. *Journal of Death and Dying* 8:305-317, 1977-78.

Nagy, M. The child's theories concerning death. *Journal of Genetic Psychology* 73:3-27, 1948.

Piaget, J. *The Child's Conception of the World.* London: Routledge and Kegan Paul, 1951.

Rochlin, G. Loss and restitution. *Psychoanalytic Study of the Child* 8:288-309, 1953.

Shambaugh, B. A study of loss reactions in a seven year old. *Psychoanalytic Study of the Child* 16:332-351, 1961.

Sigal, R. Child and adult reactions to the assassination of President Kennedy: a study in similarities and contrasts. Presented at the annual meeting of the American Psychological Association, Los Angeles, September, 1968.

Spinetta, J.J., D. Rigler and M. Karon. Anxiety in the dying child. *Pediatrics* 52:841-845, 1973.

Steiner, G.L. Children's Concepts of Life and Death: A Developmental Study. Unpublished Ed.D. dissertation, Columbia University, New York, 1965.

Swain, H.L. Childhood views of death. *Death Education* 2:341-358, 1979.

Williams, S. and V. Crane. Television Violence and Your Child: A Survey of Recent Research and Literature Regarding the Effects of Violent Television Program Content on the Behavior of Children. Lecture by the College of Marin and the Marin Association for Mental Health, Kentfield, CA, October 15, 1974.

Yarrow, M.P. and C.Z. Wexler, quoted in "Why Do Some People Turn Away from Others in Trouble?" *The New York Times*, July 13, 1981, p.C1.

5

Religion and the Child's Concept of Death

Judith S. Rubenstein, EdD and Terrence Tivnan, EdD

Editor's Note: A family's religious beliefs and traditions play an important role in the development of a child's concept of death. As they grow up and learn more about their family's beliefs, this role can grow. The degree to which very young children are affected by religious beliefs will be determined by the extent to which parents teach and try to instill their own religious beliefs in their children. In most cases, young children assume their parent's religion by birth, not by choice. The younger children are, the greater the likelihood that they are not conscious of the role that religion plays in their lives. However, these facts do not mean that religion should be ignored in a public school setting. A curriculum is a statement of priorities. To avoid creating potential conflict between the school and the parents who have their children enrolled there, these statements must take into consideration all religious beliefs. Also, with the increasing cultural diversity in our schools, educators have an even greater need to know and understand the religious beliefs and traditions of all students.

There is an important difference in public school classrooms between teaching religion and teaching *about* religion. Teachers in public schools may not teach religious beliefs. However, they must be able to teach about religion if they want to effectively answer the questions that inevitably will arise when discussing death with a classroom of religiously diverse students.

THE QUESTIONNAIRE

The subjects studied were average children. None of them were in mourning and none of them were (or had been) psychiatric patients. Both the Jewish and Protestant subjects were given a one-page, 24-item, anonymous questionnaire titled "Questions about Death" that took about 5 to 10 minutes to complete. Because the wording was deemed too advanced for children in kindergarten through second grade, a teacher read the questions privately to each of the students in these age groups and then recorded each of their answers. Those in third grade and up were given the questionnaire by the classroom teacher and read it on their own and wrote down their own answers. The teachers were given a short introduction to read out loud to the class as follows: "Our class is taking part in an experiment to discover what children really think about death. Doctors, people from the church and teachers would like to help children who are confused or having problems because someone they know has died. I am going to give you a set of questions that you are supposed to answer. This is not a test. There are no right or wrong answers, so you will not be graded. Because you will not put your name on your paper, when I look at your answers, I will not know who said what. Hopefully this will encourage you to answer honestly." The questionnaire contained the following questions:

1. When people die, what happens to their bodies?
2. When people die, does any part of them remain alive?
3. If yes, what part?
4. When people die, will any part of them come alive again?
5. If yes, what part?
6. When people die, will we ever be able to see them again?
7. If yes, when and where?
8. When people die, why do we bury them in the ground?
9. When people die, can we do things with the dead body other than burying them?
10. If yes, what?
11. When people die, are they still able to see people who are alive?
12. Why do people die?
13. Does everyone have to die?
14. What if no one ever died?
15. Which is better, life or death?
16. Why?
17. Are you afraid of death?
18. Why?
19. I am a: boy, girl (circle one)
20. I am __ years old. I am in _____ grade.
21. My religion is _____ .
22. My mother's religion is _____ .
23. My father's religion is _____ .
24. Have you known anyone who died?
25. If so, who?

RESULTS

For data analysis, the children were combined into four groups: grade one (K through 2), grade three (3 through 4) grade five (5 through 6) and grade seven (7 through 9). We focused specifically on four items from the questionnaire: questions 2, 3, 11 and 15 from the list above.

In response to the question, "When a person dies, does any part of them remain alive?" for Jewish children there was a steady and statistically significant increase with age in the belief that *part* of a dead person remains alive after death. This belief increased steadily from 8 percent of the children in grade one to 84 percent in grade seven. The remaining children in each grade responded with the statements "no" or "I don't know." The results were similar for Protestant children. Although the age curves for Jewish and Protestant children were not identical, the differences were not statistically significant.

To the question, "If yes, what part [of a person remains alive]?" the Jewish children's affirmative responses fell into the following five categories:

1. Spirit defined as "soul," "the part in heaven or hell" and "ghost."
2. Physical parts defined as parts of the body for "organ transplants" such as "eyes" and "liver," and other parts of the body, some of which cannot yet be transplanted, such as "brains."
3. Pictures defined as "photographs" or "home movies."
4. Deeds of achievement that the deceased earned during their lifetimes.
5. Memories of the deceased that the survivor can keep, defined as "thoughts" or "dreams" about the deceased.
   (For this analysis, the latter two categories were combined into a single category called "deeds or remembrance.")

Among the Jewish children, trends were noted in the two categories "spirit" and "deeds or remembrance." The belief that the deceased remains alive through his "deeds or remembrance" increased steadily from zero percent in grade one to 55 percent in grade seven. This increase was statistically very significant. Twice as many Jewish seventh graders believed that "deeds or remembrance" survived (55 percent) compared to 24 percent who believed that a spiritual part survived. Very few children answered "I don't know" to the other two categories, "physical parts" and "pictures," not creating any discernible pattern.

In contrast, among the Protestant children, there was a steady and highly statistically significant increase in the belief that "spirit" survived, but no statistically significant increase in the belief that "deeds or remembrance" survived.

Although the Jewish and Protestant first graders were similar (only 21 percent or less of either group believed that "spirit" or "deeds or remembrance" survived), the Jewish and Protestant seventh graders differed greatly. The majority of Protestant seventh graders believed that "spirit" survived (65 percent), but the majority of Jewish seventh graders believed that "deeds or remembrance" survived (55 percent). Overall, the differences between the two religious groups in their changing beliefs in "spirit" versus "deeds or remembrance" were highly statistically significant.

In response to the question, "When people are dead, can they see other people?" the Jewish children showed a steady and statistically significant increase across all grades in the belief that when people are dead, they are still able to "see." While most of the Jewish children responded, "no" or "I don't know," this belief increased from zero percent in grade one to 29 percent in grade seven. Among Protestant children, there was no statistically significant change across the grades. Although the curve for the Jewish children's answers is somewhat lower than that for the Protestant children's answers, the differences between the two religious groups were not statistically significant.

The Jewish children's responses to the question "Which is better, life or death?" showed a highly statistically significant decrease across the grades in the belief that life was better than death. This belief decreased from 85 percent in grade one to 66 percent in grade seven. Also, 26 percent of the seventh graders responded "I don't know" and 8 percent believed that death was better than life. Characteristic responses of this group included: "I don't know, I've never experienced death," and "Death might be better if you are suffering pain or unhappiness." The curve for the Protestant children was similar. For both Protestant and Jewish children, fewer seventh graders than first graders believed that life was better than death. Here again, the differences between the Jewish and Protestant groups were not statistically significant.

DISCUSSION

This study shows that the Jewish children's concept of death changed with age. There were steady and statistically significant differences across the grades in all four items. The Jewish first graders presented as earth-oriented realists. Not one child in this group believed that when people die, they continue to be able to see other people. Eighty-five percent believed that life was better than death. One Jewish first grader said a part of the person stays alive after death, but the part he was referring to was body parts used in organ transplants, not a living corpse, not spirit, memory or deeds.

The Jewish seventh graders differed from the younger group in that more than three-quarters of them had developed the belief that part of a deceased person survives through "deeds or remembrance" or "spirit." Almost one-third of the seventh graders believed that the deceased are able to see other people again. Also only 66 percent of the seventh graders believed that life was better than death compared to 85 percent of the first graders.

A comparison of the beliefs of Jewish and Protestant children reveals various similarities and differences. Among the younger children (grades one and three), there were no statistically significant differences between the two religious groups. The younger children in both groups regarded death as final and they did not believe a part of the body remained alive. Interestingly, the only statistically significant difference between the Jewish and Protestant children across all grades was that the majority of Protestant seventh graders believed that the "spirit" remained alive after death, but the majority of Jewish children responded that "deeds or remembrance" remained alive.

IMPLICATIONS FOR COUNSELORS

It is important for health care professionals who counsel children about death to take into consideration how a child's age affects his concept of death. It is also useful to be aware of whether a child has religious beliefs, and if so, what they are. When counseling younger children (grade three and below), counselors should be sensitive to the likelihood that this group has not yet absorbed the teachings of a religion. If a counselor speaks to children of this age about the deceased as living on through his good deeds, living on through a survivor's memory, or living on through his spirit, the young child may not know what the counselor is talking about. Moreover, the counselor must be careful to recognize that if the young child appears to know and to accept too readily her religion's teachings, the child may merely be covering over her grief rather than working through it and she may also just be trying to please the counselor. It is important for counselors of young children to carefully ascertain why a child may be reacting to a death in a way that seems too religiously knowledgeable, otherwise they may unwittingly do a disservice to children of this age group. For the sake of a child's mental health and to promote honest communication between counselor and child, it can be useful for the counselor to acknowledge the young child's beliefs and disbeliefs, regardless of what their religion es- pouses. This may be difficult for rabbis and ministers and, if so, they should refer the child to a counselor who believes, as very young children do, that death is final and that the belief of living on through good deeds, memories and spirit may be irrelevant. Sometimes even the mention of such a possi- bility may anger a young child who is faced with irrefutable loss. Religious advisors should accept the young child's views without feeling that a lack of further explanation of what that child's religious group believes would show that they are inadequate. It may also be dangerous to tell a grieving young child (third grade or younger) that his deceased loved one is alive in heaven. Anecdotes abound about the grieving child who kills himself so that he can join his loved one in heaven.

However, counseling the seventh grader is a different matter. After first acknowledging and accepting that death is a true and irrevocable loss, counselors may be able to help grieving Jewish children by reminding them that they may find comfort in remembering the good deeds of the deceased. On one hand, counselors should approach bereaved Jewish children differently than Protestant children, for whom a discussion of "spirit" may be more meaningful. On the other hand, although good deeds may be more important to the Jewish child, many Jewish seventh graders also believe in a surviving spirit. Moreover, the Jewish seventh graders in this study were not significantly different from the Protestant children in their belief that after a person dies he can still see others. However, the counselor should be aware that one-fourth of the Jewish seventh graders were dubious about any kind of life after death and might not have found solace in such teachings at all.

DO CHILDREN OF DIFFERENT RELIGIONS VALUE LIFE AND DEATH DIFFERENTLY?

The adolescents, represented by seventh graders in this study, showed a disturbing belief. While the first graders, Jewish and Protestant alike, stated overwhelmingly that they thought that life is better than death, the seventh graders of both religions had a much weaker belief that life is better than death. They would probably enter most of life's situations with a weaker commitment and attachment to life than their younger counterparts. They conceived of death as a legitimate alternative to life. To speak glowingly about the "spirit" and "deeds and remembrance" to this group may be even more dangerous than to speak this way to younger children. *Such an approach may unwittingly encourage thought of suicide.*

Based on this study, it seems clear that caring adults—whether parents, teachers or counselors—who wish to help bereaved children must know and understand the teachings about death of the child's religious tradition and they should learn the individual child's views of life and death.

REFERENCE

Stevenson, R.G. Religious Values in Death Education. In K.J. Doka and J.D. Morgan, eds., *Death and Spirituality*. Amityville, NY: Baywood, 1993.

6

The Forgotten Children: Adolescents with Life-Threatening Illness

Mary K. Kachoyeanos, RN, PhD

This chapter describes some of the emotional and educational problems that adolescents with chronic, life-threatening illness encounter (as identified by Havighurst 1953). Clearly, adolescence is a complicated phase of life, but for those with chronic illness—whether they have visible or noticeable physical or mental disabilities or not—this period of development can be fraught with many added difficulties that are not encountered by healthy adolescents. For chronically ill adolescents, dying is not merely an abstract topic; it is a realistic and daily threat. For most people, the idea of dying—of not existing—is almost unfathomable, and probably rarely contemplated; for chronically ill young adults, a remote possibility becomes an undeniable fact. This is a terrifying situation for anyone regardless of their age, but for adolescents, it can present a unique set of problems. This chapter explores these problems and presents some possible methods of promoting cognitive and psychosocial development in terminally ill adolescents.

DEFINITION OF TERMS

For the purposes of this chapter, the term *chronic life-threatening illness* is defined as a severe health problem that meets at least one of the following criteria at the time of diagnosis: it interferes with normal daily activities for at least 3 months out of a year and it leads to hospitalization that lasts from a month to a year (Pless and Pinkerton 1975). Some of the illnesses that fall into this category are cystic fibrosis, leukemia, diabetes, asthma, hemophilia and chronic renal disease. Despite the severity of these illnesses, some afflicted children may often show few, if any, outward signs of sickness or disability. This situation can cause many more problems than one might suppose.

SCOPE OF THE PROBLEM

If one considers all possible handicaps that a child with a life-threatening illness can have—both mental and physical—the scope of potential problems is enormous. Both American and British surveys report that 10 to 20 percent (approximately one million) of all children under the age of 15 have a chronic illness (Siegel 1987). This range has not changed significantly in the last 10 years.

Advances in medical technology have prolonged life for many sick (and old) people. For example, the symptom-free period for children with leukemia has increased and people can now have periods of remission that can last for many years. In the same way, young women with cystic fibrosis, previously condemned to an early death, are now able to live to an age when they are old enough to have children.

While this may sound promising, unfortunately, social advances have not even remotely paralleled medical advances and this causes a multitude of problems. For one, many chronically ill young people who are sick with a life-threatening disease are not brought up in an environment that encourages them to master age-appropriate tasks. This occurs mainly because some families who have a member with a chronic life-threatening illness are subject to such a wide variety of problems that they cannot always tend to everything. As a result, many parents tend to just try to do the best they can to make sure their child gets the medical attention he needs. This alone is a full-time job for parents, not only in terms of the actual time spent obtaining medical treatment and carrying out medical regimens, but also finding the necessary financial resources. Clearly, this is a very hard situation for all involved. Society (and in particular, parents, schools and hospitals) need to place much more emphasis on fulfilling the mental and emotional needs of chronically ill children.

Mattsson (1972) describes three different psychological profiles of children who are maladjusted due to chronic illness:

1. The child is fearful, inactive, markedly dependent on his family (especially his mother), and he lacks outside activities. The child is passive-dependent and his mother is overprotective.
2. The child is overly independent, often daring, and engages in prohibited and risky activities. He strongly denies realistic dangers; his mother is overly solicitous.
3. Less commonly, the child is shy, lonely and resentful of healthy people. His family usually emphasizes his defect(s) and tends to hide

and isolate him. As a result, the child often develops the self-image of a "defective outsider."

PROBLEMS OF MATURATION
ASSOCIATED WITH CHRONIC ILLNESS

What influence does chronic illness have on an adolescent's attainment of normal developmental goals? The following are examples of the problems that chronic illnesses have on adolescents as they grow up.

Accepting One's Physique and a Masculine or Feminine Role

Acquiring a good self-concept and body image may be the most difficult task for chronically ill adolescents. During adolescence, even healthy youngsters find themselves conflicted over their changing bodies; the effects of illness usually serve to accentuate ill adolescents' preoccupation with their bodies, as well as distorting their perceptions. Richardson and Hastorf (1964) found that chronically ill children felt isolated and somewhat inferior to others. Kaufman (1971) found a pronounced distortion of body image in adolescent diabetics even after the children had been taught about the etiology of diabetes and its effects on body organs.

The effects of drugs such as steroids that damage the body by promoting acne and facial hair, stunting growth and causing edema of the face and extremities, make it difficult for sick children to determine their body boundaries and have positive self-concepts. The part of the body that is not working, (the pancreas, for example) may be the target of the child's anger because its failure to function makes the child see himself as less than adequate.

The limitations that a disease places on adolescents' bodies may understandably be difficult for them to accept. Some may deny these limitations and abandon treatment in an attempt to test the reality of their condition. For example, it is not unusual for the diabetic adolescent who, during latency, was very strict about a daily regimen, to suddenly go off the diet, go drinking with buddies and neglect to take insulin. It has been suggested that such behavior may be suicidal. More than likely, however, it is an attempt to normalize life and to be like everyone else. Adults need to acknowledge rebellion and seemingly strange behavior in chronically ill adolescents for what it is. While being careful not to seem as if they are actually condoning their behavior, adults need to instruct adolescents how to moderate indiscretions when they do occur. For example, they should suggest that additional insulin be taken after drinking alcohol.

Adolescents lacking external signs of illness seem to have more problems with self-identity than youngsters who manifest visible symptoms. For example, Bergman and Freud (1965) found that youngsters with heart disease were more withdrawn than children with orthopedic problems.

The adolescent's sense of sexual adequacy and acceptability by others can be negatively influenced by a chronic disease. A diabetic male may experience impotence, and a male with cystic fibrosis will most likely be sterile (Whaley and Wong 1983). Chronically ill females, such as those with diabetes, are often discouraged by others from having children because of the physical stress of child-bearing. Increased sexual behavior among chronically ill adolescents may be a reaction to identity problems during this period of growth. The converse—delayed sexual behavior—may also be true.

Low energy levels and other limitations imposed by the disease diminish the ability to express emotions—behavior that is normally characteristic of non-sick adolescents. These youngsters may act out and become aggressive and disruptive and should be helped to find positive ways of expressing emotions.

Establishing Relationships with Peers of Both Sexes

Because ill adolescents often have negative opinions of themselves, they may shy away from peers of both sexes. They are often unable to engage in typical activities and this makes them feel abnormal. For example, young people with cystic fibrosis might not be able to attend a circus or ball game because if it is too dusty they will cough and even dancing can be too strenuous for young people with hemophilia. Dietary restrictions placed on diabetics may limit such youngsters from joining peers in social functions or feeling comfortable in situations that involve eating. The restrictions that chronically ill children are subject to are enormous.

Some adolescents may attempt to keep their sick condition a secret and may not engage in certain activities for fear of being "found out." In an attempt to keep her illness a secret, a 16-year-old girl refused to join in social events such as pajama parties. She was afraid that someone would see her injecting herself with insulin and discover that she was sick. Though atypical, some sick youngsters will do what it takes to protect themselves from being perceived as different.

Frequent, prolonged periods of hospitalization further isolate youngsters from their peer group. Even when treatment regimens can be performed at home, it may demand inordinate amounts of time; for example, chest physical therapy performed twice a day for 20 minutes can become very taxing and may exceed a young person's patience quickly.

The mere thought of the possible death of a sick friend can cause healthy children to socially isolate an ill child; potential death is threatening to healthy adolescents who are struggling to find their identities and learning how to live. They don't want to think about dying. Healthy children may retreat from their sick peers because they may perceive illness as disfigurement and this is frightening to them. Waechter (1979) found that the more knowledge healthy children have of a disease (in their study, the disease was cancer), the more they are willing to interact with sick children. During periods when their disease is life-threatening, sick children may withdraw from their peers in order to protect themselves. For example, a 17-year-old boy, hospitalized for serious surgery as a consequence of cystic fibrosis, refused to have his friends visit him: "It's bad enough that I'm sick; no use in making the other guys sick" (in other words, that they would find him repulsive to look at). It can, therefore, be very important for adults and teachers to educate healthy youngsters about the many trials and tribulations suffered by the terminally ill so that they are not further alienated by their peers because of simple lack of knowledge.

ATTAINING EMOTIONAL INDEPENDENCE FROM PARENTS AND OTHER ADULTS

Parents who have not resolved their guilt and grief over their child's illness tend to be overprotective. When parents are overprotective it is usually due to their need to control their children's activities. Under the guise of protecting their children, some parents may even attempt to enlist a teacher to impose unnecessary restrictions on them while they are at school.

Frequent hospitalizations during the adolescent's formative years with subsequent separation from their parents have been shown to have dire effects on adolescents' ego formation and on their ability to establish trust in other people (Robertson 1958). Chronically ill adolescents may continue to show immature behavior and make demands on adults that are more characteristic of younger children.

Most adolescents, whether healthy or ill, are usually relatively responsible problem-solvers and decision-makers and, therefore, should have a say in their treatment when the situation permits it. Giving total autonomy to the adolescent regarding all activities is, however, not without risk. If, for example, school teachers allow chronically ill adolescents to engage in activities that may be potentially injurious to their health, they may be considered negligent and this can have legal implications. Some parents find that it is emotionally risky for them to give their children too much autonomy. Other parents do not have enough trust in their children's ability to assume responsibility for their own care.

Achieving Economic Independence: Preparing for and Selecting an Occupation

Every child's self-esteem and self-confidence is achieved in part by his ability to control his environment, and this ability results both from formal and informal learning. Chronically ill children who miss school periodically are clearly at a disadvantage. Studies indicate that chronically ill children miss an average of 6 weeks of school per year (Sultz 1972). Additionally, this study showed that 26 percent of chronically ill children were enrolled in classes that were below the expected grade level. Academic achievement expectations for children with life-threatening illness may also be less than they are for the average population. A study of academic achievement for 17- to 21-year-olds with asthma indicated that only 14 out of 68 children had completed high school.

Obtaining jobs and demonstrating other socially responsible behavior such as getting a driver's license have become more common for those with chronic illnesses. The advances made by chronically ill people have come about mainly through social awareness, decreasing myths about the chronically ill and through legislation. However, inequities still persist: medical and life insurance rates are higher for those with chronic illness; in some instances insurance is denied; states have limitations on driver's licenses for epileptics and diabetics; and certain types of employment are sometimes prohibited to the chronically ill. Though some of these limitations may be realistic for purposes of public safety, they limit the resources available to the chronically ill and, therefore, their ability to achieve economic security and independence.

Preparing for Marriage and Family Life

All of the information above clearly points to the fact that chronically ill young adults do not have a great chance of achieving a successful marriage or starting a family. The lack of adequate preparation for a vocation and limited access to jobs decrease the likelihood of attaining the economic security more and more necessary for having a family.

As mentioned previously, certain diseases such as diabetes and cystic fibrosis can interfere with normal sexual ability, reproductive capacity or both.

Though marriage is possible, genetic and premarital counseling is imperative for young people with chronic illnesses so that they can realistically plan for the future.

THE EDUCATIONAL SYSTEM AND
THE CHRONICALLY ILL ADOLESCENT

As mentioned earlier, chronically ill youngsters have lower achievement scores and are more prone to drop out of school than students who are healthy. Though the reasons for these behaviors are multifaceted, decreased school attendance and lack of continuity in studies are certainly significant contributing factors (Cruickshank and Johnson 1975). For example, the treatment regimens that chronically ill adolescents must undergo (that can become more and more frequent during bad periods) can seriously disrupt a student's education.

It is essential, therefore, that schooling be provided to chronically ill students during the periods when they are unable to attend "regular" school. So that hospitalized school children can keep up with their studies, most modern pediatric hospitals have implemented simulated schools with classrooms staffed by teachers from local school districts. Without the pressure of meeting predetermined educational objectives, teachers who work in this environment are free to spend time evaluating each child's abilities and filling any educational gaps they may perceive. Ideally, the continuity of learning objectives in a hospital classroom should be maintained in the same way it is in a regular classroom. Unfortunately, this is easier said than done because patients with a chronic illness are frequently subject to unforseen medical problems and therefore live in a constant state of flux, adherence to any sort of regimen and continuity is difficult at best.

Children who are hospitalized in institutions that do not have school facilities or children who cannot leave their home can always try to find a tutor. However, children who are ill for only short periods of time (asthmatics for example) are not always able to benefit from this type of service; often by the time the referral procedure for a tutor is completed, the child may be well enough to be discharged from the hospital or even to go back to school. Absenteeism can spiral quickly for these students, sometimes accumulating into weeks and months of lost school time. This problem is intensified for children who, in addition to having a chronic illness, come from a deprived environment. For example, when parents don't do everything they can to assist their children, chances are that they will miss more school than they need to.

What then is the solution to the problem and who should assume responsibility? The school system? Schools routinely plan individual education programs (IEPs) for special students. Individual educational programs need to be planned and evaluated for children with chronic illness who have varying degrees of intelligence, as well as those determined to be mentally handicapped. Possibly, and just as important, we need to reexamine our attitude toward these youngsters. If the general reaction is one of pity, this needs to be replaced with empathy and realistic goal-setting. Establishing appropriate academic expectations is more constructive than being "kind" by passing a student who doesn't deserve it. When a chronically ill young adult was asked what he would like educators to know about students like him, he summed it up succinctly: "Tell them to treat me like a regular guy."

BEN: A CASE STUDY

Ben was 19½ years old when he was interviewed during one of his kidney dialysis therapies. When he was a young child he suffered several episodes of glomerulonephritis and by the age of 9 he had complete kidney failure. At the time, techniques for kidney transplants were new and donors were scarce.

During the first few years of his illness, Ben spent 6 hours on kidney dialysis, three times a week. Now, due to advanced technology, he only has to spend half that time in therapy. But years of prolonged drug therapy took their toll on Ben. He is short compared to other boys his age—he is only 5-feet-2 and has a small physique.

He was enthusiastic about talking to the interviewer because he said that he did not often have the chance to talk with many people. Ben, who reads at an eighth-grade level, quit school when he was 16 years old. He is now preparing to take the high school equivalency exam. He reports, "I missed a lot of time in school, but the teachers were nice to me. I guess they felt sorry for me. I remember one teacher gave me a 'C' for an exam I missed so that I'd pass with my class." This teacher "benevolence" became something that Ben encountered regularly during his formative years; it left him semiliterate and without the skills necessary for obtaining any sort of job later on.

Ben's social circle was small, consisting of "guys at the car shop." He has never dated: "I'd ask [girls] to go out, they kept on saying no, so I just gave up. I do go out with the guys, have a few beers sometimes [against medical advice]." Ben still lives with his widowed mother; his disability compensation is not sufficient for him to live on his own.

CASE MANAGEMENT AS A SOLUTION

It is hard not to be struck by the level of Ben's helplessness, some of which is entirely understandable; he has a chronic disease that most likely will take his life. Could the health care and educational systems make a difference for the Bens of the world? Perhaps the quality of his life could have been improved had his life been managed differently. The nature of today's health care and educational systems make it easy for youngsters like Ben to get lost in the system, but there are possible solutions, one of which is the use of case managers. Currently, the case manager system mainly assists elderly people to weave their way through the health care system and in developing and implementing goals of therapy. For some clients, the case manager is the only person with whom they have contact.

Case managers could play a critical role in working with youngsters who have chronic life-threatening illnesses. They could be especially helpful in facilitating educational goals for chronically ill children when health problems interfere with education. Usually, case managers are assigned to special education students in public schools. It must be acknowledged that adolescents with chronic life-threatening illness have special needs too and that they could benefit greatly from the case manager system.

Assisting chronically ill adolescents to achieve their developmental tasks is critical for enhancing the quality of their lives as well as for improving (if not creating) their social economics. The incidence of chronic illness doubled from 1.1 percent in 1967 to 2 percent in 1981 and rose to 3.2 percent by 1992. Because more chronically ill people are living for longer periods of time, in the future we can expect an even greater increase in those living with chronic illnesses. When we reach a point when today's major childhood diseases are cured, will our children be prepared for life? The health care and educational systems have a responsibility to make sure that they are.

REFERENCES

Bergmann, T. and A. Freud. *Children in the Hospital*. New York: International Universities Press, 1965.

Cruickshank, W. and O. Johnson. *Education of Exceptional Children and Youth*. Englewood Cliffs, NJ: Prentice-Hall, 1975.

Havighurst, R. *Human Development and Education*. London: Longmans Green, 1953.

Hirt, M. *Psychological and Allergic Aspects of Asthma*. Springfield, IL: Charles C Thomas, 1965.

Janeway, C. Adolescent patient. *Northwest Medical Journal*, February 1974.

Kaufman, R.B. and B. Hersher. Body-image changes in teenage diabetes. *Pediatrics* 48:123-128, 1971.

Mattsson, S. Long-term physical illness in childhood: A challenge to psychosocial adaptation. *Pediatrics* 95:727-730, 1972.

Nesbitt, M., W. Krvit, et al. Follow-up report of long-term survivors of childhood acute lymphoblastic or undifferentiated leukemia. *The Journal of Pediatrics* 95:727-730, 1979.

Pless, W. and K. Roghmann. Chronic illness and its consequences: observations based on three epidemiologic surveys, *The Journal of Pediatrics* 79(3):351-359, 1971.

Pless, I.B. and P. Pinkerton. *Chronic Childhood Disorder: Promoting Patterns of Adjustment*. Chicago: Yearbook Medical Publishers, 1975.

Richardson, S.A. and A.H. Hastorf. Effects of physical disability on a child's description of himself. *Child Development* 35:893-907, 1964.

Robertson, J. *Young Children in Hospitals*. London: Tavistock, 1958.

Siegel, D.M. Adolescents and chronic illness. *Journal of the American Medical Association* 257 (24)3396-3399, 1987.

Sultz, H., et al. Long-term Childhood Illness. Contemporary Community Health Series. Pittsburgh: University of Pittsburgh Press, 1972.

Waechter, E. The Adolescent with a Handicapping, Chronic or Life-Threatening Illness. In Ramona Mercer, ed. *Perspectives in Adolescent Health Care*. J.B. Lippincott, 1979.

Whaley, L. and D. Wong. *Nursing Care of Infants and Children*. St. Louis: Mosby, 1983.

7

Young People as Victims of Violence

Ronald Keith Barrett, PhD

American educators are witnessing alarming behavior among a new breed and generation of young people. Today, it seems as if many students are challenging schools by making it difficult for educators to fulfill their most basic mission—to transform young people into students and ultimately to realize the higher goals and objectives of our institutions of learning. Teachers are reporting students who appear unteachable and unable to learn because of behavioral and emotional problems that interfere with their ability to focus and adjust to the school and classroom environments. Many of today's young people are exhibiting this problem behavior in school with an alarming disposition toward indiscriminate violence. This violence is directed at other students as well as teachers. A recent criminal justice report suggests real cause for concern over two identified trends: the alarming trend toward adolescent violence, and the observation that it is younger and younger youth who are both the perpetrators and victims of violence. In schools where the budget barely provides for basics, teachers are facing the unprecedented challenge to work with a student population that few of them were professionally trained or prepared to deal with. For many educators, the metamorphosis witnessed in less than two generations of these students is overwhelming and perplexing. What is wrong with the youth today?

THE REALITY OF CONTEMPORARY CHILDHOOD

Today's youth are different because the nature of childhood is fundamentally different than it was in earlier generations. The reality of the daily challenge for sheer survival in many of today's urban school communities is drastically changing the nature of childhood for an ever-increasing number of American youngsters. For example, a large number of children now live in communities besieged by chronic violence (Garbarino, Dubrow, Kostelny and Pardo 1992). The daily exposure to episodes of violence increases children's risk of trauma and potentially undermines their psychological and emotional well-being (Pynoos 1995).

The cumulative effect of the exposure of young children to episodes of chronic violence and trauma cannot have anything but negative consequences for their learning potential and interpersonal conduct at school, at home and in the community at large. An emerging body of literature suggests a strong link between formative developmental episodes of abuse and neglect and the tendency for subsequent violent interpersonal behavior (Doyle and Bauer 1989; Brown and Finklehor 1986). The research evidence from case studies of perpetrators of sexual assault, domestic violence and manslaughter reveals a pattern of abuse and victimization of the perpetrators themselves at some earlier developmental stage (Kiser et al. 1991; Deblinger et al. 1989). While some of the research focused on adolescent homicidal violence has attempted to explain the current phenomenon of escalating violence and aggression among youth (Barrett 1993), too few researchers have empirically detailed and examined the long-term consequences of trauma and victimization of young urban children who *witness* these episodes of violence.

THE NATURE AND SCOPE OF CHRONIC VIOLENCE

The escalating incidence of lethal violence in poor, socially disadvantaged, nonwhite, urban communities often translates into trauma, distress and violence in the lives of the growing number of children who live in these communities. The incidence of homicidal violence is so significant in these communities that homicide is now the leading cause of death for adolescent, urban, nonwhite (i.e., African American and Latino) males aged 15 to 24. Over the past two decades, the persistent pattern of lethal violence in African American and Hispanic communities has continued to grow. Premature homicidal death rates have significantly reduced the total average life expectancy for African Americans and Latinos and this has caused homicide to be regarded as a public health issue (Barrett 1993).

Children in urban environments are increasingly at risk of becoming "primary victims" of homicidal violence as they are more likely to be both victims and perpetrators of lethal violence. In a major demographic study of homicides over a 12-month period in 1988 for Los Angeles County, Barrett (1991) found that African American and Latino males aged 15 to 24 had the highest risk for being victims of homicidal violence. Similar findings were reported by Barrett in 1993 after examining national statistics on homicides in a number of larger metropolitan areas that had reported a persistent pattern since 1970 with urban adolescent youth being over-represented as both victims and perpetrators of homicide. Research studies empirically support a characteristic profile of perpetrators of lethal violence as urban, adolescent, nonwhite and male. However, the most recent criminal justice statistics reveal an emerging trend of violence among urban adolescent females, especially since 1980 (Barrett 1993; Henneberger and Marriott 1993).

In recent years, it has become increasingly evident to human services workers and those who work routinely on the "front line" with young children that more and more young urban children are "secondary victims" of trauma and violence (Garbarino et al. 1992). These children face a barrage of routine acts of violence in their immediate social environment. A growing body of research (Pynoos 1995; Garbarino et al. 1992) has begun to document the consequences of community violence on the psychological functioning and well being of young urban children. Psychologically, their behavior seems to reflect both a loss of hope for their physical survival and for the future in general. The obvious contradiction is that culturally we regard children as *our* hope for the future, but our children have increasingly lost hope in a future for *themselves*. This attitude can be seen in the increasing cynicism among today's youth who engage in high-risk behaviors (smoking, alcohol and drug experimentation, gang and related criminal involvement, unprotected sex) that ultimately threaten their chance of survival. In unprecedented numbers, urban youth are planning their own funerals with the same preoccupation characteristic of those anticipating death in the later stages of life (Kalish and Reynolds 1989). The recognition that this is the emerging reality of a growing number of America's adolescents forewarns of a whole generation of children at risk (Pynoos 1995; Garbarino, Dubrow, Kostelny and Pardo 1992).

THE PSYCHOLOGICAL CONSEQUENCES AND IMPACT OF CHRONIC VIOLENCE AND LOSS

An emerging body of literature and observation in clinical settings suggests characteristic behavior of young children traumatized by violence, grief and loss. Their losses include the death of friends and significant others, a place to live, a sense of safety and protection, health, a sense of fairness and equal opportunity with others, and the possibility of a meaningful future. Many factors may influence the impact of loss on a child's grief. Among the more important are the availability of a support system for the child and access to a caring and empathetic parent or significant other and this includes teachers (Perkins and Greenberg 1994). There are some losses that are more difficult for children because of an associated social stigma (e.g., loss of a parent due to incarceration, drug or criminal involvement, abandonment, suicide, homicide or AIDS). The type of loss and the corresponding stigma can complicate the grief and recovery adjustment of the child.

Death is a frequent visitor in all violent societies. The child's response to the loss of a parent deserves special mention since it has such wide implications for the child's behavior. The following factors can affect childhood bereavement following the loss of a parent:

- The severity of the grief reaction in the surviving parent or significant others
- The nature of the parent's death (e.g., natural vs. unnatural or stigmatized loss)
- The degree of attachment to the lost parent
- The extent of the child's experience with prior losses
- The child's experience of the death (e.g., direct vs. vicarious)
- The timing and nature of notification of the death
- The degree of social support vs. social pressures that may inhibit or complicate the child's natural grief response
- The extent of the child's internalization of guilt reactions
- The degree of the impact and consequences of the loss (e.g., family role loss, economic survival concerns, labels and social stigmas)
- The extent of changes in family identity
- The child's personality and emotional maturity

The Influence of Age and Developmental Stages on Children's Comprehension of Death

Some research studies on children suggest a sensitivity to the age and developmental maturity of the grieving child (Piaget 1929; Nagy 1948), as well as the child's past experience (Piaget 1929; Bluebond-Langner 1978). Accordingly, this research suggests a conceptual framework with three age and developmental categories:

Preschool age: This is the *primitive* stage in which the child has a very limited understanding of death characterized by a basic inability to comprehend the permanence of death and difficulty with the intensity of affect associated with grief.

Age 5 to 9: This is the *primary* stage in which the child understands the permanence of death, but is unable to conceptualize death in abstract terms (e.g., that people can die physically but may exist or be with us in spirit).

Age 10 and older: This is the *secondary* stage in which the child is able to conceptualize death in adult terms and manage the affective intensity of grief.

While age is a useful framework for conceptualizing the child's comprehension of death and dying, research with dying children and with urban children who have been exposed to chronic lethal violence suggests that this experience may account for the atypical maturity in dealing with death and dying found in observational studies of these children.

SYMPTOMS OF GRIEVING IN CHILDREN

The general behavior of young children who experience the trauma of loss and grief associated with violence include a cluster of behavioral symptoms, including many that can be observed in the classroom and school environment. The following *affective* symptoms are of particular significance:

- experiencing episodic bouts of depression and sadness (intermittent grieving)
- feeling indifferent
- being unable to respond to praise or reward
- showing a lack of enjoyment from pleasurable activities
- feeling bad about oneself
- feeling guilty
- feeling pessimistic about life and sorry for oneself
- being easily tearful or crying spontaneously
- showing significant changes in facial affect and eye contact
- showing a loss of enthusiasm and excitement

Among the many *behavioral* symptoms of grieving in children are the following:

- being less talkative or uneasy and restless
- showing significant changes in normal behavior (e.g., deviations from personal norms)
- experiencing a change in eating habits (decreased appetite or overeating)
- experiencing a change in the sleep cycle (unable to sleep or constantly tired and sleeping)
- exhibiting changes in bodily functions (e.g., constipation, headaches, aches and pains)
- showing changes in play habits and interests
- experiencing low energy or chronic tiredness
- regressing to immature behaviors as a means of coping (e.g., soiling, bed wetting, frequent crying and playing with food)
- displaying clinging behaviors (e.g., intense attachments)

- showing social withdrawal or avoidance
- displaying irritability and excessive anger
- being atypically confrontational
- exhibiting hyperactivity or fatigue
- showing significant changes in personal appearance, including grooming and dress
- displaying accident proneness or forgetfulness

Cognitive symptoms of grieving can be manifest in any of the following behaviors:

- unfocused, repetitive thoughts or preoccupation and daydreaming
- loss of ability to concentrate, think clearly or focus one's attention
- difficulty in making decisions
- preoccupation with death or talk of "being with the deceased"

Grieving in the School Setting

In the school setting the behavioral symptoms of grieving may be shaped and elicited in response to the social and ecological environment of the school and classroom. The following symptoms are of particular significance and should not be overlooked by the teacher:

1. Decline in academic performance
2. Poor concentration and interest
3. Daydreaming and absentmindedness
4. Atypical confrontations and fighting
5. Social withdrawal, isolation and avoidance
6. Hyperexcitability, hyperactivity or fatigue

Grieving in the Home Setting

At home, parents and caretakers, as well as educators conducting home visitations or conferences with the parents about the children, should be alert and watchful for the following behavioral symptoms:

1. Change in appetite
2. Sleep disturbances (including nightmares, night sweats, bed wetting, extreme fatigue or insomnia)
3. Social withdrawal, isolation or avoidance (possibly by spending long periods alone)
4. Clinging behaviors

5. Regression to immature behavior as a means of coping
6. Loss of enthusiasm and apathy
7. Accident proneness, forgetfulness or absentmindedness
8. Increased irritability, confrontations and fighting

INFLUENCES ON CHILDREN'S MOURNING

Family Prototypes

It has been observed that the coping adjustments and the support of the parental figure(s) and caretaker(s) during the child's grief may play an important role in the mourning and recovery of the grieving child (Perkins and Greenberg 1994). It has also been observed that the type of family in which the child has been socialized can make a difference in the expressive nature of that child's grief and mourning behaviors. Family prototypes can be divided into two main groups. *Internalizers* are family members who are more covert in mourning. They are the keepers of secrets. They consider family business and affairs as private and not for public display. *Externalizers* are more overt in the expression of mourning behaviors, less inhibited, less guarded and less secretive. Children with an internalizing family are more stoic and their concealment of feelings can lead to depression, while children with an externalizing family show their feelings and are more prone to displays of emotion and release.

Gender

It has been observed that children are securely sex-typed as early as 24 months of age and boys are more securely and rigidly sex-typed than girls. The emerging gender differences between boys and girls are evident as early as preschool. One of the most pronounced behavioral differences between the sexes is that young boys can be observed to externalize their grief more during mourning. They are also more likely to act out their anger, show a tendency for confrontational behavior, have more conflict in interpersonal relations and fight more frequently when experiencing trauma, loss and grief. In contrast, young girls are socialized to internalize feelings. Girls generally suppress feelings of anger and rage and consequently are more likely to turn them inward. These gender differences are relatively similar throughout much of the life cycle.

CLINICAL INTERVENTIONS FOR CHILDREN IN MOURNING

Many children experiencing trauma, loss and grief do not receive help because adults either don't know what to do or fail to recognize the

symptoms of grief and mourning. Among the common myths about grieving children are the following:

- "They will outgrow it."
- "They are too young to understand."
- "If we don't talk about it, in time they will forget."
- "Talking about it only upsets the child."
- "It's time to grow up and get over it."
- "Only babies and sissies cry."

In many ways the grief of children and adults is similar, but there are some
important differences. Most characteristically the grief of children is intermittent. It seems to come and go unpredictably, moving the child in and out
of sadness and grief. Many of the recommendations for clinical interventions
with children are similar for adults who grieve. However, because the young
child may lack the verbal capacity to express feelings and identify internal
states, conventional counseling can be quite awkward and uncomfortable.
The use of creative art mediums may be helpful for both assessment and
therapeutic purposes. It is also important to note that young children who
have no sense of the normal expectations of the roles in a counseling relationship may also feel a bit uncomfortable. A children's support group has been
observed to be especially helpful for children of all ages as it takes the focus
off the individual child and allows identification with other children who are
also grieving. A grieving child's sense of isolation and alienation can also be
eased by the social interaction of the group.

A number of therapeutic intervention strategies have been suggested for
children. These include: grief recovery support groups; micro-counseling;
psychopharmacology; art therapy; bibliotherapy; play therapy; puppet
therapy; music therapy; movement therapy; and journaling. The four essential psychological tasks of grief work are generally held to be understanding, grieving, commemorating and moving on. In an individualized
case management approach, a combination of therapeutic clinical interventions may be employed to assist the child's grief recovery. Without the
assistance of the educational community in the grief recovery process of
young children, the primary objective of educating and socializing children
will become increasingly difficult. As more and more young children are
experiencing dimensions of loss, educators must be aware that grieving
children who are experiencing trauma, loss and grief are now more the
norm than the exception.

CONCLUSIONS AND RECOMMENDATIONS

Educators as Caretakers

Educators have traditionally been regarded as secondary caretakers of the young. The uncomfortable reality of our contemporary dilemma of coping with escalating violence requires that educators extend their roles to help support and enable young children to learn. Helping students deal with their pain is an essential task of the teacher. Educators must restore a sense of safety within educational settings so that children are able to learn in an atmosphere of tranquility, free of concerns of personal safety from violence. In addressing the societal task of curbing violence, schools must be a part of the solution. Educational institutions have always been focal points for social change within communities. The present situation requires that a school's role must now be one of leadership to help transform a violent society through working with children impacted by violence, trauma, loss and grief (Lee 1994).

Understanding Community Violence

Schools are an integral part of the sociocultural context in which they function. Schools must take seriously the task of being connected with the communities they serve and in doing so they must understand the issues and concerns of the pupils and their community. Knowing the nature and scope of violence as well as other social concerns is an important part of staying in touch with the community.

Professional Development

Educational institutions must include a fundamental commitment (i.e. school budgets, professional resources and staff development) to the professional preparation, training and development of teachers so that they are able to work with and meet the changing demographic needs of the community. An ongoing effort for staff and volunteer training should be an essential component of any plan for professional development.

Professional Referrals

The identification of professional resources and personnel to assist with staff development objectives as well as with the critical service needs of the student population is an emerging reality. The ability to work with other professional service providers is an essential part of meeting the needs of students.

Children's Support Groups

Because so many issues now complicate the lives of many young people, they should not be further encumbered because the safety of traditional boundaries that separate school from home and community is compromised. Many of today's children are dealing with extraordinary conditions (e.g., hopelessness, dysfunctional families, alcohol and substance abuse, domestic violence and abandonment) and these issues need to be addressed as they increasingly find their way into the classroom. Attempts to organize support groups for children should be sensitive to the unique issues inherent in different types of losses, along with ethnic, cultural, age-related and developmental concerns. With the identification of children in need and the careful structuring of groups with a skilled facilitator, effective interventions can begin.

Creative Therapy

The use of creative art therapies is especially recommended for work with very young and ethnic minority children who may have difficulty with the clinical counseling situation and who also may have limited language skills. Caution should be used in attempting to clinically interpret children's art and drawing because the clinician may make the serious error of overprojecting into the child's experience. Concerns regarding clinical interpretations and projection errors are particularly problematic when working with urban inner-city children who come from multicultural environments. It is suggested that expressive arts be used primarily as a lens and as stimulus for dialogue with the child about the child's feelings and experiences.

Holistic Intervention

Research literature and clinical experience suggest the wisdom of establishing a partnership with a child's parents or other caretakers. Work with children should match home-based (primary caretakers) and school-based (secondary caretakers) intervention. With a collaborative partnership, all of the principal caretakers can work together to support the child's grief recovery. Any intervention started at school must be supplemented with aftercare at home in order to maximize the impact and benefit for children.

Educational Supportive Services

Children in crisis cannot be expected to function normally. Consequently, they may fall behind in their schoolwork. If this happens, they will need remedial supportive assistance. When children in crisis begin to do poorly in school, it causes them to suffer an additional loss. This extra burden makes more difficult the grief recovery of the child experiencing trauma, grief and loss.

Helping Children with Their Grief

Adults who wish to assist grieving children may wish to do the following:

- Acquaint themselves with the grief process by reading literature on the subject or talking to a counselor or spiritual advisor.
- Allow children to talk about death.
- Use the proper name when speaking of the deceased person.
- Use direct language when talking about the death. Say "dead" instead of "he's passed on."
- Let children express their fears.
- Offer children loving, touching support.
- Allow them to cry and to be sad.
- Let children ask questions and answer them as simply as you can. (No one is expected to have *all* the answers. When you don't, it's okay to say, "I don't know how to answer that.")
- Encourage children to talk about dreams at home right after they happen. If you wait until morning, they are usually forgotten.
- Reassure children that you are healthy and will be around for a long time, but avoid unrealistic statements such as the promise that you will "always" be there. However, say that *someone* will always be there and remind children of other adults who know and care about them.
- Explain the ritual of funerals and allow the children to participate *if they wish to do so.*
- Offer support and structure in helping children complete their homework.

REFERENCES

Barrett, R.K. Urban adolescent homicidal violence: an emerging public health concern. *The Urban League Review*, 1993, pp. 67-75.

Bell, C. Traumatic stress and children in danger. *Journal of Health Care for the Poor and Underserved* 2(1):175-188, 1991.

Bertoia, J. and J. Allan. Counseling seriously ill children: use of spontaneous drawings. *Elementary School Guidance and Counseling* 22:206-221, 1988.

Bluebond-Langner, M. *The Private World of Dying Children.* Princeton, NJ: Princeton University Press, 1978.

Brown, A. and D. Finklehor. Impact of child sexual abuse: a review of the research. *Psychological Bulletin* 99:66-77, 1978.

Costantino, G., R. Malgady and L. Rogler. Storytelling through pictures: culturally sensitive psychotherapy for hispanic children and adolescents. *Journal of Clinical and Child Psychology* 23(1):13-20, 1994.

Deblinger, E., S. McLeer, M. Atkins, D. Ralphie and E. Foa. Post-traumatic stress in sexually abused and nonabused children.*Child Abuse and Neglect* 13:403-408, 1989.

Doyle, J. and S. Bauer. Post-traumatic stress disorder in children: its identification and treatment in a residential setting for emotionally disturbed youth. *Journal of Traumatic Stress* 2: 275-288, 1989.

Dubrow, N.F. and J. Garbarino. Living in the war zone: mothers and young children in a public housing development. *Child Welfare* 68(1):3-20, 1989.

Fox, S.S. *Good Grief: When a Friend Dies.* Boston: New England Association for the Education of Young Children, 1988.

Garbarino, J., N. Dubrow, K. Kostelny and C. Pardo. *Children in Danger: Coping with the Consequences of Community Violence.* San Francisco: Jossey-Bass, 1992.

Garbarino, J., K. Kostelny and N. Dubrow. *No Place to be a Child: Growing Up in a War Zone.* Lexington, MA: Lexington Books, 1991.

Guy, T.N. Let's talk it over: dialoging between children and adults on death. *The Forum,* January/February 1992.

Heltherington, E.M., M. Cox and R. Cox. Effects of divorce on parents and children. In M. Lamb, ed., *Non-traditional Families.* Hillsdale, NJ: Lawrence Erlbaum, 1982.

Henneberger, M. and M. Marriott. For some, rituals of abuse replace youthful courtship. *The New York Times,* July 11, 1993.

Kalish, R. and D. Reynolds. *Death and Ethnicity: A Psycho-cultural Study.* Amityville, NY: Baywood.

Kamerman, S. and A. Kahn. *Mothers Alone: Strategies for a Time of Change.* Dover, MA: Auburn House, 1988.

Kiser, L., J. Heston, P. Millsap and D. Pruitt. Physical and sexual abuse in childhood: relationship with post-traumatic stress disorder. *Journal of the American Academy of Child Adolescent Psychiatry* 30(5):776-783, 1991.

Kotulak, R. Study finds inner-city kids live with violence. *Chicago Tribune,* September 28, 1990.

Kübler-Ross, E. *On Death and Dying.* New York: Macmillan, 1969.

Kübler-Ross, E. *Living with Death and Dying.* New York: Macmillan, 1981.

Kübler-Ross, E. *On Children and Death.* New York: Macmillan, 1983.

Lee, W. Preparing the school community to cope with violence. In R. Stevenson, ed., *What Will We Do? Preparing a School Community to Cope with Crises.* Amityville, NY: Baywood, 1994.

Losel, F. and T. Bliesner. Resilience in adolescence: a study on the generalizability of protective factors. In K. Hurrelman and F. Losel eds., *Health Hazards in Adolescence.* New York: Walter de Gruyter, 1990.

Matter, D.E. and R.M. Matter. Developmental sequences in children's understanding of death with implications for counselors. *Elementary School Guidance and Counseling* 17:112-118, 1982.

McLeer, S., E. Deblinger, M. Atkins, E. Foa and D. Ralphie. Post-traumatic stress disorder in sexually abused children. *Journal of the American Academy of Child and Adolescent Psychiatry*. 6:650-654, 1988.

Nagy, M.H. The child's theories concerning death. *Genetic Psychology* 73:3-27, 1948.

Ochberg, F., ed. *Post-Traumatic Therapy and Victims of Violence*. New York: Brunner/Mazel.

Ogbu, J. A cultural ecology of competence among inner-city blacks. In M.B. Spencer, et al., eds., *Beginnings: The Social and Affective Development of Black Children*. Hillsdale, NJ.: Lawrence Erlbaum, 1985.

Oklander, V. *Windows to Our Children*. Moab, UT: Real People Press, 1978.

Perkins, Q. and M. Greenberg. Children's experience of life stress: the role of family social support and social problem-solving skills as protective factors. *Journal of Clinical Child Psychology* 23(3):295-305, 1994.

Piaget, J. *The Child's Conception of the World*. London: Kegan Paul, 1929.

Pynoos, R. and S. Eth. Children traumatized by witnessing personal violence: homicide, rape or suicide behavior? In S. Eth and R. Pynoos, eds., *Post-Traumatic Stress Disorder in Children*. Washington, DC: American Psychiatric Press, 1985.

Pynoos, R. and K. Nader. Psychological first aid and treatment approach to children exposed to community violence: research implications. *Journal of Traumatic Stress Studies* 1(4):445-473, 1988.

Sameroff, A., R. Seifer, R. Barocas, M. Zax and S. Greenspan. Intelligence quotient scores of 4-year-old children: social-environmental risk factors. *Pediatrics* 79:343-350, 1987.

Solnit, A. *Working with Disadvantaged Parents and Their Children*. New Haven, CT: Yale University Press, 1983.

Terr, L. Forbidden games: post-traumatic child's play. *Journal of the American Academy of Child Psychiatry* 20:741-760, 1981.

Vygotsky, L. Play and its role in the mental development of the child. In J. Bruner, A. Jolly and K. Sylva, eds., *Play: Its Role in Development and Evolution*. New York: Basic Books, 1976.

Werner, E.E. and R.S. Smith. *Vulnerable But Invincible: A Longitudinal Study of Resilient Children and Youth*. New York: McGraw-Hill, 1982.

Wohl, A. and B. Kaufman. *Hidden Screams and Silent Cries*. New York: Brunner/Mazel, 1985.

8

The School Nurse as a Student Bereavement Counselor

Eileen Stevenson, RN, CSN

For a student who has suffered a loss and is bereaved, to have to go to school can be a very uncomfortable experience. Often, other students don't know that someone in their classmate's family has died and the bereaved person often does not know how or may not want to broadcast this information. On the other hand, when schoolmates do know that a death has occurred, the bereaved student may feel paranoid that his peers are scrutinizing him to see how he is reacting. Bereaved students may feel that this "interest" by their classmates is only morbid curiosity, not a show of sympathy or an attempt to help. As a result, it is not unusual for bereaved students to feel that there are few people at school with whom they can discuss their loss and they may not know who to turn to for help.

One staff member who is in a highly advantageous position to help bereaved students is the school nurse. Most students do not feel hostility or dislike for the school nurse. Perhaps one reason for this is that some of the emotional barriers that are present in the classroom do not come into play in the nurse's office. It is important that nurses keep the lines of communication with students free from unnecessary static because, as is evident from the following information, the school nurse has a very important role in helping bereaved students.

With all of the difficulties that students face today, they need a place where they can go when the pressure gets to be too much; a smart and caring nurse can make her office just this sort of "safe place." Because the nurse usually sees students on a one-on-one basis, they may feel more relaxed than they do in other school settings. The privacy of the nurse's office makes it easier for students to talk openly about personal problems and because of this, school nurses can get to know the person behind the student. Nurses should be willing to help students deal with a wide variety of emotional issues that they may be grappling with. They cannot and should never try to take the place of parents, but because schools act *in loco parentis*, nurses should try to be there if students need them.

In recognition of the special role that school nurses can fill, a number of contingency plans have been developed. The protocol established at River Dell Regional Schools, for example—making the school nurse an available resource for students who need help dealing with various emotional upheavals—was nationally circulated by the National Association of Secondary School Principals (Stevenson and Powers 1987). If school nurses accept this role, they must be willing to help students when necessary and to act in their behalf if students want and need this help.

The chief responsibility of school nurses is to care for the health and welfare of students. Medical care must be provided in a professional manner, and to do this effectively, a certain amount of personal distance is necessary. However, when nurses extend their roles to include the provision of emotional support, they will quickly find that they need an entirely new set of qualifications. For example, before school nurses can help others deal with loss and grief, they must first examine their own emotional state of mind regarding certain issues. For example, to be able to help others cope with the death of a loved one, nurses must attain a personal understanding of their own feelings on the topic of death. Also, nurses must have a full and thorough understanding of grief and bereavement and a knowledge of what should and what should not be done. This requires that they have a good handle on the losses they themselves have experienced and that they have come to terms with these situations. What could be worse than a bereaved student pouring her heart out about how much pain she is in because her father just died, to a nurse who is still tackling—or even worse, denying—her own problems regarding the death of her own father. A nurse's goal should be to make students trust in her and not experience confusion and disillusionment.

PROVIDING A SAFE PLACE FOR STUDENTS

Students must first feel that they can trust the nurse before they will feel comfortable enough to be open and talk to her about their problems. Methods for gaining the trust of students vary among nurses. Because students have nothing to prove to the nurse in terms of academic achievement and school nurses are not usually asked to offer their judgment regarding students' ability or behavior, nurses can get to know students on a personal level, one that is entirely outside the realm of academic performance. Certainly, this is to a nurse's advantage and her independent, nonteaching status can facilitate the kind of open and trusting relationship that can be helpful to students in need.

Oftentimes, students cannot discuss certain issues with their parents. They may need to talk to someone who is objective, someone like the school nurse. (One complicating problem is that school nurses have so much paperwork—something they have no choice but to complete—that it is extremely hard to strike the right balance between filling out forms and caring for their students. In some schools, if the nurse does not achieve this balance, her job may be in jeopardy. A sympathetic administrator can play a key role in helping the school nurse provide emotional as well as physical care to students.)

A nurse should never underestimate students' emotions; they can tell if a nurse places paperwork before a problem that to them seems like a matter of life and death. If she gives this impression, in no time students will probably write the nurse off as just another uncaring professional, and she will rapidly lose her unique position to help students who are in need. In summary, a school nurse can best provide a safe place for students who are bereaved in the following ways:

- Address physical needs in a caring and supportive way.
- Create an attractive (nonjudgmental) physical environment.
- Listen to the concerns of students (both spoken and unspoken).
- Develop a knowledge base concerning the needs of bereaved students and the behaviors they may exhibit in school settings.
- Be open to your own past pain and to the present pain and concern of your students.
- Seek administrative and staff support.
- Develop and maintain counseling skills for working with grieving students. The Association for Death Education and Counseling (ADEC) can be a valuable resource in facing this task, as can articles circulated by M.A.D.D. (Mothers Against Drunk Driving) and the National Association of School Nurses.

ANSWERING STUDENTS' QUESTIONS ABOUT THE DEATH OF A CLASSMATE

Our school was recently forced to confront the issues surrounding the death of a sixth-grade student who died suddenly when struck by a car on a Saturday. The principal used the emergency phone list and notified each of the school's staff members. On Monday, half an hour before school opened, there was a faculty meeting to discuss the situation and to decide which measures should be taken. At the regular opening exercises, the principal announced to the students that the boy had been killed suddenly and that it seemed appropriate to have a moment of silence to remember him. It was suggested to students who knew Bill to think of his special qualities that they had admired, and those who had not really known him were asked to think about someone who was still alive whose friendship they cherished. The children were then told that if they wanted to, they could bring up any questions they had during the day with the principal or the school nurse.

And students did indeed avail themselves of this opportunity. Their questions and concerns were very down-to-earth. To each of their questions we provided simple, concrete answers:

- *What is a wake?*

  A wake is a special event when people can show how they feel about the loss of someone they knew.

- *What is a casket?*

  A casket is a box that holds the body of a dead person.

- *Do I have to look at the dead body?*

  You do not have to look if you do not want to or if it makes you feel uncomfortable.

- *What should I wear to a funeral or a wake?*

  Wear something that shows respect, something you might wear to a religious service. (One student said he would wear his sweatsuit. In his case, coming from a poor family, this athletic wear represented the "best" he had. It was the way in which he could show respect and after speaking with the nurse, he felt comfortable about it.)

- *How should I act?*

  Be on your best behavior. It is all right to ask questions about what you see, or to talk about other things with your friends, but don't forget the main reason you are there is to remember and show how you feel about your classmate.

- *What should I say to Bill's parents?*

  You don't *have* to say anything. If you want to say something, just say what you remember about Bill. (We explained that sharing memories with others who loved Bill was a good way of giving a special gift.)

The students also voiced concern about Bill's parents and expressed how sad they must have felt. When they "put the shoe on the other foot," transferring these feelings to their own lives and parents, it made them think. They tried not to do or say anything that would cause their own parents sadness or worry. The children were less anxious about discussing these concerns with the nurse not only because she was not directly involved with the family but also because they saw her as someone who had faced these issues before, and therefore, knew what she was doing. Even though there was a close relationship between the nurse and the students, allowing students to feel free to ask these questions, there was still a distance because the nurse was not *their* parent. The teachers also experienced a wide range of reactions from students.

TEACHER CONCERNS

Some teachers needed to be reassured that the way they were dealing with the students was appropriate. Teachers who were effective when dealing with intellectual issues were afraid of doing something wrong and potentially hurtful to the child when approaching emotions related to grief. They did not want to be too demanding. They were also concerned that they might be enabling students to use the grief process as a means of taking advantage of the situation: "I'm too sad to work," for example.

After Bill's death, the students' visits to the principal's and nurse's office persisted for a few days. Teachers asked if this was OK and how long they should allow this to continue. Students simply wanted to talk about their feelings and to ask questions and if this access to a caring listener had been denied them, their anxiety might have made learning impossible. The nurse and administrator can serve as support for classroom teachers. Teachers want to help. They just want to be sure that what they are doing is appropriate.

THE ISSUE OF RISK

Even in the best of school settings, there is an issue of risk that must be considered. It has been said that it is no longer safe for teachers or staff to physically touch students. It is a matter of public record that in New Jersey in one year there were over 100 cases of alleged child abuse by educators. The vast majority of these accusations were found to have no substance. However, whether or not these charges have any basis in fact, the damage has already been done to one or more careers in every case.

The nurse cannot avoid "touching" students both physically and emotionally. We must remember that there is a clear line between "good" and "bad" touching of which even the youngest child is aware. It is the nurse who is often counted on to stress this difference to students. Further, an unfounded charge can be leveled at anyone, whether they have had physical contact with a student or not. As is the case with office procedure, each nurse must face this issue individually and be prepared to live with the consequences of her choice.

CONCLUSION

When I started work at my school, students were sent to the nurse's office when they were being punished. However, before I knew it, students seemed to start looking for reasons to come to my office to "talk about life"—to discuss their problems or concerns. I am hoping that the way in which I communicated with students made them want to talk to me and maybe they didn't always feel that it was such a "punishment" to have to come to my office. The way that students feel about the school nurse is determined in large part by how the nurse presents herself. By their behavior, students will make it clear whether you, as the school nurse, have made your office a place in which they feel safe enough to talk. They are the final judges.

At the end of the school year there are always fond farewells and some tears as the students move on. When I have the opportunity to see them several years later, I feel a sense of pride and awe at their development. Because I have really known these children as people, it is as if, in some small measure, they were "my children" and it always pleases me when they are doing well. They all have made quite a journey and hopefully in some small measure, the "safe place" that students found in my office helped them along the way.

REFERENCES

Fassler, J. *Helping Children Cope*. New York: Free Press, 1978.

Kavanaugh, R.E. Children's Special Needs. In P. Chaney, ed., *Dealing with Death and Dying*. Horsham, PA: Intermed, 1980.

Lochner, C. Helping ourselves to help others. *Archives of the Foundation of Thanatology* 14(1), 1986.

Schaefer, D. and C. Lyons. *How Do We Tell the Children?* New York: Newmarket Press, 1986.

Stevenson, R.G. and H.L. Powers. How to handle death in the school. *The Education Digest* 52(9), 1986.

9

Helping Elementary Schoolchildren Cope with Grief: What Teachers and Parents Should and Should Not Do

Robert G. Stevenson, EdD and Kit Wallace

When children are very young, they usually have no concept of death. However, by age 10, most psychologists and educators agree that most children have knowledge of the biological reality of death and are aware that someday they, too, will die. It is now 40 years since Maria Nagy first published her landmark work, "The Child's View of Death" in the *Journal of Genetic Psychology*. Her article discusses the stages children go through in achieving a "mature" understanding of death. Children, she explains, go through periods in which they view death as something different: first, as separation from loved ones, then as a reversible condition, a person, place or thing (as opposed to an event or concept), and finally as a biological reality. However, when a sudden death occurs, even the best theories can sometimes be difficult to put into practice and these neat stages do not always follow each other in such an organized manner. For this reason, Nagy's theory is not particularly useful for individuals who have experienced a sudden death. In fact, when a sudden death occurs, young children may be completely confused. They have probably not yet contemplated what it means to be alive, let alone dead (this can be just as true with older people). Therefore, when children must suddenly face the reality of death, it is essential that caring adults provide explanations that are appropriate to the age and developmental level of the child. Parents are the first adults to face this challenge, but as soon as the child enters school, teachers also become an important part of this process of explanation.

Chapter 4 of this book explains how death can intrude on young lives suddenly and without warning and Chapter 5 shows how death is such a large part of life for many of today's children. For this reason, it is important that teachers and parents know *beforehand* how to handle the delivery of the news of the death of a classmate and how to cope with the problems that such a death can create.

The following case history is about a kindergarten teacher whose student died in a fire. She kept a detailed account of how she and her colleagues at school handled the situation. Understandably, dealing with her young students was no easy task and it needed to be approached with extreme care. Because these were kindergarten-age children, many of whom probably didn't fully understand the meaning of death, the teacher—Kit Wallace—needed to explain the tragedy to her class with extreme care. The information provided is very useful for teachers whose class is confronted with the sudden death of a classmate. Parents, too, whether or not they have a child in a class in which a child dies, and even those parents whose own child dies, will benefit from this first-hand account.

Near Christmas, Hannah, a kindergarten student, and her younger brother were asleep in their rooms. Her parents were not at home, and she and her brother were under the care of a babysitter. Workmen were redecorating their house when a fire was suddenly discovered spreading rapidly through the building. The babysitter ran through the flames and managed to save the little boy. A painter tried to save Hannah, but he wasn't able to get through the flames, and both he and Hannah perished. Kit Wallace, Hannah's teacher, had to tell the class of youngsters about the terrible tragedy that had occurred. Some of her reactions and those of her colleagues follow:

> Oh, help! was my first thought. How I wished for someone, or some organization, to guide us. The first thing we decided to do was to send a letter to each member of Hannah's class so that the parents and children would know about the death before school started a few days after the New Year. The child's father was contacted by an associate to find out if there were any details that he wanted to pass on to the class. The family arranged for a memorial service at a nearby Episcopal church. I asked the young curate who conducted the service to come visit with the children on their first day back to school. Perhaps he could do "something"—at that time we had no clear idea of exactly what—maybe sing a song, say a prayer, maybe just talk to the children—anything to help them find a focus and a way to understand just what had happened.

Because we never know when an accident that causes a death will occur, it is important for both teachers and parents to be prepared in case such a tragedy occurs. The following guidelines can be implemented by educators and parents so that they can be prepared for the tragedy of a death of a classmate before it occurs. Of course, not everyone will have the advantage of knowing the following information *beforehand*; however, it is equally useful to those who suddenly find themselves in this situation and need immediate help.

POST-DEATH PROCEDURES

Know What Local Support Systems Exist

Many areas have developed organizations with programs that provide assistance for just this type of situation. There are, for example, The Center and Helping Children in Crisis, both of which work with schools in the New Jersey and New York City metropolitan area. The Good Grief Program helps schools in the Boston area and there are countless other programs across the country that offer similar help. Schools and concerned adults should learn where they are and how they can be contacted should the need arise.

Inform the Class as Soon as Possible When a Death Occurs

The National Association of Secondary School Principals has established a system that can be used in all schools when there is a need to inform the school community of a death. The news will be painful no matter what is done; however, prior planning for such an event can help keep that pain to a minimum because it will prevent mistakes—mistakes that are usually well-intentioned, but which could make a child's reaction much worse. This is important for children of all ages. It has been decided by The Association, among others, that classmates should be notified as soon after the death as possible. (A detailed discussion of the teacher's role in helping elementary school students cope with the death of a classmate can be found in *Instructor* magazine [Cohn 1987].) One particularly anxious parent called to say that he was not going to tell his child himself. He felt that it would be better for all of the children to be told when they were all together in school.

Home and School Should Work Together

Myra Lipman, a member of the New York Parents League, states in Chapter 12 that schools cannot assume the entire responsibility for a child's death education, but neither can they ignore the matter entirely. There should be effective home-school communication so that parents know what information is being presented to their children at school. Successful death education courses exist across the country for helping concerned parents with any specific needs they may have. The school can also point parents toward appropriate support groups in their community with whom they can communicate for further help. Wallace tells us:

On the first day [that the children were] back in school, I met with parents while the teachers met with the children. I wanted to let the parents know what the teachers were saying to the children and to share information I had gotten from [a therapist] and from a teacher that she had referred me to.

Parents Should Not Hesitate to Confront
the Issue of Death with Their Children

Some children will feel more comfortable discussing the topic of death with their parents who have known them all their lives and certainly are better acquainted with their personal experiences than any outside "expert." This is an area where the home and school should reinforce each other. Both parties should try to help the children involved, because parents can sometimes do what schools cannot and vice versa. It is usually appropriate for parents to tell their children what they believe about afterlife and to at least let their children know what they believe in; whether they expect their children to follow their faith is another issue altogether. This type of discussion cannot be conducted in a school setting without the risk of violating the respective beliefs held by the many different faiths of the students (or at least those of their parents). Students can speak of their beliefs when they are at school, but this is not the same as a discussion with a caring parent who can answer the "Whys?" that often follow such explanations. One of the best examples of such a parent-child talk can be seen in the David Susskind film, *All the Way Home* (1964). In this film, a mother tries, with varying degrees of success, to explain to her little boy what death is as they discuss the illness of his grandfather. This film can be a valuable tool to facilitate discussion in a classroom or home setting. It may be difficult to obtain a print of this film, so a next-best source would be the book on which the film is based, *A Death in the Family* by James Agee, available though Bantam Paperbacks.

Children Should Not Be Deprived of the Sight of Adult Grief

The experience of seeing their parents openly grieve can be an extremely effective way for children to learn how to deal with the sadness of death. Parents can show their children that grief hurts, tears are normal and that emotions need not be avoided. Such an experience can reduce both children's and parents' fears.

Silence is the Worst Enemy

Social critic Phyllis Schlafly has been quoted as saying, "Anything [teachers] do is apt to be far worse than doing nothing at all" (Bordewich 1988). It has been shown that silence can magnify the feelings of helplessness, hopelessness and loneliness, all of which are part of grief reactions and can add feelings of worthlessness (Stevenson 1987). In this way "silence" can strengthen all of the often confused emotions felt by many youths who attempt suicide. The silence which Ms. Schlafly sees as preferable can cause children to feel as if they must confront the topics of dying, death and the feelings they generate all by themselves.

> The teachers talked to the children about Hannah and had them draw pictures and write letters to her family. All of the children drew pictures of red-headed angels or Hannah looking like "Sleeping Beauty."

Be Aware of the Power of Nonverbal Communication

All of us should be aware of the many different ways in which we communicate. Our attempts to speak with children can be influenced by location (where we speak), time (when we speak) and space (distance between us when we speak). We should be aware of all of these factors because they have an impact on our communications with children.

> The teachers decided to keep Hannah's "cubby" as it had been—dance shoes, smock and all. Some days later, one child was seen showing Hannah's shoes to her mother. It was important for the children to have something of Hannah's to hang on to for a while. It was important for the teachers, too, to see a visual confirmation of their loss.

Schools Should Also Offer Support to the Parents of Students

Because of its death education program, River Dell High School in New Jersey regularly receives calls from parents and organizations throughout the area. They are seeking assistance in providing help for bereaved children and families. It is clear that schools do not have all the answers to any problem, but they do have information that many parents find useful. When the school can act as a clearinghouse, there is no need to reinvent the wheel. Kit Wallace describes her meeting with the parents of her class:

> I told them not to be surprised if their children were sick more often than usual. That they might even speak of feeling some "blame" for the death if they had a spat with her. Actually, Hannah was the sort of child whom everyone loved. Even though she was very talented and was perhaps the best reader in the class, no one seemed to have been jealous of her. We spoke of the possibility of nightmares and I said we'd keep the conversations and formal support going at school for as long as was necessary. The parents stayed at school for a long time that day—needing each other and the support that comes with togetherness.

In Times of Bereavement, It is Important for Children to Feel They Have Some Control Over Their Lives

With one part of life "out of control" because of a death, children need to be able to feel there is still control in other areas of life. It is fairly common for school children to attend class immediately after a loss and to try to go through the day in as normal a manner as possible so that they can feel they still have control over this part of life. However, to imply to children that they should try to behave as if nothing out of the ordinary has happened after a death when they do not wish to do so usually tends to remove the very feelings of control that need to be instilled. The individual child is *always* more important than the general policy. Wallace wrote:

> After its unusual start, the rest of the school day was just as it had always been for the children—filled with reading and math. It seemed as though everyone believed that a familiar routine would be best for everyone.

Memorials and Ritual Can Be Very Important After a Death

Memorials need not be traditional or formal, but it is important to show children that a death does not occur without other changes taking place as well. By taking the time to acknowledge and mark this change with some type of ritual, we confirm that this change has happened and that the child's reactions to that change are important and justified. If teachers and parents deny that a change has taken place, don't be surprised when children adopt coping mechanisms that attempt to make it seem as if nothing has happened.

> I told the parents that we had arranged for an Episcopal priest to come to school at the end of the day to perform a short memorial and that their children could attend if they wanted to. Parents were kept informed of all that was taking place so that they could be the primary support for their children.

> The priest arrived at the school in the afternoon. He was a casual person, more at home in lay dress than in clerical garb. He sat on one of those little chairs and the children sat on the floor around him. He told them that it had been hard to lead the service at the church because he had not known Hannah— could they tell him about her? How tall was she? The children pointed to a classmate about the same height. They then told of Hannah's red hair, her purple down-filled coat, her ready laugh, her good reading, her likes and her dislikes. He helped them put their images of Hannah into words. Then he strummed his guitar and taught them the song, "Kumbaya, Lord: Kumbaya." They all sang with hand motions and then they added two verses of their own: "We Miss Hannah, Lord" and "We Love Hannah, Lord."

> To conclude on a positive note, he asked the children to tell him something that they were thankful for that day. He set the tone by saying that he was thankful for being with them. They said they were thankful for family, for

God, for having known Hannah, thankful that she'd been at their school and that she had been their friend. After singing one more song with the priest, the children sang some of their songs for him.

In the lower school assembly a week later, a prayer from the Presbyterian Prayer Book was read and the kindergartners led the older girls in their song, complete with hand motions. This served as a sort of memorial for the benefit of the older girls. They, too, had been affected by the tragedy which had taken this funny little girl from them.

The letters that the girls wrote were very touching. After the writing, the children talked about Hannah. One girl asked the nurse if she knew that they had Hannah in a box over at the church. She wondered if it had a cushion. Another girl told her mother that Hannah had died, but she wondered when Hannah would be coming back to school.

Help Children at Their Individual Developmental Levels

In any group, young children will have reached a variety of developmental levels. This mix is more pronounced in elementary schools. A "formula" approach toward conveying information may help some children but will miss, or even confuse, others. The classroom teacher plays a key role in listening to the questions of each child and seeing that an answer is provided in a manner appropriate to the developmental level of that child.

A Child's Death: Impact on Teachers

To say that the death of a student has a clear impact on that child's teacher is only to belabor the obvious. However, teachers in the roles of caregiver and educator may have difficulty taking time to tend to their own needs. When a child dies, teachers often spend such long hours helping their students and the parents and also seeking personal training that they often have little room for their own grief. It is important that the school administration acknowledge the fact that the death of a student places a great deal of strain on teachers; therefore, the administration needs to take time to acknowledge that a change has occurred for staff as well as for students.

Time passed and we got through the tragedy and its aftermath. It would have been easier had we not had to reinvent the wheel. If there was one area we did not address, it was to help the teachers with their heartache. All three of the teachers of the young children were deeply affected. The youngest teacher was often out sick and experienced episodes of depression for a long time. Another may have suffered a nervous breakdown. They ran their classes well enough, but they suffered.

REVIEWING THE MAIN POINTS

In looking back, the following points should be kept in mind when attempting to help students deal with the death of someone close to them:

1. Before the need arises, find what local support systems exist in your area and how and who to contact.
2. When a death occurs in the school community, inform the class and talk about it. Silence can be very damaging.
3. Because parents are a child's primary support, schools should do all they can to assist parents at this difficult time.
4. Children are helped most when home and school cooperate.
5. In the long run, being silent about a loss is more likely to hurt a child than speaking about it in an open and caring manner.
6. Nonverbal communication can sometimes convey more than words alone. Both methods of communication should be used by teachers and parents.
7. When memorials and rituals are held following a death, they acknowledge that a change has occurred and this in turn validates children's feelings of loss. Also, memorials and rituals let children know that when someone dies, life does not just continue as if nothing had happened and that each of us is important.
8. With proper preparation, schools can offer support to students of all ages, but each child must be helped in a manner appropriate to the child's developmental level.
9. When a death occurs (especially an accident), a person's feelings of control over life are put in serious jeopardy, so it is important to affirm those areas in which the person still has control.
10. A student's death has an impact, not only on other students, but on teachers too. School administrators at all levels must remember to make time to help the helpers.

RECOMMENDATIONS

Children who have suffered the death of a relative or a friend clearly have special needs. A well-known psychologist once said of her own grief that knowing why you hurt won't make you hurt less. It should be added, however, that knowing the reason for your pain can keep you from hurting more than you have to. If this is true for adults, it is even more so for bereaved children. To keep the hurt from being worse than it has to be, schools and parents have found it helpful to create a plan to respond to such a situation *before* the need arises. If this is done, plans are formed when the pressures of time and emotional distress are at a minimum and will therefore probably be better composed. School policies, staff training programs and even appropriate readings for use by (or with) students can be put in place in advance of need. There are many things that can be done by both parents and educators *now* to help children when they are faced with the need to cope with a death. If, as a parent or educator, you had been faced with the situation of Hannah's death, what would you have done? If you are able to take the time now to think of an answer to that question, it may be the first step toward helping a child in the future. To approach this type of situation before it happens—one that can happen when you least expect it—will ensure that you will do a better job of helping your student or child cope than you will if you must deal with these issues in the midst of the chaos that so often surrounds a death.

SUGGESTED READINGS

Bordewich, F.M. Mortal fears. *The Atlantic,* February 1988.

(A balanced discussion of the pros and cons of actual courses on death education which take a proactive approach rather than waiting to react to a crisis.)

Cohn, J. *I Had a Friend Named Peter.* New York: William Morrow, 1987.

(This book is intended to be used by parents as a support for those who may need to help their child deal with the death of a friend.)

Cohn, J. The grieving student, *Instructor,* January 1987.

(This article discusses the role of the elementary school teacher in helping a child to understand death and grief.)

Fassler, J. *Helping Children Cope: Mastering Stress Through Books and Stories.* New York, The Free Press, 1978.

(Joan Fassler's book examines children's literature by topic and age and is considered by many parents to be a very important aid in helping them select books with which to help their children deal with developmental problems, including death, in an age-appropriate way.)

Levin, S. Lessons in Death. *The Dallas Morning News,* April 17, 1988, Section F.

(This is a beautifully written, balanced discussion of the growing area of death education in public schools.)

Nagy, M. The Child's View of Death. In H. Feifel, ed., *The Meaning of Death,* New York: McGraw-Hill, 1959.

(This brief article gives an excellent overview of the developmental process children go through in reaching a mature understanding of death.)

Stevenson, R.G. The Fear of Death in Childhood. In J. E. Schowalter et al., eds., *Children and Death: Perspectives from Birth Through Adolescence*, New York: Praeger, 1987.

(This article discusses the differences between fear and anxiety and the role that each plays in the child's understanding of death. It also presents implications for a school curriculum.)

Stevenson, R.G. and H.L. Powers. How to handle death in the school. *Education Digest*, May 1987.

(This protocol has been adopted throughout the United States and Canada and can provide a good starting point for teachers and administrators who wish to establish guidelines for dealing with such an event.)

Stevenson, R.G., ed. *What Will We Do? Preparing a School Community to Cope with Crises*. Amityville, New York: Baywood, 1994.

(This recent work helps schools to build a support network before crises occur and to draw upon all of the resources available in the community.)

10

Crisis Intervention Teams:
A Model for Schools

Jack Kamins, PsyD and Henry Lipton, PhD

The youth of today are frequently exposed to tragic incidents involving violence and death. In response to the growing opinion that schools should help students deal with the problems that result from these incidents, the Region IV Division of Special Education of the Board of Education of the City of New York has trained teams of clinicians (consisting of a psychologist, a social worker and a clinical supervisor) to serve as a resource to elementary schools in times of crisis.

The purpose of the teams is to serve as consultants to the administration, to work with the school staff and students and to help school-based support teams and guidance counselors when a traumatic event occurs that affects students. The teams are prepared to be deployed to schools immediately whenever the need arises. The teams provide both direct and indirect service to students and faculty and they also teach school staff how to handle the aftermath of a loss situation once the crisis intervention team has left the site. However, should the need arise, the team members remain available for consultation, both in person and by phone.

TRAINING

Region IV consists of seven school districts encompassing the eastern half of Brooklyn and the entire borough of Staten Island, and serves approximately 200,000 elementary and junior high school students. For approximately 6 weeks, one team from each district and an additional team from the regional office (24 clinicians in total) underwent four sessions of approximately 14 hours of intensive training. The training was conducted by Dr. Janice Cohn, a noted expert and author in the area of the childhood grief process. The following is an outline of the four training sessions that were offered to the clinicians.

Session I

1. Participants explored their own feelings and experiences regarding death and loss. Particular emphasis was placed on remembering personal childhood experiences with loss that they may have had and how they reacted and coped with feelings of grief.
2. Participants discussed previous situations in which children in schools were confronted with death and loss:
   a. What was done?
   b. What problems or frustrations were encountered?
   c. What questions did children of various ages typically ask?

Session II

1. Research and clinical findings regarding how children are affected by death were explored. Journal and newspaper articles and extensive bibliographies on these topics were distributed.
2. The impact of a child's age, sex, culture and socioeconomic status on the grieving process was examined.
3. Differences between normal and abnormal grieving were discussed. Four stages that children must go through to achieve successful healing were conceptualized. These were:
   a. Understanding what happened
   b. Being allowed to grieve
   c. Commemorating
   d. Going on (investing in new relationships)
4. Also discussed was how to identify children in the school who seemed to be at particular psychological risk. Examples include:
   a. Siblings
   b. Children who have experienced a recent loss
   c. Children with previous emotional problems
   d. Children who feel they have some responsibility for the death
5. The crisis team's role in the school was conceptualized within a consultative framework.

Session III

1. The consultative model of intervention was outlined. Strategies for assisting the school community to deal with the aftermath of a death were explored through various scenarios and role-playing.

2. A principal and teacher from a school that had recently worked through a crisis situation discussed how they felt our teams could be the most useful. This included effective ways for the team to gain entree and specific areas of need where the team could be of most assistance.

Session IV

1. A review of the literature and research on childhood and adolescent suicide was presented. Risk factors and symptomatology were explored. A video on teen suicide was viewed and then discussed.
2. An examination was made of children's increasing exposure to violence. The effects of modeling and its use by children as a means of conflict resolution were studied.
3. A general review was conducted along with group feedback.
4. An end of the year meeting was scheduled for the sharing of field experiences and the evaluation of the program's effectiveness.

IMPLEMENTATION OF THE CRISIS INTERVENTION TEAM MODEL

A conference was held with community school district superintendents and their designees to launch our Crisis Intervention Project. The unique contributions that clinicians can make in assisting schools to deal with traumatic events were outlined. Each representative was provided with a packet of information that included the following:

1. Hotline numbers and contact persons from the Committee on Special Education for each school district. (Backup numbers and contacts at the Regional Office were provided as well in case the local team could not be reached.)
2. Recent articles from newspapers and journals highlighting not only the level of incidence of traumatic events, but how schools can best serve as resources of support for the children.

An overview of the Crisis Intervention Project and its range of services was outlined at the conference. District representatives and crisis team leaders discussed how the project could best be implemented in each district. After a question-and-answer period, plans were made for future district follow-up that included presentations at district meetings for principals, workshops for other school-based support team members and guidance personnel, as well as overviews for parent groups. Brochures were also prepared for distribution to the school principals who worked within the region (approximately 180).

SUMMARY OF CRISIS TEAM INVOLVEMENT

In the 3 months following the inception of the project, our crisis intervention team was utilized at least 16 times. Because of the uniqueness of our training, our services were employed by two other regions of the Division of Special Education, the Division of High Schools and a private nursery school.

Our teams provided support to schools in six incidents in which children died. On two of these occasions, children were run over by cars in front of their classmates. In another incident, a student committed suicide on school grounds and this was followed by serious attempts at suicide by four of his classmates. Also, after a child drowned during a class trip, we provided service to the two schools whose students were on the trip.

Crisis intervention teams were also utilized for other reasons. There were two instances when parents died while their children were at home, one of which was front-page news for several days. This wide coverage made it particularly hard on the children. It was also an especially hard case for intervention because the two siblings involved attended two different schools in two different school districts. Our teams also provided service to schools where staff members died unexpectedly from illness, when a child was attacked by a pit bull in front of his classmates and when a teacher was slashed in a school lavatory during a robbery attempt. These cases have been mentioned not for shock value, but to illustrate the tremendous need our school children have for this type of clinical support.

Upon reaching the school, the teams generally perform the following range of activities:

1. Consult with the administrative staff
   a. Explore what has already been done
   b. Establish the facts surrounding the incident and find out what information has been conveyed to others
2. Consult with and serve as facilitator for the school's support personnel
3. Help the school identify "at-risk" groups of students
4. Help the school compose a letter to parents to discuss levels of possible parental involvement in crisis intervention
5. Conduct group counseling sessions for staff and students
6. Conduct individual counseling sessions for staff and students
7. Help the school plan to properly commemorate deaths when appropriate
8. Put the school in touch with local community resources
9. Perform follow-up as necessary

CASE STUDY

The following case illustrates the full scope of services that crisis intervention teams can provide.

"Couple Murdered in Apartment" read the headline in the local newspaper. Two surviving children found the dead bodies of their parents. One
of the children, a 7-year-old girl (who we will call Sarah) was a student in
an elementary school in the local school district. On the day following the
murders, the crisis team in the district was contacted by the principal of
Sarah's school in an effort to help the children in Sarah's first-grade class,
as well as their teacher, work through issues raised by the death and the
circumstances surrounding it.

What could be more devastating to a child than being in her own home,
in her own bed, asleep with her parents in the next room, when suddenly
her life is turned upside down by the murder of her parents? As well, the
effect that an incident like this could have on Sarah's classmates, many of
whom were probably wondering when something like this would happen
to them, could be very serious.

The crisis team was called upon to help deal with the issues that these
murders had on Sarah's classmates. First, a plan of action had to be
developed with the school administration and the classroom teacher. Since
the principal had initially contacted the team, there was full cooperation
and easy access to all parts of the school. A meeting was held with key
people and the following plan of action was developed as a result:

1. A letter prepared by the principal was to be sent to the parents of the
    children in Sarah's class alerting them to what happened and advising
    them to be aware of possible changes in their child's behavior. Sug-
    gestions were offered on how to deal with these changes, should they
    occur.
2. A session would be held with the students in Sarah's class.

The principal was willing to offer whatever she could to help make the
school function again in a normal manner and as soon as possible. She
prepared the letter and it was sent home with the students at the end of the
day. The principal was willing to offer whatever services she could to assist
the team in meeting with both the teacher and the class. For example, she
agreed to take over the first-grade class during the time the team met with her.

Meeting with the Teacher

Mrs. A., the teacher, was extremely upset about the incident and was
preoccupied with two issues in particular. One was her personal concern

for Sarah. The other was her uncertainty about her own ability to deal with her students' reactions to the death of Sarah's parents, the impact it had upon them and whether she could deal with these matters. Mrs. A. admitted that on the day following the murders, her students had asked her many questions about what had happened and why it had occurred. She said that in an attempt to keep them focused on their school work, she kept her responses to their questions short. She noticed that throughout the day that her students were becoming increasingly restless and as the day progressed, some of them even started to become physically aggressive. Their behavior made her worry that she had not handled the situation well.

As a result of her concerns, the members of the crisis intervention team met with the teacher. The school-based support team also attended as observers. They would have the responsibility of follow-up in the school after the crisis team had completed its work and left, so it was important for them to be present.

After some discussion, Mrs. A. realized that she had been reluctant to deal with her students' questions because she was fearful that she would say something to the children that would only upset them further. Moreover, she had not yet had the opportunity to resolve her own reactions to this particular situation.

The team discovered that Mrs. A. had in fact been able to offer a great deal of support to the young students, but she was being asked questions that she herself could not answer: "Why did this happen to these people?" and, by implication, "Could this happen to me?"

Classroom Meeting

The class consisted of approximately 30 children from extremely diverse racial, religious and cultural backgrounds. When the team entered the classroom, they were introduced by the principal. The principal had been covering the class for Mrs. A. so that the teacher could brief the team in person. When Mrs. A. returned to the room with the team, the principal introduced the team members as friends who had come to talk about what happened to Sarah's parents. The whole class, with the exception of Sarah, was present. The principal was leading a discussion that had veered onto the topic of drugs. The students felt this was one of the areas of speculation as to why the murders may have occurred. Even though these children were very young (5 and 6), they were aware that something terrible had happened and they wanted to talk about it.

The members of the team—a psychologist and a social worker—worked along with Mrs. A. by situating themselves in different places in the classroom. They asked the students some general questions to break the ice: "Do you have any idea why we are here talking to you?" The incident had received so much coverage by the news media in the 24 hours since it occurred that all of the students had some knowledge of what had happened.

The greatest concern the students expressed was for Sarah's safety. In fact, there was an underlying tone among the students that seemed to question whether the little girl was still alive. Because Sarah may have had some knowledge of the people responsible for killing her parents, she was in protective custody and therefore had not been seen by anyone in school since the murders. Her classmates expressed a desire to do something to help Sarah. They wanted to give her tangible items, such as food, dolls and jewelry. Implicit in these feelings were the questions: "Who is taking care of her?" and "Is she being fed?"

At this point, the principal left the classroom to attend to other activities and it seemed a propitious time to break the class into smaller groups, each led by one of the three people from the crisis team. The classroom teacher, Mrs. A., now felt more confident in her ability to help her students and led one of the groups herself. The psychologist and social worker led the other two groups. The small-group format allowed the children who were unable or unwilling to speak in the larger group an opportunity to share their feelings and concerns. Small groups also made it easier to identify children who might be at a high risk for further difficulty later on. A number of students continued to raise questions about why or how such a thing could have happened to "good" parents. We could only support their concerns and suggest that what had occurred was very unusual and that there was little likelihood that it would happen again, or to them.

The children were trying to gain control and make sense of the irrational things that happen in this world. In one group, the discussion focused on what the children would do when they grew up. This may well have carried the double message of "I *will* grow up!" and "I will become capable of caring for myself." It was ascertained that one little boy who appeared extremely agitated lived in the same building one floor below the couple that was murdered. He believed that he had heard the shots that had killed the parents. Furthermore, his family had encouraged Sarah's family to move into the building. Our follow-up team was notified of this student and of children who were close to Sarah and her family and about several other students in the class who had experienced losses due to death.

The small-group sessions along with the follow-up by the school's team helped the students in Sarah's class and her teacher work through a great deal of their immediate anxiety. However, it became clear that one important element was still missing that would help provide closure; the children needed to see Sarah again. Because of the circumstances of the deaths, Sarah had to remain in protective custody and was eventually placed with other family members outside of the community. However, with the help of the police we were able have Sarah brought into the class for a party at the end of the school term. When the children were finally able to see their classmate and exchange gifts, a terrifying incident began to close and the children were able to begin to move on with their lives.

CONCLUSIONS

We feel that the model that has been established in Region IV for both training and service delivery has been extremely successful. From the feedback received, it appears that through the training and prompt intervention, a crisis team can be very effective and may even save lives. We have expanded our training since the early days of the program and similar programs have now been established in other school systems.

11

Impressions from an Englishman on Death Education in the United States

David Willcock

Several years ago, I traveled from England to New Jersey to film a 50-minute documentary for BBC television. The documentary, called "The Facts of Death," was aired as part of the Everyman series and was shown in Britain, Canada and Australia in 1988-89. It was presented on American public broadcasting stations in 1993-95. It was the first and, as far as I know, remains the only treatment of the subject of death education on British television. The show reflects the realization of the importance of educating children about death.

Journalists have the advantage of approaching a subject with a fresh eye. Personally, I was reporting on a subject that I was no expert on; I came from outside the sphere of American education in general and death studies in particular. I offer my first impressions with the hope that they may be of use to those who teach or study death education.

My road to Oradell, New Jersey began in Battyeford, Yorkshire where I studied for the Anglican priesthood. I was not ordained, but in the pastoral training I received, there was a great deal of emphasis on loss and bereavement. Kübler-Ross's work *On Death and Dying* was standard course material. I used to go visit the newly bereaved with the clergy who made funeral arrangements. I sat with the dying who were tucked away in the corner rooms of hospitals where they were least visible to others. In short, I came face-to-face with the blind eye that society turns to the universal fact of death. My work since has often reflected an interest in the ways in which the taboo of death is exposed and the efforts people have made toward helping others come to terms with loss due to death.

The idea for "The Facts of Death" came from the program editor who flicked a copy of *The Atlantic* magazine across my desk. She indicated a fascinating investigative article that contained an idea that no one I spoke with had ever heard of before—death education. The most alluring parts of the article were the tales of excesses and abuses that this new subject had seemed to provoke: lurid stories of how schools make children lie in caskets so they can "imagine" what it "feels like" to be dead; school trips to the city morgue; lessons in sepulchral gloom given by teachers who were probably doing nothing but off-loading their own hang-ups and inhibitions about death to their students. This would be excellent material for a documentary if we could find real evidence to film.

There is a long (and a not altogether honorable) tradition in Britain of smirking at American innovations and eccentricities, particularly things that originate on the West Coast. This is especially true regarding American attitudes and rituals concerning death. Evelyn Waugh's *The Loved One* and Jessica Mitford's *The American Way of Death* were recommended to me as compulsory reading by others when they heard about the program we were planning on doing. I must admit that my first opinion was that death education was another wacky aberration from abroad. Educators in America seem to have identified that most people have trouble coping with death—but it also seemed that their "remedy" of "teaching" children in school (including those who are very young) was possibly misguided and maybe even dangerous. Initially, we planned to do a satire of the American attitude toward death, lumping death education with the ghoulish cryonicists in California who carry the denial of death to the absolute extreme, and including a look at the phenomenon of pet morticians.

That, however, was in the first stage of planning. After just a few preliminary telephone calls, it became clear to me that this was not a wacky story at all. Apparently, there was some evidence of the abuses mentioned above, but it was clear that these practices were not characteristic of the American death education movement. The first people to admit that these abuses had taken place were death educators themselves who were anxious that their own credibility not be damaged by a handful of spectacularly inept teachers. The fact that we could not find significant examples of these incidents speaks for itself; it is easier to create an impression in an article by citing a number of isolated instances than it is to prove on film that these practices occur by showing such abuses actually happening. It soon became clear that death education deserved to be treated as a serious academic and educational discipline. Armed with this understanding, I began to explore the American phenomenon of teaching school children about death.

The first impression I got was that there was confusion over the extent and nature of death studies. It was difficult to see death education as a homogeneous entity. The term "death education" seemed more and more like an inclusive name for a belief—a common approach to the question of which subjects should be included in a school curriculum. Although the theories and published works in the field were well known to most of us, the practical application of theory in high schools throughout the United States appeared shrouded in mystery. There seemed to be little communication between each state and between school boards on whether the subject should be taught as a subject within other disciplines or treated as a separate subject. There seemed to be little communication or agreement on the percentage of schools that offered death education to their students; few of the academics I spoke to were willing to even hazard a guess at this number or which states had most firmly established the discipline as a real part of the curriculum. There have been attempts to collate information on the spread of the subject, but these have been conducted for the most part by death educators themselves and, as a result, though certainly not falsified, their opinions are perhaps subject to idealism or optimism.

I also discovered that incorporated into death education are suicide awareness programs that have sprung up in an attempt to reduce the frightening increase in the incidence of adolescent suicide. Suicide awareness and death education, however, are not synonymous. Death education has far broader aims. It can be misleading when any topic even remotely connected with death is included under the umbrella of death education.

I do not mean to imply that the fragmental and independent growth of death education is a bad thing. The subject is—and should be—highly personal in its presentation. To try to straitjacket this groundswell into a rigorous orthodoxy with strict definitions and narrow curricula would destroy its strengths and deny its essential nature. However, it is important to draw some broad lines of reference in order to present to the unconverted a convincing case for including death education in the curriculum of all schools.

The need for points of reference is especially clear in light of the intense opposition that the topic of death education has aroused. Personally, I was not impressed by the opposition. Although they are vociferous, they seem to possess little ammunition other than hysteria and hearsay. Phyllis Schlafly's conservative cable television show,"The Eagle Forum," was unable to provide any instances of abuse that had occurred in death education classes other than those mentioned in *The Atlantic*, nor were they able to point us to a single school in America where those abuses are still taking place. Instead, the opponents seemed to object to the proposition that the subject of death be taught to school children at all. This controversial subject is ammunition for those who make it their work to assault the education system. Ironically, because of their irrationality on the subject of death education, the opponents may well turn out to be death education's greatest allies. Educators in favor of teaching this subject must prevent opponents from gaining the high ground and setting the agenda with their allegations about the problems of teaching death to children. The supporters of death education that I was aware of seemed reticent about starting a discussion about the *benefits* of death education; instead, they approached the topic defensively by trying to state what it is *not*, rather than promoting its positive points.

My own personal experience with death education was far from sensational. With a camera crew in tow, I attended two classes in death education taught by Dr. Robert Stevenson at River Dell High School in Oradell, New Jersey, as well as two classes at a grammar school in New York's North Bronx that was participating in an experimental program funded by the New York City Board of Education.

SECONDARY SCHOOL DEATH EDUCATION

Robert Stevenson has been teaching a death education course in one form or another at River Dell since 1972. The one-semester course he created as an elective for 11th and 12th graders is entitled "Contemporary Issues of Life and Death." It is now open to 10th graders as well. The course was developed and promoted with the consent and support of the staff and the parents of students who took the course. Actually, I was surprised at the extent of their cooperation. For the purposes of presenting a balanced program, I wanted the arguments against death education to be advanced by a local opponent. It is usually possible to find at least one parent in a school who disagrees with most parts of school life—the type that finds fault even with the color scheme of the front entrance. It is a testament to the way Robert Stevenson has instituted his course that we were unable to find one single parent who refused to let their child take the course. A researcher who had been dispatched to America in advance of our main production team telephoned back in despair because of her inability to find "the opposition." (We ended up having to resort to interviewing a number of local pressure groups who had no direct contact with River Dell.) An *argumentum ex nihilo* is understandably suspect, so we augmented it with our first-hand and objective impression of the course.

The students at River Dell are given an extensive curriculum that covers many aspects of death. The course is preceded by a test that assesses student's vulnerability to what can be a highly charged subject. The course proper includes sections on coping with loss, definitions of death and associated philosophical and ethical implications of these definitions, the five stages of grief, rituals of death and rites of passage, and a discussion about life after death. Death is examined in its many forms—from a purely medical perspective to a literary and an artistic interpretation. The classes we attended depend in large part on the input of the students who are encouraged to discuss with the class their subjective experiences with issues related to death. The classes we attended were concerned in large part with rites of passage such as funerals. In addition to discussing the philosophical importance of marking the times and places of the deaths of friends and relatives, students were given the opportunity to talk about funerals they were not allowed to attend and the deaths they were not told about until far after the fact. It was a chance for students to voice in safe surroundings, among trusted classmates, any unconscious feelings of resentment they may have. In spite of the presence of the camera, many students spoke openly. Others were silent. There were no feelings of uneasiness and the teacher did not need to coerce discussion among students. The education classes at River Dell made the production team, who were initially skeptical about the subject, aware of how important death education is and what it is trying to accomplish.

YOUNG CHILDREN AND DEATH EDUCATION

The other example we saw of death education in operation was, in my opinion, more dubious. At the public school we visited in Co-op City, New York, children as young as first graders were taught about death. The experimental course was designed by Dr. Janice Cohn for the New York City Board of Education. Dr. Cohn (also a contributor to this book) teaches the course at different schools, although this particular death education class is also taught at these schools by their own regular teachers. The lessons taught in primary school and, as Dr. Cohn hopes, eventually at a pre-school level, are meant explain to children that most all of the varying emotions they have when someone close to them dies—even the death of a pet—should not be considered abnormal, that most everyone feels some form of loss, even though it may be displayed in various ways. Also stressed to the students is that it's important for them to reach out to others when they are confused or frightened. Dr. Cohn believes that an ideal approach is to use the prepared lessons in response to an actual death that one child may want to talk about, one that might then encourage other children to reveal any hidden anxieties they may have. However, my impression is that the lessons go beyond this. It seems that oftentimes the subject of death is brought up in a way and at a time when some of the children may not wish—or may not be ready—to consider the subject.

The two classes I saw in New York were given to 6-year-olds and 9-year-olds. There were about 25 pupils in each class—surely too many for a single teacher to be able to watch for important individual reactions to this sensitive subject. The first class taught to the younger children took the form of a story about a cat named Barney who dies. This provided an invitation to the young students to talk about their own experiences with the death of pets or relatives. The class finished with the children drawing pictures of these experiences: among others, there was a drawing of a dead goldfish in a bowl and a grandfather's funeral. The second class was asked to write answers to three questions that the teacher wrote on the board. The questions were about the children's perceptions of death, such as What is death? (there is no right or wrong answer), and questions about their own experiences of loss. The pupils were then asked to read aloud what they had written.

It was instructive to hear the young children's responses. They were certainly willing to talk about death, and were sometimes even entertaining. Some common misapprehensions came to the fore ("Death is a horrible thing, but I think it won't be so bad if you can come back again"). In my opinion, the lessons didn't seem to do any harm. They were taught by a class teacher who knows her students and they in turn know and trust her. However, I have my doubts about how much can really be achieved in classes such as this one, comprised of such young children. Students in the upper grades of high school are more skilled in analyzing and, to some extent, objectifying personal experience. They can switch with little difficulty from theoretical discussion about death and its psychological effects to the emotional repercussions of death in their own lives. Very young children cannot deal with the abstract in the same way. They sometimes have only a tenuous grasp on concepts such as past and future, reality and fantasy. In addition to that, their emotional reactions to death are rarely articulated at the time a death occurs and as a result, their after-the-fact feelings are often much more difficult to express. As well, if a death occurred sometime in these students' past, it means that they were *very* young and this would also complicate their ability to understand death. This is why I think it is ineffectual to have very young children express their feelings of loss from death. Moreover, an emotional response to a loss is often dissociated from the actual event. A child may not show any feelings about the death of a beloved grandparent, but may appear unreasonably angry or frightened about another, unrelated incident. I fail to see how discussions about death in the classroom can help young children make such connections. As far as I could see, in discussions about their feelings, children rarely went beyond the "Yes, I was sad and I cried" stage.

Perhaps the key to teaching younger children about death is not to give them structured lessons, but instead to have teachers who are specifically trained to deal with very young children and loss maintain a sensitive vigilance and to deal with a death situation *when it occurs*. If a child comes to school distraught (or morose) because his pet hamster has died, the teacher could take that child aside (along with some friends, if it seemed appropriate) and answer any specific questions. These questions would be limited to those the children asked, as they occurred to them. The whole stated aim of the course was to answer the questions that parents ignore or are afraid to answer. The possible danger, as I see it, seems to be that by addressing 20 or more children at one time, the teachers may raise questions that *they* think children ought to be asking, while ignoring the real needs of one or more of the most vulnerable pupils.

ADOLESCENTS AND DEATH EDUCATION

From what I saw at River Dell, it is obvious that death education can serve a very important emotional function. Despite the demanding curriculum set for students, there is a noticeable fluidity about the way the actual lessons are worked through. If a particular topic provokes discussion, Dr. Stevenson allows a fairly wide margin for digression before setting the lesson on course again. This gives the students room for the sort of self-revelation that I think is important. It also means that the lessons are, to some extent, dictated by the needs and interests of students who take part in the discussion. In spite of the large number of students in the class, they do feel able to make frank confessions of bewilderment, anger and anxiety regarding grief and loss. I was struck by the emphasis on loss, rather than bereavement alone. With the rise in the divorce rate, today's children are more likely to "lose" a parent through the breakdown of a relationship than through death, and the emotional ramifications of this kind of loss can be just as traumatic as death. I was impressed when doing "vox pops" (short, off-the-cuff interviews) by how often the students would talk about the long-term impact of the course on their personal development. One student explained how, through the course, he had made sense of his feelings about his father's suicide 7 years earlier. Others spoke of how the course had given them a heightened awareness of other people's problems, and perhaps more significantly, how it had shown them a new perspective on the value of life and the importance of the quality of relationships. It is these affective elements that the students give as their reasons for appreciating the course rather than any purely cognitive achievements.

DEFINING DEATH EDUCATION

Is death education primarily an academic discipline or a pastoral undertaking? This is an important question because it has implications for the way in which death education courses are taught.

The course at River Dell was not an academic "soft option." One of the more cogent charges leveled at death education by its opponents is that it trespasses on areas usually reserved for the church or for parents and that by spending time teaching about death, the school is ignoring more important intellectual nourishment needed by students. However, the interest and enthusiasm with which the students I observed approached the psychological, anthropological and philosophical aspects of the course seem to confirm the contention of death educators that this subject can indeed enhance overall education rather than detract from it. On average, students at River Dell who had taken death education courses achieved better results at a higher academic level in that subject than they did in their other courses. This academic benefit could be invaluable if it can be carried over to children in urban settings. Their need for information about life and death issues is certainly as great as that of the River Dell students. Given the rise in violent behavior and death among urban youth, the need of city children may actually be far greater. In the example I saw, a balance was achieved. (Editor's Note: There is clearly an ongoing bond between the intellectual and emotional aspects of grief and recovery. In educating the whole person, the public schools do give greater emphasis to the academic dimension, but the affective component of death education should not be ignored.)

It must be said here that we chose River Dell because it is known to be a good example of a school that actively offers death education to students. Dr. Stevenson is held in great esteem and affection at the school. It is clear that he has that indefinable quality that makes some teachers stand out, that causes them to be remembered long after students have left school. He has a touch that enables him and his students, quite unconsciously, to transcend the generation gap and the standard student-teacher relationship without compromising respect on either side. This is not intended as a eulogy to enhance Dr. Stevenson's next pay review. I think that the natural ability to switch sensitively from listening to students' long-repressed anxiety to giving them the next week's reading homework is rare. Death educators need to be aware of a possible tension between the tasks of professor and pastor and, if necessary, choose one or the other, rather than run the risk of doing both badly. Also, by recognizing that there is a tightrope to be walked between the two poles of fact and speculation in death education, its supporters could dispel the impression that the subject is rather amorphous.

ANOTHER JURY'S VERDICT

I think it is worth mentioning the reaction of the camera crew—two men and one woman—who had been assigned to us for this one production. The subject matter was not necessarily their concern. Before they came to us, they had been working on a film for *Reader's Digest* and after we finished, they stayed in New York to do a feature on Picasso. Strictly speaking, their sole responsibility was for the technical quality of sound, lighting and framing. However, as any producer will tell you, the reaction of the crew is the acid test for any documentary. Because of the sheer variety of topics that they cover, it is harder to engage a crew's interest and to scrape through the veneer of professional cynicism than it is to appeal to the interest of the general public. They came to the first day's filming at River Dell with a fair degree of skepticism, but left, if not totally sold, then at least interested enough to become engaged in a heated conversation about death education that night. They also were very concerned about teaching very young children about death.

The documentary was aired in England and also in the United States starting in the spring of 1993. Although generally favorable, reviews reflected the same dubious feeling about teaching very young children about death that I discussed above. Unfortunately, for the sake of a couple of column inches of entertaining prose, most seized on the controversial aspects rather than considering the wisdom conveyed in the other 90 percent of the film.

Of far greater value were the letters from viewers and from groups such as those who deal with suicidal young people who praised the program and encouraged the idea of teaching children about death in Britain. One young woman wrote a moving letter expressing her regret that she herself had never been given any preparation for dealing with death and bereavement. In the last year she had suffered the deaths of her mother, her sister and a close friend. She described watching the program with great pain, but with the hope that there were others making moves to break down the dreadful isolation that society imposes on the bereaved.

CONCLUSION

It is evident that something must be done. At a deep level my experience of death education has led me to believe that it can provide some important answers; however, regarding some points, it seems to me to lack clarity. This is something that educators will have to sort out, but I was left with the feeling that something positive was definitely taking place.

It was only after returning to England that I realized that I had been thinking about Ashley Paton. Ashley was a dare-devil I knew at school when we were both 12. He spent most of his time just on the wrong side of school rules. Bigger than most of us, he was willing to stand up to gang leaders and bullies. After one summer holiday, we returned to school to hear a buzz of speculation and rumor. "Paton's dead" was the whisper in the playground. There was a terse announcement at morning prayers: Ashley Paton had been killed; the school sends its sympathies to his parents. Friends managed to piece together the whole truth. Locked out of a hotel room in Spain, Ashley had tried to climb up the outside of the building and had fallen to his death. His closest friends were allowed to attend the funeral. For the rest of us there was little to say and even less to do. Schooled in the best tradition of the British stiff upper lip, we were not encouraged to grieve or even talk about the event. Any emotion channeled itself into a sterile, angry mocking of Paton's stupidity in attempting the climb.

I went to a "good" school. It turned out many gifted students, excellently qualified for academia and the working world. Yet the gulf in personal and emotional education displayed by our school's reaction to Paton's death indicates clearly why death education can be relevant and valuable. There was a real need for help among the students at my school and absolutely no effort was made to meet it. There is a greater need for death education today and I feel this will only continue to increase in the future. AIDS and the growing incidence of suicide, random and accidental deaths and teen-age violence will make bereavement a far more common experience for young people today than it has been in the past. If death education can be true to its role and be led by the needs of the students rather than the whims of educators or the voices of critics, it will be able to provide an important resource needed to meet the emotional crisis that threatens today's youth.

REFERENCES

Cohn, J. *I Had a Friend Named Peter*. New York: William Morrow, 1988.
Kübler-Ross, E. *On Death and Dying*. New York: Macmillan, 1969.
Mitford, J.L. *The American Way of Death*. London: Hutchinson, 1973.
Waugh, E. *The Loved One*. London: Chapman and Hall, 1948.

12

Death Education in School: What Parents Want

Myra R. Lipman, PhD, Judy Sussman and Arlene Shneur

Editor's Note: The way that parents feel about the pros and cons of including death education in schools is critically important to everyone involved in determining whether students should be offered death education in school. This chapter contains three brief comments on death education from three parents, each with a different background. Myra Lipman is the former head of the Parents League, a parent group with children in private schools in New York City. Judy Sussman is the former head of the Parent-Teacher Organization of River Dell High School in New Jersey. Both of her children attended that school's death education course. Mrs. Arlene Shneur, a parent whose husband had recently died, wanted her son to take the death education course that was offered at his school with the hope that it would help him deal with his grief.

MYRA R. LIPMAN, PhD

Before one can understand what parents want from death education programs in schools, it is necessary to determine what parents know about death education in general. We might paraphrase a well-known question and ask, What do parents know about death education and when do they know it? The answer is that most parents know very little and what they do know, they usually learn only *after* they need the knowledge. For example, parents learn—often incorrectly—how to deal with the death of a beloved pet but this knowledge usually comes only *after* the pet has died. Perhaps "learn" is the wrong word. Parents react to a death and, with the best of intentions, they attempt to meet their children's needs concerning the death, but many parents do not have the "death skills" needed to help their children cope with what may be an extremely traumatic event.

The ways in which people react to death vary according to their age and which developmental stage they are in and, perhaps most significantly, how their parents and backgrounds prepared (or didn't prepare) them for dealing with death. Personally, I am part of the generation that tended to protect children from a single, individual death, but at the same time, my childhood was saturated with the unspeakable horrors of the Holocaust. This is an indication of the crossed signals I received from my parents regarding the subject of death. My parents would go to the funerals of relatives and friends while I, being "only" a child, was left at home. In fact, I was 22 when my aunt, to whom I was extremely close, died and that was the first funeral I had ever attended. It was clear to me then that I was not prepared to deal with death or the grief that inevitably follows a death. I am still having a difficult time with this subject. What do today's parents want from death education programs? I cannot speak for all parents, but, both personally and from talking with many families from the Parent's League, I have culled the following information:

1. *Schools cannot assume the entire responsibility for a child's death education and neither can they ignore the matter entirely.*

Parents tend to expect more and more from schools. As awareness of the importance of death education proliferates, schools have realized that there is a need to train their teachers how to deal with students and death. As mentioned in other chapters in this book, there are programs designed to train professionals that have already been or are being implemented. In the same way, parents also need training and guidance. They, too, need to know about the "cycles" of grief and how to explain some of the inexplicable issues that will inevitably arise as their children encounter death or perhaps parents will chose to discuss the subject beforehand. In other words, parents need to know just what their roles as parents should be regarding death and how they can best fulfill those roles.

To be any real help to children, it is important for parents to first take a hard look at their own style of parenting. Are you emotional in front of your children or do you hold in your feelings? If you are the type that vents your feelings without reservation, then your reaction to death, or at least the way you respond to a traumatic situation, will be very different from parents who tend to suppress their feelings. It is important to realize that there is no one correct way of reacting to death or one set of rules that parents feel they should follow and this is true for many other aspects of parenting. In fact, a parent's gut reaction may turn out to be the most appropriate way to handle certain situations regarding their children. Nevertheless, parents need a death education. Not only will it help them uncover some real truths about themselves (such as their own attitude toward death), but it will also help them help their children. If parents can sort through their own emotional baggage regarding death, they will be less likely to pass any harmful information on to their children. Therefore, it is important that parents learn as much they can about how to best cope with death and how to assist their children do the same.

Many of the parents I have spoken to would like to see, when possible, an integrated, interdisciplinary approach to death education at all grade levels, elementary through high school. Unlike sex education, which is offered only to certain grades, death education should be taught to all children of all ages in all grades. I believe it need not be a separate course, but integrated into other topics responsibly and sensibly according to the discipline or the event.

2. *Parents would like guidance on how to approach and talk with their children about death.*

The book entitled *I Had a Friend Named Peter* by Janice Cohn is a good example of how the parents of a young child can begin a dialogue about the painful and complicated issue of the accidental death of a friend. The death of a peer is shocking to all of us, but it is compounded when young children lose a friend who is their age. Children feel every loss keenly, from the death of a grandparent to the death of a gerbil. Parents require guidelines for helping children express their grief and cope with the event.

3. *Parents need assistance in dealing with the confusing and often contradictory way in which the media presents death to both children and parents.*

The emotional context in which death is presented by the media to children is often confusing to parents. Think of the Western movies you and your children may have seen in which hordes of pioneers or Indians die in a decidedly impersonal, but thoroughly gory manner. Most children appear to be unaffected by the mass slaughter. But then there are the "tear-jerkers," movies that are deliberately meant to draw an emotional response to the death of a single individual, someone the viewer develops feelings for and perhaps relates to. How do we explain death and loss to our children when we react so differently to different kinds of deaths, seemingly unaffected by mass death in one movie and tearful over the death of a single person in another?

There is no question or doubt that parents need extensive training in death education. Two specific areas can be defined. The first is concerned with the death of a relative, a close friend or a pet; in other words, someone close to the family. The second, which also poses a big challenge for educators, is when death takes place in a school setting or affects the members of the school community. (The rash of teen suicides that sometimes occurs after the suicide of someone that children relate to comes to mind immediately, as does the sad case of Elizabeth Steinberg, the little girl who died of abusive treatment by her father.) In the school where I teach, the seniors watched as one of their classmates with cystic fibrosis grew weaker daily, until one weekend she was finally hospitalized, her only hope being to find a donor who could provide her with a lung for a transplant operation she needed to live.

4. *Teachers must be willing to maintain an ongoing dialogue with parents to ensure that together they can maintain death education curricula that will benefit the children and families of their community.*

How can parents work together with teachers and administrators to make sense out of something that seems so senseless? The more people involved in this process, the greater will be the potential for confusion. As mentioned earlier, each of us (each teacher, each parent, each administrator) has a unique set of biases concerning death that is the result of our upbringing, religious views and experiences. If we have no clear guidelines to follow and no predetermined plans of action, there is little hope that our children will be receiving the kind of consistent and intelligent guidance they need.

Furthermore, this "death education" is not a simple process; it is not a subject capable of being learned in two easy lessons and then imparted to children. Education, whether at home or at school, is a *process* and needs to be slow and deliberate. As such, we should not expect to be provided with magical answers that will answer all questions, but we *should* expect death education to offer us strategies, suggestions and specific information to help us help our children.

5. *Death education programs should be in place in our schools now.*

What parents want from death education programs, first and foremost, is that they be implemented by the schools and put in place as effectively and efficiently as is feasible. As a parent, I applaud the efforts of educators who are attempting to do just that. I eagerly anticipate reentering the classroom to expand my death-related knowledge as I attend the death education classes they will surely be offering to parents in the not-too-distant future.

JUDY SUSSMAN

Both of my children took a death education course when they were students at River Dell High School. We often discussed classroom lessons at home. We found that death education was a good "icebreaker." The teacher encouraged students to talk about death issues with their families. Material from class was brought home to be shared and from there it was possible to talk about the loss of a relative or a parent or grandparent. The course made it easier to speak openly about death. Also, it reminded all of us just how precious life is. My daughter Karen once said that if someone died, she never knew how to react when speaking to loved ones. After her death education course, she said that it didn't feel so clumsy when she tried to talk to them. The details of a particular class or unit should be worked out by professional educators. The greatest value for me, as a parent, was the process of communication, often about difficult topics, that the course helped our family to develop. I know that death education programs come in many forms, but whatever the particulars, I see the most important component as parental involvement. Parents should be aware of what is going on in school so they will be able to offer informed support. Death education is a difficult task for any individual to attempt alone, whether teacher or parent. It is best carried out as a team effort.

ARLENE SHNEUR

Before my son, Robert, took a death education course we did discuss death. It was very open in the house. But when you have a course about it, it is much more structured. I tried to discuss the topic by "feel" more than anything else.

We like to think that we're going to live forever, or at least for a very long time, a kind of thinking that usually begins when we were children. We don't teach enough of the truth about death to our children. Because, as children we were not taught about death, we don't know enough about it ourselves. Death was and still is hushed up and pushed under the carpet until it happens in your family. Then every lesson becomes a potential crisis. My children and I have become stronger people by coming through the grief that followed my husband's death. By learning to deal with death and grief, my children can face the world with more strength. My children and I are survivors and we can come through any situation that is put upon us. Having a death education course available to my children meant that we didn't have to face this difficult task alone.

CONCLUSIONS

Editor's Note: From the comments of these three women there are a few points that are clear about what parents want from death education programs:

1. Most parents want to be part of the process of death education and must be given the opportunity to know what is being taught in the death education course. They also want this process to be ongoing

and not simply something done once or twice a year at parent-teacher meetings.

2. Parents want to develop effective communication with each of their children. They are often afraid of saying or doing "the wrong thing" and believe the school can offer guidance in this area.

3. Parents feel that death education courses have helped their children face the reality of death and grief by offering accurate information in a structured environment. This information can be used by parents as an "icebreaker" for discussion of the topic of death or as a supplement to ongoing family support.

4. The parents of children who have taken death education courses believe that such courses should be available to all students who wish them and that such courses should be available now.

13

Death Education: Teaching the Teachers*

Mary Ann Morgan, MEd

Since the early 1960s, teaching about death, dying and bereavement has become more and more popular. Today, there are hundreds of workshops, seminars, conferences and courses available on these subjects. Course curricula have been published, media resources have been extensively reviewed in journals, countless books and articles have been written and many associations have been formed. Most of these initiatives have been extremely informative and helpful in developing the field of thanatology.

Death education was first introduced into the educational system at the undergraduate college level. Later on, palliative and hospice care became a focus of study for health care professionals. Still later, death education was brought into the elementary and secondary school systems and has been offered there ever since. Since its initiation, the formal study of death, dying and bereavement has mainly been associated with adults who intended to teach.

Throughout its history, little attention has been paid to those adults who specifically want to learn how to teach death education. This chapter discusses the demands of the field of thanatology integrated with the needs of those adult learners who assist educators in developing death education program design, structure, implementation and evaluation. Finally, several techniques for accomplishing this goal are provided.

---

* An earlier version of this chapter appeared in M.A. Morgan, ed., *Bereavement: Helping the Survivors* (London, Ontario: King's College, 1987) and is reprinted with permission.

DEMANDS OF THE FIELD OF THANATOLOGY

As one begins to organize a death education program, several unique components demand attention. A number of the recognized leaders in the field have cogently addressed the requirements of the discipline (Wass 1979; Wass, Corr, Pacholski and Forfar 1985; Feifel 1959, 1977; Fulton, Markusen, Owen and Schieber 1978; Shneidman 1980). Their findings reveal that this area of study is both multidisciplinary and interdisciplinary. The subject cuts across the fields of psychology, sociology, biomedical ethics, suicidology, theology, philosophy, and even art, literature and music. Students are confronted with seeing the reality of death from different perspectives and must consider the relationships among the differing views. Even when a program has a very narrow focus, such as pain control or counseling the bereaved, teachers must be aware that they will have to address issues that are generated by the particular student at hand and may deviate from the original focus of the program. The teacher will need to help the learner integrate new material into other ways of thinking about information generated by another discipline. If need be, the focus of a program can be designed to be narrow. Teachers, however, must be broad in their understanding of the field. It is a tall order for both program developers and educators.

Death education is also a field in which there are cognitive, affective and behavioral components (Stillion 1979). If educators truly believe that the study of death is life-enhancing, then death education programs must address the whole person. Kastenbaum (1977) indicated this clearly when he wrote:

> I would encourage an approach in which both emotional and intellectual, individual and socially oriented, experiential and scholarly facets of the educational process are welcomed. A course in death education can make its most significant contribution if it helps us to integrate our total selves, rather than lead to either 'emotional trips' on the one hand or aloof intellectual analysis on the other. There is no better area in which to bring our thoughts, skills and feelings together.

Kastenbaum is supported by Benoliel (1982) who writes: "a broad goal of death education programs is creating a learning situation that fosters awareness of the multidisciplinary nature of death in human experience and encourages a fusion of cognitive and affective learnings." Corr (1978) states it more simply: "Death education concerns [are] theoretical and practical, conceptual and pedagogical, humanistic and scientific." This appeal for "whole-person" death education programs is directed to everyone who is involved in thanatology, whether undergraduate or graduate, professional or nonprofessional. However, death education that addresses the whole person is harder to accomplish than it may sound. Sinacore (1981) believes that professional health education in particular avoids the humanistic aspect of dying. "Death education has crystallized out of a need for a more humanized approach toward the dying person. Yet the forces that have influenced this need have not been conceptually linked to the study of death and dying. The practices of health education and death education have been running [on] parallel tracks with little, if any, points of intersection." Unlike many other educational programs, death education cannot easily be compartmentalized into intellectual, rational, cognitive, affective or behavioral components. Yet, when educators are designing a program, they tend to think in these terms because to do so makes it easier to articulate goals and objectives. Perhaps it is more important for program developers to think holistically as they design death education programs.

The study of death takes place in a death system (Kastenbaum and Aisenber 1976). Any program about death, dying or bereavement occurs within the context of the culture which influences the program, the content, the methods of presentation, what is taught and how it is taught. If it is true that North America is a death-denying or death-ignoring culture, then teachers and learners in death education programs are engaged in counter-cultural education. Consequently, it is important that teachers be well acquainted with how they personally feel about the subject of death and the demands of the field and the reactions of the community as they begin to initiate programs.

Death education attracts diverse individuals with diverse interests. At the 1987 conference of the Association for Death Education and Counseling (ADEC), Darrell Crase profiled the typical learner based on his nine years of university teaching about death and dying: The average age of the participants in death education courses was higher than in other undergraduate courses; the ratio of female to male was nine to one; and the students cut across every academic discipline (Morgan, personal communication 1987). This profile does not differ all that much from that of students in the undergraduate or continuing education non-credit courses at King's College in Canada (Morgan 1987). A significant consideration in death education programs is the expressed and unexpressed needs of the participants. More than 50 percent of the students at King's College indicated that they registered for the courses in death, dying and bereavement for professional reasons. Later, over 60 percent of these students disclosed that they had personal learning needs which they chose not to reveal at first. Learners come to programs about death for many different reasons; some will easily articulate their needs, others will not disclose this information or will be vague about their personal reasons for enrolling in death education courses. How then does the educator know which areas to concentrate on and which areas to avoid? If everyone has different needs, how will the teacher know the right material to cover? It is a dilemma that must be addressed by all death education instructors.

In summary, death education is interdisciplinary in nature. Even when a program is carefully designed and organized, the teachers must be prepared to address the diversity of issues. Learning takes place within the culture in which it is set. Most of the students in this field are adults who come with personal and/or professional learning requirements. It is true that death education does involve all the aforementioned components and these cannot always be separated. It is also true that educators who initiate, organize, prepare and deliver death education courses, workshops, seminars and conferences need to articulate clearly their orientation to the subject. They need to orient their students to the specific focus of the program they will be teaching. However, they must also be aware that because programs about death and dying are popular and well-attended, they will attract people with many different needs.

Like any other educational course of study, certain fundamentals of good teaching and learning must be recognized. These include the setting of goals and objectives and the selection of the style and methods of presentation and evaluation (Knott 1979; Draves 1984). Because this chapter is concerned with the integration of the needs of the field of thanatology with those of the adult learner, these aforementioned components will not be addressed; however, a brief look at the needs of the adult learner will help address some of these issues.

ADULT LEARNING AND TEACHING

Pedagogy—the art, science and profession of teaching children—is the usual model on which most educators build programs of study. This methodology developed in the monastic schools of medieval Europe and was based on the idea that the purpose of education is the transmission of knowledge and skills (Knowles 1980). The focus was on the teacher who was the expert, who enlightened and filled the empty slate with information. Clearly the teacher was in control. In more recent times, a very different view emerged. In 1950 Gilbert Highet wrote: "There are thousands of different things to learn and teach; so many that you may well ask whether they could all be taught under the same system." Thus, decades ago the door was opened to the possibility of more than one way to view teaching and learning.

Today it is believed that learning is a life-long process. If this is true, then educators must realize that not all learners are children. Consequently, the pedagogy of adult education is a contradiction in terms (Knowles 1978), especially in view of the changing demographics of the Western world. The new reality is simply that there will soon be more adults than children engaged in learning activities. Perhaps, then, it is time to question the traditionally accepted pedagogical paradigm. Because adults differ from children in their readiness to learn, their life experience and their orientation to learning, perhaps pedagogy should be replaced by *andragogy*—the art and science of helping adults learn (Knowles 1978), which may be more appropriate term when referring to the needs of the adult learner in the field of thanatology. In the andragogical paradigm the emphasis is changed from a focus on teaching to a focus on facilitating learning. Consequently, the role of the teacher changes from that of a conveyor of information to that of one who helps the student engage in the learning process.

In 1987, at a congress held in Waterloo, Ontario, the following story was related. Unlike many stories, the moral is presented clearly at the beginning: You will only learn what you already know.

> A wise, elderly Native woman was invited to be the guest speaker at a celebration in a neighboring village. When she arrived, she asked the group in front of her, "Do you know what I am going to tell you?" "No," they replied. She told them that they didn't need her and she went away. Well, this group was determined to avail themselves of her wisdom so they invited the sage to return. This time, when she asked the same question, the villagers were smarter and they replied, "Yes." The sage said, "Then you don't need me," and she went away.
>
> The community issued a third invitation. When the sage arrived, she again asked the question, "Do you know what I am going to tell you?" By now the group was well prepared for this question. Half of the group lined up on the left and said, "Yes," and the other half lined up on the right and said "No." The wise old lady responded, "Good, then the left side can tell the right side."
>
> Later, in a dream, one of those who had invited the sage solved the puzzle and recognized the wisdom of the invited guest speaker. People who desire to know something already possess knowledge and experience on which they can base their reflections in order to come to a different, broader or more in depth understanding of their problem.

Many people are clumsy at learning and teaching, not because they are stupid, but because they have not thought about it (Highet 1950). Teachers regularly subscribe to the accepted pedagogical paradigm without reflecting or thinking about the basic assumptions of teaching and learning. The following discussion, based on the work of Knowles (1978, 1980), Kidd (1973), and Cross (1983), reviews basic presumptions about teaching and learning. In pedagogy, the role of the learner is dependent and the teacher takes responsibility for what should be taught and how it should be taught, and then decides if it has been learned. In andragogy, the assumption is that adults become increasingly independent and self-directed as they mature. Therefore, educators need to help adult learners direct their own enquiry while they balance the demands of the discipline, the institution and society with the needs of the learner.

Adults bring a wealth of life experience, background, ethnic heritage and upbringing to the learning situation (Draves 1984). In a course about death, dying and bereavement, they bring their personal and professional experiences with dying patients and children and their experiences with survivors of anticipated, unexpected, accidental, suicidal and homicidal deaths. Educators who recognize such experiences as a valuable resource can tap into them for teaching and learning. It is possible to help adult students to reflect upon and develop broader, deeper understandings of their own life experiences. Teachers must be willing to help students to come to a different understanding of the life experience, rather than being satisfied with the role of expert conveyor of information. In order to accomplish this, teachers must be experienced in the subject matter of death, but also committed to addressing the varied needs of their students.

Children are compelled to attend school until they are 16. They must learn what the educational system dictates is proper for them to learn at their particular ages. Adults come to a learning situation because they have experienced a problem or difficulty or because they have curiosity or a concern (Knowles 1979). A personal need to learn is the motivating factor in their attending school. Therefore, educators must give up their notions that they are solely responsible for designing, structuring, implementing and evaluating programs of study. If students recognize their learning needs, then they should be allowed to have some input into the learning process. This is particularly true in the field of thanatology. While some educators may have difficulty allowing their students to take an active part in the program design, they ought to remember that people tend to feel more committed to a decision or activity if they have participated in making or planning it (Knowles 1980). By allowing students to play a role in the structure and design of their courses, educators actually facilitate an environment where the demands of the field, the institution and society are all more likely to be met.

Children are expected to use much of the information they receive in school later on in their lives. Children's curricula are usually designed around subject-matter units and proceed from the simple to the complex. On the other hand, adults see education as a means of developing increased competence. Generally, they desire to apply their newly acquired knowledge immediately (Knowles 1979). Therefore, adult educators must change from an orientation that is subject-centered to one that is performance-centered.

One could question whether andragogy and pedagogy are mutually exclusive paradigms. Perhaps the best education occurs when the teacher recognizes that some subjects are better suited to the pedagogical methodology, while others lend themselves better to the andragogical approach. It is not so much the age of the students, but rather the subject matter that is the significant variable. It now appears that the andragogical paradigm is a better model on which to build death education programs. Death educators should recognize that students will enroll in their course because they have experienced a need or have a problem or dilemma in their personal or professional lives; they will want to apply their new knowledge immediately and are likely to be seeking an understanding of personal experiences. In New York City, Janice Cohn helped design a death education curriculum for third and fourth graders. Shortly after the program began, curriculum changes were made in order to allow students to discuss their own responses to death and loss. The field of death and dying, with its emphasis on holistic education and on cognitive, affective and behavioral variables, fits easily into the andragogical paradigm which stresses the experience of the student, the immediate application of knowledge and skills, and the uniqueness of each student.

There are obviously a whole array of teaching techniques that could be applied to death education courses. Issues such as physical comfort, good lighting, program planning which is sensitive to various learning styles, learning contracts, having the learner participate in course goal-setting, ongoing evaluation and a learner-centered environment all help contribute to dynamic adult education programs. For further elaboration on these points, see Knowles (1978, 1980), Kidd (1973), Draves (1984), Cross (1983), Thomas (1983), and Tough (1979). More important, however, is the death educator's commitment to the principle and assumptions of adult learning and the demands of the field of thanatology. This commitment will result in course design, structure, implementation and evaluation that address the needs of the adult student while maintaining allegiance to the discipline.

CONCLUSION

The fields of thanatology and adult death education are still in their infancy, but both are developing at a rapid pace. Education about death, dying and bereavement is at its best when it is taught holistically; when the teacher clearly understands the interdisciplinary nature of the subject; when students are involved in the teaching process, especially when they are invited to help decide the course content; when the teacher adapts the course agenda to suit the learning needs of the particular participants (while adhering to the demands of the discipline, the institution and society) and when the students learn enough practical information that they can apply their new knowledge immediately.

Andragogy is based on the assumption that the deepest needs of the adult are attended to when the course material is based on what each individual wants to learn and when students are treated with respect. As such, andragogy is learner-centered and problem-oriented (Kidd 1973). But this is not new. All the greatest teachers—from Confucius to Socrates to

Jesus—made assumptions that learning is a process of discovery by the learner. Consequently, these historic teachers used appropriate procedures, methods and dialogue to engage their learners. They were the first adult educators. Today, death education provides the perfect vehicle for transforming andragogical theory into practice.

REFERENCES

Benoliel, J.Q. Death influence in clinical practice: a course for graduate students. *Death Education* 5:327-346, 1982.

Corr, C.A. A model syllabus for death and dying courses. *Death Education* 1:433-457, 1978.

Cross, K.P. *Adults as Learners.* San Francisco: Jossey-Bass, 1983.

Draves, W.A. *How to Teach Adults.* Manhattan, KS: Learning Resources Network, 1984.

Feifel, H. *The Meaning of Death.* New York: McGraw-Hill, 1959.

Feifel, H. *New Meaning of Death.* New York: McGraw-Hill, 1977.

Fulton, R., E. Markusen, G. Owen and J.L. Scheiber. *Death and Dying: Challenge and Change.* Reading, MA: Addison-Wesley, 1978.

Highet, G. *The Art of Teaching.* New York: Vintage, 1950.

Kastenbaum, R. *Death, Society and Human Experience.* St. Louis: C.V. Mosby, 1977.

Kastenbaum, R. and R. Aisenberg. *The Psychology of Death.* New York: Springer, 1976.

Kidd, J.R. *How Adults Learn.* Chicago: Follet, 1973.

Knott, J.E. Death education for all. In H. Wass, ed., *Dying: Facing the Facts.* Washington, DC: Hemisphere, 1979.

Knowles, M.S. *The Adult Learner: A Neglected Species.* Houston: Gulf, 1978.

Knowles, M.S. *The Modern Practice of Adult Education: From Pedagogy to Andragogy.* Chicago: Follet, 1980.

Morgan, M.A. Learner-centered learning in an undergraduate interdisciplinary course about death. *Death Studies* 11:183-192, 1987.

Pine, V.R. A socio-historical portrait of death education. *Death Education* 1:57-87, 1977.

Pine, V.R. The age of maturity for death education: a socio-historical portrait of the era 1976-1985. *Death Studies* 10:209-232, 1986.

Shneidman, E.S. *Death: Current Perspectives.* Palo Alto, CA: Mayfield, 1980.

Sinacore, J.M. Avoiding the humanistic aspect of death: an outcome from the implicit elements of health professions education. *Death Education* 5:121-133, 1981.

Stillion, J.M. Rediscovering the taxonomies: a structural framework for death education courses. *Death Education* 3:157-164, 1979.

Thomas, A.M. *Learning in Society.* Ottawa: Canadian Commission for UNESCO, 1983.

Tough, A. *The Adult's Learning Projects.* Toronto: The Ontario Institute for Studies in Education, 1979.

Wass, H., ed. *Dying: Facing the Facts.* Washington, DC: Hemisphere, 1979.

Wass, H., C.A. Corr, R.A. Pacholski and C.S. Forfar. *Death Education II: An Annotated Resource Guide.* Washington, DC: Hemisphere, 1985.

14

"If This is Supposed to be the Best Time of My Life, Why Do I Feel So Rotten?" Questions and Answers about Adolescent Suicide and Loss

Robert G. Stevenson, EdD

In recent years, the topic of adolescent suicide has pushed its way into the national spotlight with frightening force. The reasons that adolescents attempt and commit suicide vary so significantly from one youngster to the next that many professionals believe that adolescent suicide is, as Lester (1993) has called it, a true enigma. There are few patterns in the motives behind adolescent suicides and no fool-proof methods for successful suicide prediction or intervention. It is generally recognized, however, that adolescence is an exceedingly difficult period of life for today's youth and that this may contribute greatly to the problem. Despite the enormous number of studies that have been conducted and the growing amount of literature that now exists about the tragic issue of young people taking their own lives, most people have more questions than answers.

Because most of us cannot comprehend how a young person who has his entire life ahead of him could feel so hopeless that he chooses to kill himself, anything that can help facilitate communication with and understanding of adolescents is very important. Certainly a good place to start is by making an effort to understand life from an adolescent's point of view. To this end, this chapter is a collection of questions that directly or indirectly deal with adolescent suicide. The questions were asked during suicide prevention programs that were conducted over the past several years for and with high school students, their parents and teachers. This chapter addresses some of the important questions that adults (parents, teachers and anyone else who works with teenagers) may have about adolescents. The answers and the discussions that follow each question should help adults understand adolescents a little bit more. This information should help adults help young people make their way through this very difficult period of life.

The title of this chapter is a question that was asked by a teenage student who was confused about the way he felt about his life. His question is important to consider because it bluntly addresses the way many of today's young people feel. Addressing this question and others like it may be an extremely helpful task for parents and teachers as well as teenagers.

Because today's teens have more material wealth and more opportunities than previous generations, why do many of them they say they feel unhappy and pressured?

It is true that many of today's teenagers do have more opportunities, but as a result, more is expected from them—by society, their parents and their teachers—and they also expect more from themselves. In addition, there are various issues unique to adolescence that young people must contend with, a list of which follows:

- Biochemical changes. Sudden mood swings are common and sometimes, because adolescence is a period of rapid growth, these many physical changes can make a teenager's own body seem alien to him. These new and sometimes disorienting feelings can be further complicated by substance use and abuse. Drugs and alcohol are readily available (despite laws in most states prohibiting the purchase of alcohol by those under 21). Teenagers often get involved in substance use because of peer pressure and because drug use may provide entry into a clique that a teenager thinks is "cool."
- Intensive self-examination. As children become teenagers, many of them realize that they are no longer merely an extension of their parents. They realize that they are their own person and that this requires taking a good long look at who they are. This realization often brings with it a need for others to recognize their individuality and independence. This in turn often results in a tendency for teenagers to ignore the respect they had for those they used to see as authority figures—people whose direction they formerly accepted without question (in particular, their parents and often teachers, too).
- Emerging sexuality. This means more than making decisions about whether or not to engage in sexual activity. Teenagers must learn what

it means to become a man or a woman and to become sexual beings. They must also try to learn to be comfortable with the many different things that these roles carry with them.

- Reforming relationships with parents. Because young people change as they become teenagers, so too do the relationships they have with their parents. The relationship will change from what it was during childhood and both children and parents need to adapt to a relationship that is more equal. Teenagers need parents to do more than tell them what they can and cannot do; they need a friend and someone they can talk to. This period is also hard for parents: some simply do not want to let go and allow their kids to grow up and others simply do not know how to relate to their "new" child who they have only known as their offspring, not as a separate person who may be developing different—and sometimes opposing—opinions, attitudes and behavior. This time is often accompanied by arguments and hurt feelings on both sides.

If many of today's teenagers have futures that hold so much potential, why do they say they feel helpless?

One important thing to realize is that it is pretty hard for anyone to think about the future all the time. Most people live in the present and some in the past, but no one can live in the future. For adolescents, the present is often very difficult. They go through many changes and these changes often cause them to feel as if they have no control of their own lives. Change always causes some sort of loss and every loss tends to magnify this feeling. The following are typical losses that many young people experience:

- One in 20 children lose a parent to death by the time they reach the age of 18.
- One in 750 high school students dies each year. The top three causes of death, all of which can be sudden and violent, are accidents, homicides and suicides. In other words, many of today's students frequently lose friends to death.
- More children die in the first year of life than at any other time in their childhood and this does not include miscarriage or stillbirth. This means that many children will lose a young sibling to death.
- Separation and divorce parallel the death experience, but to make matters worse, these losses usually do not reach the same sort of closure that is possible with a loss due to death.
- A sudden "community loss" can occur, such as the Challenger tragedy (in which a classroom of students watched as the space shuttle carrying their teacher exploded, killing all of those inside).

- Adolescents generally spend more of their waking hours in school than at home. Therefore, school is a very large part of life and the death of a teacher can be very traumatic and will affect everyone in the school community in some way.
- Other changes that can cause losses may include an increase or decrease in popularity, losing old friends and changing "groups," a change in appearance and a loss of the emotional security that often accompanies life as a younger child.

How does a teenager's reaction to losses such as those just mentioned affect his behavior?

Loss causes stress and we know a good deal about the ways in which young people react to stress. In terms of school, stress and anxiety can impair a student's academic performance. Grief takes energy and attention, the effects of which can best be seen in areas that require cognitive problem-solving. Adolescents react to anxiety and loss in many ways. Some of these reactions include:

- Apathy and withdrawal from life.
- Punishment-seeking due to feelings of guilt and anger.
- Imitating the lost loved one's behavior in an attempt to keep part of that person "present."
- Changing one's values because the *quality* of life may now seem more important than its *quantity*. Also, some youngsters may feel so low that they think nothing is important enough to worry about.
- Acting "humorous" in a way that may seem inappropriate or taste-less, or joking about losses and fears. Laughter can restore a measure of control and tears can be effective tension-relievers.
- Another important point for teachers and parents to realize is that grief caused by loss takes a lot out of students and may not leave them much time for schoolwork. Even when students exert a great amount of effort at school, it may not yield the expected results and this can cause them to feel confused and even guilty. This may become more emphasized if their grief reaction is delayed. Studies show that even a "normal" reaction to loss may be delayed for as long as five years and it is not abnormal for people to deny their true feelings toward some losses for a very long time.

How big of a problem is adolescent suicide today?

Because of the exploitative attention that the media always gives to adolescent suicide, one would think the problem is bigger than it really is. In fact, adolescents are not the group most at risk; senior citizens are. There are some important facts about adolescent suicide that should be known by all adults who take care of and have contact with young people. Many young people *contemplate* suicide as a possible solution to life's problems and pains. Of the many young people who contemplate suicide, few actually *attempt* it and of those who attempt the act, even fewer *complete* it. Between 10 and 14 years of age there is about one death per 100,000 young people. Between the ages of 15 and 18, about eight young people in 100,000 die by their own hands each year. However, these statistics provide little consolation because even one death is one too many, especially if it is someone we love. Additionally, thoughts of suicide should *never* be considered unimportant and ignored. In fact, if a youngster talks about suicide (that is, in relation to himself), it should always be considered a "red flag" and should be dealt with immediately.

How can the problems that young people have be identified and by whom?

Adults must assume the responsibility of being aware of what their actions or lack of action may mean. To fail to act when there is some evidence of a problem, no matter how slight, is usually worse than reacting when there is no real threat. Such inaction can have lethal consequences. Parents may notice changes in their children, but they are not always sure what they mean. If parents think that their child needs help, they should do whatever is necessary to obtain help. Schools can help parents to reach this goal. While parents have a right and a responsibility to inform schools of their children's needs, schools cannot fulfill a parent's role. Educators have their own roles to fill. Seeing students every day for nine months a year, they are in a good position to notice changes and sometimes have the objectivity that parents may lack to identify problems when they exist. Parents must be willing to look at objective evaluations of their children and admit when they are true. Finally, young people can help one another if they realize that sometimes they have to be willing to break the adolescent code of silence. Telling a parent or a teacher if they are worried about a friend can be very helpful, even life-saving. Adults should point out to young people that providing such information does not imply "informing" on a friend.

Where do young people learn coping skills?

Children watch the way their immediate role models act and usually adopt their methods of coping—whether they are effective or not. For this reason it is important for caring adults to think about how well they themselves deal with loss and to identify their own coping strategies. Parents who have difficulty dealing with loss can help their children by first helping themselves. By identifying and employing more effective coping styles, they can become positive role models for their children. If this is not possible, family counseling can assist all family members to identify and work on coping styles together.

Are there groups in my area with people and programs that can help concerned parents and teachers?

There are now resources throughout the country, in just about every city and town. For example, in Bergen County, New Jersey, the Mid-Bergen Regional Counseling Center has a program called the Adolescent Suicide Awareness Program (A.S.A.P.). In addition the CENTER for Help in Time of Loss provides adolescents and adults with support groups and individual counseling. The American Institute for Life-Threatening Illness and Loss in New York City offers symposia on grief and consulting services to schools and community groups. You can also obtain names and phone numbers from state clearinghouses to directly contact locate local self-help groups. The Association for Death Education and Counseling (ADEC) in Hartford, Connecticut can provide a list of groups and agencies in most areas. Clearly, there are many places you can contact when you need help with loss. You need never feel alone.

Are there things about a death by suicide that cause it to have a greater impact on survivors than other sudden deaths?

There are several points that should be remembered when a suicide occurs:

- Suicide is sudden and seldom anticipated. Sudden loss is more likely to complicate the grief process than a death that is anticipated. Sudden death may be "kinder" to the deceased but it exacts a greater toll on survivors.
- Suicide is often violent and even when it is not, it violently rips apart our ideas concerning the natural order of things.
- Suicide most often takes place in an environment where there is other stress. In other words, problems existed before the suicide attempt. Sometimes, for those who contemplate, attempt or complete suicide, the act is not a "problem" but a "solution."
- Suicide often causes feelings of regret and guilt in survivors. Survivors think back to see if there were signs of the suicide that they may have missed, or even worse, signs they noticed but did nothing about. Many feel "if only I had done this" or "if only I had said that." Regret for the comment left unsaid or the deed left undone can aggravate guilt and complicate grieving.

- What we *believe* is true can often be more important than reality. Our internal thoughts and fears may not be based on fact, but we feel them nevertheless and they can be very real and painful. The silence imposed on survivors often limits the chance to talk about these thoughts and feelings and can increase the certainty that these beliefs are, in fact, real.
- Survivors' grief following a death by suicide can be complicated by the fact that for the most part, society looks down on suicide (attempting suicide remains technically illegal in most states). People often look to the family of the suicide to see what it was that they did to make the child kill himself. The support systems that are available to survivors of other types of deaths are often not offered to suicide survivors. Funerals and interment rituals, for example, may be withheld.
- Survivors may become isolated by the distancing of others. Communication often breaks down because survivors see the silence of others as an act of judgment. Sometimes people do not want to discuss a suicide because they believe survivors will be too sensitive.
- Even when most of the above things do not occur, survivors may still believe them to be true. Just as there may have been options other than self-imposed death that the deceased could not see, survivors may believe that all possible negative reactions are taking place, even when they are not.

What sorts of things do young people find helpful after a death has taken place?

The students in the River Dell High School course "Contemporary Issues of Life and Death" offer the following suggestions to educators who try to help bereaved students. They are in no special order, but they are sincere and may be helpful to concerned educators.

- Talk about the death and allow students to initiate discussion when they feel the need. Because curriculum has been defined as a "statement of priorities" when students are touched by a death, that event should be given a place in the curriculum because it occupies an important place in our lives.
- Provide students with a "safe place" and allow them to go there when they need to. Feeling "trapped" in school or in a classroom can exaggerate the feelings of helplessness that are part of the grief reaction.
- Allow for changes in the environment. Students should have a say about seating and other things that may need to be changed after the death of a classmate.

- Many students react to anger with violence. Teachers should try to help students to avoid violent responses, but they should also try to understand such reactions if they do occur.
- Teachers should point out that at some point following a death, the time will come to get on with life. This point will be different for each student and teachers should never try to force students to make this decision.
- Teachers should provide students with a contact person for times when others might not be available. For example, a teacher could provide a sure-answer phone number and a place where students can be together. Open time in the gym can bring people together and help them let off steam at the same time.
- A good way for students to deal with feelings of helplessness after a death is by helping those who want to offer organized help, such as doing jobs for others.
- Teachers should listen to their students because they are the ones who know best what they need. Sometimes the best thing a teacher can do is to be quiet and listen.

Are there some guidelines that educators should try to implement in our schools?

The following points may prove helpful when a death occurs:

- Do not try to shield young people from life. Explain what you can and remember that talking about a problem does not make it worse and just might help.
- Things may be "all right" at some point after a death, but they will never be the same as they were before the death.
- Don't block emotions. Boys cry and so do adults.
- Maintain open lines of communication. Be sure everyone involved understands what is really happening.
- Try to promote a greater feeling of control among students. Allow them some flexibility in choosing the time and place to discuss problems. Students in death education courses often report feeling less anxious following this type of experience. It is true that knowledge can sometimes give the illusion of control, but this is not necessarily bad.
- By marking the event, rituals such as funeral services, wakes and viewings can help people accept the fact that a death has really occurred.
- Be patient. Healing takes time and we cannot rush the process.

As was stated at the beginning of this chapter, we do not know much about adolescent suicide and we certainly do not know how to make people "suicide-proof." However, by talking to young people—especially to young survivors—and attempting to understand what they are experiencing and what their reactions to situations may mean, parents and teachers and all those who work with youngsters will be better equipped to help them cope with the difficulties of adolescence. If we cannot make them "suicide-proof," perhaps we can help make them "suicide-resistant."

It has been said that the only foolish question is the one that has not been asked. Young people must be encouraged to ask questions and to investigate the feelings they have. By listening carefully, adults can help them seek the answers.

15

Starting a School Suicide Prevention Program

Edward Stroh, PhD

This chapter is presented in two parts. The first addresses the issues that make it difficult to establish suicide prevention programs in high schools. The second is a description of the successful establishment of one such program, the Adolescent Suicide Awareness Program at River Dell Regional High School in New Jersey.

FACING THE DIFFICULTIES

We now have solid data that documents the fact that adolescent suicide has risen dramatically during the past 20 years. Indeed, suicide is now the third leading cause of death among persons under the age of 24. Clearly this includes a large number of school children. For this reason, suicide prevention programs have been established in schools for students at risk and for their classmates.

Even though certain individuals and groups try to justify or rationalize it, suicide is an act that is frowned on by most people. Suicide is generally viewed as a secret and private act and is seldom a topic of discussion among the general public. Certainly, a person's suicide is not a pleasant thing to be a part of—whether it is someone you are close to or someone you didn't know. People feel very uncomfortable about being associated with a person who killed himself. It is much more difficult for a parent to tell others that his child killed himself than it would be to say that he died as the result of a car accident.

Understandably, suicide generates strong anxieties and other mixed emotions among the general population and, in particular, among direct survivors. For a variety of reasons that we will discuss, immediate survivors of a suicide are often ashamed of the act and therefore deny to others that the death was self-inflicted. They pretend that the death was the result of an accident or provide no explanation at all. Because suicide is a subject that few people are prepared to deal with, this sort of denial is relatively easy to achieve.

This attitude is precisely why people are *opposed* to the establishment of suicide prevention programs. When one first hears that certain people are opposed to something like a suicide prevention program, it seems almost inconceivable. Who in their right mind would not want to do everything possible to stop this tragic trend, especially among young people who have their whole lives ahead of them? The answer is that the people who personally have had an experience with an attempted or completed suicide (perhaps their own, or perhaps their child's or sibling's) are afraid that an open discussion—whether they are a part of it or not—will reveal certain truths that they are nervous about exposing.

Even though we may understand why someone might not want everyone to know a secret of this sort, the effects of hiding the fact of a suicide and covering up the circumstances surrounding it are far more harmful to others than those who practice this denial may realize. For one, hiding the actuality of suicide has an obvious detrimental effect on the official statistics of deaths by suicide. There is no question that the actual number of suicides is probably *far* above the recorded figures.

The Special Case of Adolescent Suicide

When a person of any age commits suicide, it is painful to hear about and accept, but the suicide of an adolescent seems even more tragic and harder to comprehend than the suicide of an older person. It is a particularly disturbing thought that young people—with their entire life ahead of them—would feel so hopeless about life that death seems to be the only answer. Many people do not understand what adolescence is like for today's young people. Many adults do not see that there is a significant difference in being a teenager today compared to life when they were teens. Many people erroneously believe that today, adolescence is a period of worry-free existence. As well, some people assume, also incorrectly, that today's middle- and upper-class teenagers typically do not have much to fret about; life for them is a series of episodes without consequences. While this statement is greatly exaggerated and general, it is probably safe to say that there *are* teenagers who are protected from the harshness of reality because the nature of their lives shields them from the reality of these events. Of course, the same cannot be said for the huge numbers of under-privileged youngsters who do not have the luxury of caring parents and schools to shield them from a harsh world. Often, these children and teenagers have terribly dysfunctional home lives. Many inner-city schools do not offer the same kind of one-on-one care that smaller, more affluent schools do. Sadly, it is often just these children who need the most help because they come into contact with more losses than their upper- or middle-class counterparts. As Ronald Barrett points out in an earlier chapter, losses due to violent death are increasingly common occurrences. In summary, those who believe that today's young people "have it easy" are mistaken. In fact, as described in other chapters in this book, today's teenagers may have a *more* difficult time than teenagers did in earlier times. Today's teens think about suicide, attempt it and complete it with alarming frequency.

Most parents feel agonizing guilt when their child commits suicide. They are afraid that their child's suicide reflects a failure on their part. When the fear of parental failure is added to the shame that is usually experienced when a person in ones family commits suicide, it becomes apparent why certain people hesitate or object to high school suicide prevention programs—they don't want anyone to know about their personal lives because they are ashamed.

The Myth About Predictability

Some people believe that those who talk openly about suicide are not at risk of committing the act (Conger 1977). In other words, if they verbalize thoughts about suicide, chances are that they would never kill themselves or at least that they are not presently at risk. This is a terrible mistake! Indeed, various studies of different age groups have shown that those who openly discussed suicide often ended up killing themselves. Verbalizations are good clues to a person's feelings and must be listened to carefully. Unfortunately, many potential suicides do not verbalize their problems and therefore, the quiet person's suicide attempt is very hard to predict and prevent. Those who believe that if people talk about suicide, they are not in danger of committing it also believe that there is nothing we can do for those who keep quiet, and therefore, in their opinion, a suicide prevention program could not work and is a useless scheme. The truth is, of course, that verbalizations about suicide are often a plaintive cry for help and they can be clear signals that the chance of suicide is real. Those who say little—the quiet ones—can absolutely be assisted by suicide intervention programs; they can be watched and with the help of sensitive counselors and listeners, they can usually be helped. Not only would a prevention program dispel these myths, but it would also provide the help that potential suicides—whether overt or silent—so desperately need.

Additional Misconceptions

The problems and misconceptions mentioned above must be taken into account when establishing a suicide prevention program, especially because there are so many people who believe these myths. Klagsbrun (1976) pointed to another misconception related to suicide that is probably not so universal, but which may have bearing on the question of the support of suicide prevention programs. Certain segments of the general public believe that suicide is a problem faced only by the very poor, the very rich, that suicide is hereditary and that it "runs in families." At this point in time, no research data support the notion that suicide makes any class distinctions whatsoever. All types of people with all different personalities, from a variety of backgrounds, take their lives each year. There is also no support for the idea of a biological/hereditary factor for suicide.

Shneidman, Farberow and Litman (1976) list still other myths that add to the problem of establishing a suicide prevention program. For example, many persons feel that when a suicidal person makes an attempt to kill himself, that he is always fully intent on dying. To the contrary, when most people attempt suicide, they are in intense pain and are undecided about just what they want the outcome of the suicide to be. Suicide attempts are frequently a way of letting others know just how much pain they are actually experiencing. In other words, many suicides are just a cry for help: the person does not really want to die, but he *does* want someone else to know about his pain. Perhaps this is also true for completed suicides, except for them, the attempt worked. Admittedly, the idea of telling even a very close acquaintance—especially for a young child or a teenager to tell a parent that "he hates his life so much that he wishes he were dead"—is not exactly an easy thing for him to do. For this reason, among many others, it is critical that teenagers and their parents have a suicide prevention program to attend.

The belief that once a person is suicidal, he is forever suicidal is another myth. The truth is that most people remain suicidal for only a limited time. For this reason, immediate intervention is critical. Because young people attend school every day, the school is an ideal place for a suicide prevention program.

Finally, a widely held belief is that suicide is the act of a mentally ill person. Despite the fact that many studies indicate that some suicidal persons are mentally ill, the presence of mental illness is not always a factor in suicidal behavior. In fact, research shows that fewer mentally ill people commit suicide than those who are mentally sound.

Professional Considerations

Assuming that suicide prevention programs in the schools should be organized and presented by professionals (i.e., counselors, psychologists, social workers), certain philosophical issues of liability may pose barriers. One of these potential barriers is the question of client rights (Morgan 1981). In the United States, there are basic social values that allow individuals to decide whether or not they want to seek treatment. In the case of a suicidal person, the intervention of the professional is usually a decision made by the helper, not the "victim." While professional codes of ethics leave no doubt regarding the action of a helper, this philosophical problem must be recognized and addressed.

A different but related issue is the use of force. Under certain conditions, suicide prevention programs advocate the use of force to restrain people from inflicting injury to themselves. For those professionals opposed to involuntary measures, the advocacy of approaches including the use of force is an issue that must be recognized.

Some professionals regard the entire issue of treatment for the prevention of suicide as a frustrating, if not hopeless, undertaking due to the lack of reasonable accuracy in the techniques of suicide prediction. It is not difficult to relate the inaccuracy of current prediction techniques to the quandary introduced by certain facets of legal responsibilities. Fujimora, Weis and Cochran (1985) feel that within the counseling relationship, the proper application of legal and ethical concerns should be when the probability of suicide can be reasonably predicted. Specifically, liability problems can arise when a counselor fails to take preventive action (such as neglecting to obtain a diagnosis), or takes an action that inadvertently promotes the act of suicide (such as breaching a very damaging confidence).

Economic Considerations

The organization and operation of a suicide prevention program costs money. Staff personnel must be specially trained and must have coverage for their regular duties. Outside consultants, when needed, must also be paid. Audiovisual materials must be purchased or rented, and maintenance services for the location of workshops must be provided. Most current boards of education are closely examining the allocation of limited funds. In many districts, state and federal aid to education has been cut. Although most boards recognize the value and need for programs designed around mental health concerns such as suicide prevention, the fight for the dollar is almost always won by administrators and building committees.

A SUCCESS STORY

River Dell Regional High School is a good example of a school system that was able to overcome the many difficulties discussed above by establishing the Adolescent Suicide Awareness Program (ASAP). Under the leadership of a physical education/health department chairman and a county mental health supervisor, those involved in planning were able to convince school administrators of the need for such a program. A series of carefully organized meetings that provided convincing information together with informed parents and staff and trained personnel who wanted to join the effort, enabled River Dell Regional High School to implement a successful adolescent suicide awareness program.

The River Dell Regional School District is located in the middle- and upper-middle-class suburban community of Oradell, New Jersey. Approximately 780 students are enrolled in grades 10 through 12 at the high school and it is these students who can be part of the suicide prevention program.

Although the literature is filled with articles and books about teenage suicide, little has been written about the specific establishment of school teenage suicide prevention programs and the difficulties involved in creating these programs. The development of most programs seems to be in response to teen suicides that occurred in a particular school district. Examples of school systems that developed teenage suicide prevention programs in this way include the Fairfax County Schools in Virginia and Golden High School in Colorado (Vidal 1986). The Fairfax Schools arranged educational suicide programs for school personnel, parents and students and were helped by community agencies. Involvement of students, peer counselors and parents also helped to overcome the difficulties of starting this teenage suicide prevention program which was implemented in 1983. With the help of community resources to develop an in-school response time, the Golden High School program also offered seminars and training sessions for school personnel and parents.

Fortunately, more recent developments indicate that schools are establishing suicide prevention and intervention programs in districts in which teen suicides have not occurred. Konet (1986) points to the establishment of the program in Westfield, New Jersey. Ryerson and King (1986) report that the South Bergen Mental Health Center helped schools initiate teenage suicide prevention programs in the northern Bergen County area in New Jersey. The success of these programs was contingent on the school's ability to overcome the barriers that blocked the addition of mental health programs in schools.

The development of a suicide prevention program in River Dell Regional High School began in 1980 as a response to the national teenage suicide problem. A full suicide awareness program was in operation by 1982. The program involved administrators, staff, parents, community resources and students, and this helped ensure the successful implementation of the suicide program at the high school.

Two general meetings for interested faculty members of nearby schools were conducted by the staff at Hackensack Hospital Community Mental

Health Center. These meetings provided basic information regarding teenage suicide. The presentation of statistical data, myths of suicide, signs of depression and suggestions for faculty action served to provide a sense of the overall problem. As a result of the general meetings, the principal of River Dell Regional High School asked a counselor, the school nurse, and the school social worker to conduct small group meetings for the high school staff in order to provide the same information to the entire faculty.

The small group meetings, consisting of four periods per day for two days, took the place of the monthly principal's meeting and teachers gave up their conference period to attend. After becoming aware of the problem, faculty members expressed concern, interest, and a desire to assist in identifying students whose behavior might place them at risk. The small group setting also provided an opportunity for the staff to ask questions that might not have been possible at a large meeting.

Shortly after the small group meetings were held, Frank Acocella, who was the chairman of the Physical Education/Health Department, decided to include "teenage suicide awareness" in the health curriculum. Working with Diane Ryerson, education director of the South Bergen Mental Health Center, Acocella convinced the Director of Pupil Personnel Services and the Superintendent of Schools that such a program was important and belonged in the school. A district-wide inservice meeting on adolescent suicide and depression helped advance staff awareness. After a large group address by the school's consulting psychiatrist, key faculty members led small-group discussions.

An evening meeting was held for parents and other interested adults in the community and members of the Parent-Teacher Organization. Its goal was to alert parents and teachers to the teenage suicide problem and the intentions of school administrators to initiate a suicide awareness program for students. The format of the meeting provided ample time for questions from concerned parents after a presentation by school officials and the consulting school psychiatrist. This meeting further convinced school administrators to provide the time, staff, and support to implement the program.

The school counselors and members of the child study team then visited the South Bergen Mental Health Center to become familiar with the program developed by Diane Ryerson and Barbara King. A review of program content and methods of presentation to be used enabled school personnel to obtain the information necessary to be comfortable with the first presentation to the students. The first pilot program would serve as a training program for River Dell staff who would assist the mental health center staff and subsequently take over the program.

The presentation of the first program was followed by a meeting of all involved personnel to evaluate the program in terms of scheduling, organ-

izing, content, techniques used, and followup with students. Student evaluations were also a consideration in the evaluation process. River Dell
counselors and child study team and staff conducted the second pilot
program and followup session. After positive responses from involved
students, staff, administrators and parents, the last barriers to the program
were eliminated and River Dell implemented a full teenage suicide awareness program in 1982. A student peer counseling group called PLAN,
organized in 1986 by Robert Stevenson and Claire Marino, a school counselor, was added to the program. The students who are members of PLAN
conduct sessions directly with students on one of the days of the program.

As a result of the River Dell pilot program, Ryerson and King upgraded
and renamed the program. The Adolescent Suicide Awareness Program
(ASAP) is a comprehensive guide for educators that includes both curriculum and specific guidance examples. Acocella designed an extensive
program to overcome difficulties in starting a teenage suicide awareness
program in schools and currently serves as a consultant to interested
schools. River Dell found that to start a suicide prevention program it was
essential to have the following:

- the leadership of a person committed to its establishment
- the dissemination of basic information to the right people
- the utilization of all available community resources
- the involvement of people who have the authority to make decisions
  in the school and the community

Mental health programs of this type can be established in schools, as River
Dell has shown us, but careful planning is needed to overcome the strict
psychosocial and economic barriers that exist and to gain administrative,
staff and community support.

REFERENCES

Conger, J. *Adolescence and Youth, 2nd Ed.* New York: Harper & Row, 1977.

Den Houter, K. To silence one's self: a brief analysis of the literature on adolescent
suicide. *Child Welfare* 15:2-9, 1981.

Fairfax County Schools. Preventing adolescent suicide. *Children Today* 14:4-5, 1985.

Fujimora, L.E., D.M. Weis and J.R. Cochran. Suicide: dynamics and implications for
counseling. *Counseling* 63:612-615, 1985.

Klagsbrun, F. *Youth and Suicide.* Boston: Houghton Mifflin, 1976.

Konet, R.J. Developing a suicide intervention program in your school. *National
Association of Secondary School Principals Bulletin* 70:51-54, 1986.

Morgan, L. The counselor's role in suicide prevention. *Personnel Guidance Journal*
59:284-286, 1981.

Ray, L.Y. and J. Norbert. Adolescent suicide. *Personnel Guidance Journal* 62:131-135, 1983.

Ryerson, D. and F. Acocella. Recognizing and preventing the self-destructive behavior of adolescents. *Education Viewpoints* 5:10-13, 1984.

Ryerson, D. and B. King. *Adolescent Suicide Awareness Program*. Lyndhurst, NJ: South Bergen Mental Health Center, 1986.

Shneidman, E., N. Farberow and R. Litman. *The Psychology of Suicide, 2nd Ed.* New York: Jason Aronson, 1976.

Vidal, J.A. One school's response in establishing a suicide prevention program. *National Association of Secondary School Principals Bulletin* 70:68-71, 1986.

Wekstein, L. *Handbook of Suicidology*. New York: Brunner/Mazel, 1979.

16

Suicidal Thoughts:
The Importance of Listening
and Reaching Out

Ed Gallagher

Editor's Note: Ed Gallagher was a successful student athlete until an attempt to commit suicide left him a quadriplegic. Ed has not let his paralysis prevent him from living a full life. To the contrary, he has turned the incident into something positive. Because he wants others to learn from his mistakes, he frequently participates in suicide prevention programs for high school students. When he talks with students, he wants them to know that if they are feeling down or suicidal, that other people *can* help even if it doesn't seem possible at the time. He wants young people to know that talking to someone can possibly save their lives. Ed's story has helped many troubled young people realize that they *must* seek the assistance of others when they are in trouble.

This brief chapter has been included in this book to make sure that readers (both parents and those who work with young people) realize that there very well may be a young person in their midst who needs a friend, a young person who may be reluctant to discuss his problems with another, but who seriously needs someone to listen to him. And it is important to remember that while some young people may be able to reach out for help when they need it, others do not know how to do this, and they may need someone to try to reach *in*. Think about what may be going on inside your children or your students; what you see on the surface is sometimes very different from what is going on inside—as is the case with the boy who wrote the following suicide note. Maybe someone seriously needs a helping hand and if you are tuned to this way of thinking, perhaps you will notice someone who is in need of a friend—and perhaps this is something you ordinarily might not realize. If you yourself cannot provide help, maybe you know someone who can. It is hoped that readers will be inspired by Ed's story to listen carefully and to look beneath the surface words and behaviors of young people and to offer help when it is needed.

INTRODUCTION

Some people think about death frequently. When a person does not openly discuss and deal with obsessive thoughts of death, wild internal thoughts of fear, isolation and confusion can occur. When negative forces prey upon us and we choose to keep our doors closed to others, this internal pandemonium grows and may even lead to the ultimate self-destructive act—suicide.

In the suicide prevention programs and workshops for high school students in which I often participate, I discuss my own crippling suicide attempt in March 1985. I explain how I was preoccupied and fascinated with death. My goal in these talks is to influence children of all ages to avoid repeating my introverted suicidal style of locking out everyone who might have helped. I would often write down my feelings, but pen and paper are not, by themselves, a sufficient outlet for such serious feelings—feelings that need to be expressed to others and feelings that require feedback. During the dark days before my own suicide attempt, just finding a non-judgmental individual and candidly speaking about the reality of death and its effects, may very well have been the medicine I needed to prevent my horrible mistake.

Death education is essential for all ages in schools and beyond. Sometimes, the less a subject as vital as death is openly and honestly discussed, the more some people will dwell on it by themselves, in their own minds. This can cause—as it did to me—fear and confusion.

The following selection is a written version of an audio will by a fictitious, suicidal adolescent. I created this document to use in my work with high school students in suicide prevention programs.

AN ADOLESCENT'S SUICIDE NOTE

Hi, Mom and Dad!

Well, here it is, November 24, 1995 at 9:27 in the morning. I thought that leaving this tape to both of you might be a bit better than dropping a note on the bed, like a lot of other kids do.

It was a real good Thanksgiving, Mom. You had a new caterer this year, right? It was nice getting most of the family together again, too. Dad, it's too bad you could only stay for one quarter of the Green Bay-Detroit game. Did you really have that much pressing work down at the office?

Bill and Donna sure are doing well at school, huh? I guess he's going to have his own law office next year downtown somewhere. And she's right on the road to becoming a certified psychologist. It was good talking to Donna the other day. I can talk to her about a lot of things. I miss not having her around much.

Uncle Jack and Aunt Peg make me kind of tense. They always playfully shake me and tell me how handsome and bright I am and how I should be making the girls beg for me, right? That nothing's going to stop me from being a success. Then you and Dad (if he's there) encourage them, and heap on more praise. I wonder sometimes if you both really mean it, or whether you just want to shut the two of them up by agreeing.

I tell you, my stomach turns to knots whenever anyone compliments me like that. It gets tighter and tighter and I just feel like busting...like there's a huge wall around me. If they *ever* knew the truth about me! Sometimes my feelings change so often that I don't even know the truth about myself. If anybody ever saw inside me or found out some of the things I've done—GOD!

I always like to smile at people—even when things are tearing me apart inside. Putting on a public mask makes me like everybody else, at least in my own mind. I wish I could be like so many of the kids I know. It always seems like nothing in the world bothers them. A lot of them are so cool. I'm really not friendly with any of them though. They all kind of accept me as a casual acquaintance.

I don't have any "close" friends, you know, including the two of you. I don't hang out with anybody in particular at school either—nobody I'd really call a true friend. That's something, huh? Almost 3 years at the same school with the same kids, and not one close friend. I just can't open myself up to them. I want to, but I can't. Donna's the only one who comes close; though she's my sister. I'm even afraid of what she might think of me if only she knew the real me.

I'm still going to keep those things secret, even now. All I'll say is that I have many, many strange feelings and thoughts. Nobody but nobody could be as weird as me.

I bought everybody's Christmas presents already. I did some early shopping and wrapping this year. You can find them on the top shelf of my closet, in the left corner. They're not much, as usual, but they're something.

Don't worry about a present for me this year. I sure hope you didn't buy anything yet. I know how you feel about *wasting* money, Dad.

Maybe the two of you can get back on track again, now that you'll be alone. Don't blame each other for my leaving like this, either. It's just something I have to do. Maybe it's the only way I'll ever get in touch with myself. You know, to simply do that and *love* myself has always been a great dream of mine. Maybe I can make it happen. Already, I can feel a great weight off of my shoulders.

Mom, Dad—have a good holiday. I expect to see you both down the road sometime.

BANG!!!

DISCUSSION

There are some critics of death education who might not want a young person to read this book, or this chapter. They are afraid of what might result. I would ask these well-intentioned people to broaden their minds and to break their silence about this subject. I would ask them if they are really prepared for *all* of the possible consequences of their silence. After all, young people don't have to read the note above; faced with the kind of silence that I encountered, they just might write their own. Please listen to your children, talk to your children, and turn to other caring adult professionals—to do all that is in your power to see that this never has to happen to anyone you know, including yourself.

17

Parental Denial of Adolescent Suicide

Richard R. Hansen, MD, Ozzie Siegel, PhD
Stanley Shapiro, MD and Fred Rosner, MD

One of the most difficult issues facing society today is adolescent suicide; since 1970 there has been a dramatic increase in suicide among youths. According to the National Center for Health Statistics, suicide is the second leading cause of death in persons under 24 years of age (accidents, many of which may very well be unrecognized suicides, are the leading cause of death among this age group).

There have been many community surveys about suicide among adolescents. Dubrow and co-workers (1989) discovered that 36 percent of all junior high school students had thought about suicide at some time in their lives and 7 percent had attempted suicide. Friedman and co-workers' 1987 study of high school students reported that 53 percent had contemplated suicide and 7 percent had attempted it. Kashini and co-workers (1989) report that 7 percent of young people and teenagers currently think about suicide and that the incidence increases steadily from 8-year-olds to 17-year-olds.

It is estimated that more than 400,000 adolescents will attempt to kill themselves in the coming year and more than 8000 will succeed. Despite major efforts to reverse the growing number of adolescent suicides, the rate of attempted and completed suicides has continued to increase.

Various theories have been offered to explain the increase in incidence of adolescent suicide. For today's young people, life can be very hard. The increasing lack of a solid family unit, the breakdown of communication between parents and children, drug and alcohol abuse by adolescents and their parents, the ever-increasing divorce rate, domestic and community violence and the demands of a highly technological and mobile society may all be related to the recent increase in suicide rates among young people. All of these issues and problems cause stress. Stress, especially recently experienced and increased stress, may be a reason that many young people try (and some succeed) to kill themselves. As well, from the suicide notes that have been left by adolescents who have attempted or completed suicide, interpersonal problems appear to be a main reason for suicidal thoughts and actions (the notes left by older people, in comparison, discuss internal problems).

While we realize that the finality of suicide is a tragic testimony to the unbearable pain and suffering felt by the attempter, there are no universally agreed-upon explanations for this act. Suicide has no class distinction; it occurs among all types of people and all age groups (with the exception of infants), nor can it be explained by any one set of descriptors. Shneidman (1985) states that "the search for a single, universal psychodynamic formulation [for adolescent suicide] is a chimera, an imaginary, nonexistent conceptual monster" (p. 236).

In order to improve prevention there is a need for greater understanding of the demographics and dynamics of suicidal adolescents. Shneidman's formulation is a warning against oversimplification. The clinician's desire for specific predictive criteria is understandable in that accurate prediction, assessment, proper intervention and effective treatment may save a life. On the other hand, the search for a "universal psychodynamic formulation" may result in the omission of important individual clinical data. Suicide and suicidal intent must be studied in the context of the dynamics of each individual adolescent, within each family.

Despite the fact that there is no single diagnosis, set of circumstances, or family dynamic that can sufficiently predict or explain adolescent suicide, there are some recurrent themes in the histories of suicidal adolescents and their families. One such theme is the pervasiveness of defensive denial.

DENIAL AS A DEFENSE

The wish to deny is an organizing principle in understanding (1) the adolescent's choice of committing suicide as a solution; (2) the emotional climate within families; and (3) the reason for resistance to treatment.

The relationship between denial and aggression is well-documented in the literature on adolescent suicide (Litman and Tabachnick 1968; Litman 1983; Hendin 1985). The classical psychodynamic formulation is that the suicidal act is the result of aggression that the adolescent cannot or does not vent; this aggression is then turned inward against the self. On the other hand, little attention has been given to the relationship between denial, dependency and loss (Litman and Tabachnick 1968).

This chapter examines the role of denial as a defense against loss and the role of denial as an intrapsychic and interpersonal element within families of suicidal adolescents. The clinical examples below, taken from actual treatment sessions with adolescents who attempted suicide, illustrate how denial is used as a defense mechanism. These examples also assist in the development of a model for treatment.

Jim: A Clinical Case Report

A 17-year-old high school junior named Jim was referred for consultation by a school psychologist who noted a decline in Jim's grades and evidence of depression with "possible suicidal potential" in his psychological test results. During the consultation, Jim revealed that he had been "very depressed" for a "few years" and for the past two years he frequently thought about suicide. He had made one suicidal gesture about a year earlier (he ingested six aspirin tablets) because he had been upset about his lack of friends and because he had feelings of worthlessness. He stated that he was "pretty sure" that the aspirin would not kill him but that he wanted to see what it would do to him. He told no one. Although he currently had no definite plan to commit suicide, he said that if he did want to kill himself "it would be easy. I'd just take a bunch of the pills from the medicine chest at home."

Jim was verbal, motivated and had some degree of insight into his difficulties. It was determined that he was not acutely suicidal, did not require hospitalization and that he could be managed on an outpatient basis. Because he had previously acted on a suicidal feeling, he presented a somewhat greater risk than if he had only thought about it.

The therapist explained to Jim that in order to successfully help him with his sadness and resignation, he needed to see him regularly. The therapist also suggested to Jim that his thoughts of suicide were of concern and needed to be taken seriously and that although the foundation of psychotherapy is confidentiality, the therapist wanted Jim to discuss his suicidal thoughts with his parents in the therapist's presence. The purpose of the conjoint session was to inform the parents of Jim's suicidal thoughts and gesture, his need for treatment and the strong recommendation that the parents be seen by someone to address the longstanding degree of isolation within the family that involved Jim, his parents, and his two older sisters. It was also suggested that for a while it might be a good idea for all medications to be removed from the medicine chest and kept by his parents. Jim readily agreed.

Jim's mother, who had accompanied him to the session, was called in and informed of the foregoing discussion. She became tearful and said she could not believe this was happening. Throughout the session she did not look at Jim, nor did she address him in any way. She asked if this was a "phase" and if treatment was really necessary. A subsequent session with Jim and his parents resulted in their reluctant agreement to treatment. They also agreed to see a referred colleague to get help for themselves.

Jim responded well to treatment. Within a few months his grades improved, his affect brightened and suicidal ideation lessened. He became aware that there was a great distance between him and his parents. He also said he felt that his parents tended to be "pollyana-ish" and had very little idea of what he felt or who he was. He reported that his parents were impatient with his treatment and that they complained about the time and money and also the traffic they had to drive through on the way to his sessions. They began to pressure him about stopping.

Jim and his parents were seen again in a session that turned into both a desperate plea and an insistence that Jim be allowed to remain in treatment. They agreed, but expressed surprise that after three months Jim still needed therapy.

A few weeks later the therapist received a message from a member of the family that Jim would be unable to keep his appointment that evening. Fearing the worst, the therapist returned the call to find that Jim's 19-year-old sister had just died of an overdose while away at college. The therapist learned later from the mother that the family felt the girl's death was a "tragic accident" and not a suicide, despite the fact that she had ingested an entire bottle of pills. Contrary to the police investigative report, the parents thought their daughter's death was the result of a "college prank gone too far."

Discussion

This sad case dramatically reveals the extent to which denial was exercised by this family in an attempt to avoid some painful truths. Denial is a ubiquitous, intrapsychic defense and interpersonal theme for suicidal adolescents and their families. In another case, when an 18-year-old high school student told his parents that the only thing that had prevented his death by hanging was the fortuitous breaking of the closet pole he had tethered himself to, their first question was whether he could still go to college. In yet another case, when told that their 15-year-old son was depressed and had considered suicide, the parents took a spur of the moment four-day vacation, informing no one, leaving him home alone, unattended.

The incredible emotional detachment and lack of responsiveness in these parents seemingly defy logic. When another set of parents was told by a professional whom they had contacted for consultation that their child was in serious danger, their response was so blasé, it seemed to the therapist that they hadn't really heard what they were told. The frustration this causes the therapist is immense; this is a life-or-death situation for the therapist's client just as it is for the parent's child. The parent's denial is a repetition of the frustration and panic in the family and is also a prominent countertransference paradigm.

The Function of Denial

To more fully understand this parental reaction one must understand how denial is a defense mechanism and how the act of denial functions for suicidal adolescents and their families. Denial is not a single defense; it refers to a broad spectrum of defenses arranged along a continuum based upon the degree of reality distortion. Included are negation, minimization, intellectualization and repudiation. At higher levels, there is less distortion of either external or internal events. At lower levels, "there are significant distortions of reality to the point that a segment of subjective experience, or of the external world, is not integrated with the rest of experience" (Lerner and Lerner 1980).

With repression, unacceptable drives and drive deviations are prevented from entering consciousness and, as such, are subject to symbolization and symptom formation. This prevents more serious disruptions of the synthetic function of the ego, a function that is responsible for organizing experience.

In contrast, under the aegis of denial, two separate but opposing ideas enter consciousness simultaneously. To defend oneself against full awareness of a painful and unacceptable idea, a split is effected within the ego. In order for denial to be successful, contradictory affects and experiences must be kept separate and therefore cannot be integrated. This situation severely interferes with thought processes involved in making connections between data and affects as well as in drawing logical conclusions in situations that pose a threat to the emergence of that which is denied.

Denial is a bottom-line, primitive defense. It is utilized when all else fails. In the extreme, it is at the root of psychotic delusions. Denial is a common initial reaction to shock. It is used to buffer the ego from the threat of overwhelming assault on sense and sensibility. The extent to which denial is utilized in noncritical situations is in direct proportion to the degree of psychopathology.

Denial helps to explain why these otherwise reasonable, intelligent parents were unable to appreciate the severity of their children's suicide threats. In a very real sense, they were not listening. The information being presented was not analyzed and synthesized but was processed through a system designed to minimize, intellectualize, extract and reverse any painful affective connection.

It could be argued that these parents were reacting with shock and disbelief. This may be one component of their reaction, but it is neither a sufficient nor a satisfying explanation. All suicidal gestures and attempts are serious. Although they may differ in degree of lethality, *there is no such thing as a nonserious suicidal gesture.* The progression from ideation to action is an indication of growing desperation resulting from an inability to manage and contain increasingly intolerable amounts of pain and frustration. There is the threat that defenses are going to be overridden. The suicidal gesture then is always serious and is an index of defensive failure.

To understand adolescent suicide and its unconscious meaning for the adolescent and its message within the family matrix, it is not enough to know which defenses are employed. It must be determined what these defenses are being marshalled against. Much of the literature cites aggression at the apex of the dynamic hierarchy (Sabbath 1969; Teicher and Jacobs 1966). The thesis is that aggression toward the mother is denied and instead turned against the self and is related to the mother's denial of her anger toward her child. Litman and Tabachnick (1968) state that in dynamic formulations about suicide, there is an overemphasis on aggression and guilt and an underemphasis on hopelessness and helplessness.

Another way to understand an adolescent's choice of suicide as a "solution" is to see it as their way of putting an end to feelings of abject hopelessness and helplessness that have arisen as a result of needs they feel have been unmet. The gradual escalation of acting-out behavior that frequently precedes a suicide attempt can be seen as an attempt to communicate their wish to be protected and understood, as well as an expression of anger over unmet needs. Shneidman (1985) states that the interpersonal act in suicide is the wish to communicate intention.

The thesis here is that an important component in the parent's failure to respond to the adolescent's dependency needs is the legacy of the denial of dependency within the family and the threat of loss of love. Pfeffer and co-workers (1979, 1980) have observed that the extended families of suicidal youths tend to be unusually close and that the relationship between the parents and their suicidal child is characterized by a symbiotic, mutual dependency. The parents' wish to deny dependence in their child is a function of their denial of their own unmet dependency needs and feelings of overwhelming powerlessness dating back to their childhood. The alarming urgency of the suicidal adolescent's despair and hopelessness does not fully register in certain parents because it threatens to evoke fears of their own overwhelming neediness. If, as Shneidman states, "suicides are born, negatively, out of needs" (1985 p. 34), the familial climate that promotes adolescent suicide is organized according to the need to deny and the denial of need.

Defensive denial is the prime reason that parents of suicidal adolescents are unable to understand the seriousness of their child's behavior. The barriers that they erect to ward off their own feelings of hopelessness, helplessness and fear of loss also compromise their ability to process information from external sources and this seriously interferes with their judgment and logic.

For this reason, a supportive, educative approach is not sufficient to help parents in defensive denial to cope with and understand the despair felt by their suicidal adolescent. These parents must be seen, concurrently, in their own treatment. To become receptive and responsive to the desperation within their child, they need to be taught how to experience and tolerate their own fears of loss and feelings of helpless abandonment.

Treatments that focus only on the suicidal individual, or treatments that are available for only a short, intensive time period are not going to be effective in coping with family members who are so deeply invested in denial. Helping a suicidal teen may require intervention and support from a number of sources, given the depth and scope of defensive denial in some families. Mental health professionals can work with the schools and the assistance of teachers and professionals in a holistic approach to dealing with this problem.

REFERENCES

Dubrow, E.F., D.F. Kausch, M.C. Blum and J. Reed. Correlates of suicidal ideation and attempts in a community sample of junior high school students. *Journal of Clinical Child Psychology* 18:158-166, 1989.

Frederick, C.J. An introduction and overview of youth suicide. In M.L. Peck, N.L. Faberow and R.E. Litman, eds., *Youth Suicide*. New York: Springer, 1985.

Friedman, J.M., G.M. Asnis, M. Boech and J. DiFore. Prevalence of specific suicidal behaviors in a high school sample. *American Journal of Psychiatry* 144:1203-1206, 1987.

Hendin, H. Suicide among the young: psychodynamics and demography. In M.L. Peck, N.L. Faberow and R.E. Litman, eds., *Youth Suicide*. New York: Springer, 1985.

Kashini, J.H., P. Goddard and J.C. Reid. Correlates of suicidal ideation in a community sample of children and adolescents. *Journal of the American Academy of Child and Adolescent Psychiatry* 28:912-917, 1989.

Lerner, P.M. and H.D. Lerner. Rorschach assessment of primitive defenses in borderline personality structure. In J.S. Kwawer, ed., *Borderline Phenomena and the Rorschach Test*. New York: International Universities Press, 1980.

Litman, R.E. Suicide as acting out. In E.S. Shneidman, N.L. Faberow and R.E. Litman, eds., *The Psychology of Suicide*. New York: Jason Aronson, 1983.

Pfeffer, C.R., H.R. Conte, R. Plutchik and I. Jerrett. Suicidal behavior in latency-age children: an empirical study. *Journal of the American Academy of Child Psychiatry* 18(4):679-692, 1979.

Pfeffer, C.R., H.R. Conte, R. Plutchik and I. Jerrett. Suicidal behavior in latency-age children: an outpatient population. *Journal of the American Academy of Child Psychiatry* 19(4):703-710, 1980.

Sabbath, J. The suicidal adolescent—the expendable child. *Journal of the American Academy of Child Psychiatry* 8(2):272-289, 1969.

Shneidman, E.S. *Definition of Suicide.* New York: John Wiley and Sons, 1985.

Teicher, J. and J. Jacobs. Adolescents who attempt suicide: preliminary findings. *American Journal of Psychiatry* 122(11):1248-1257, 1966.

18

Loss of Love: Its Role in Adolescent Suicide Attempts

Maria J. Paluszny, MD and William A. Rowane, MD

Come obscure death,
And wind me in thine all embracing arms.
Like a fond mother hide me in thy bosom,
And rock me to the sleep from which none wake.

—Beatrice Cenci, from "The Cenci" by Percy Bysshe Shelley

The current psychiatric literature cites numerous issues that may influence adolescent suicide attempts. They include peer rejection, problems at school, health problems, social isolation, drug use and abuse and cognitive and psychological problems. Interestingly, however, the factors most consistently mentioned as being related to adolescent suicide attempts are problems associated with family disorganization (Petzel and Riddle 1981; Hawton 1986). For example, young children who lose a parent through death, separation, divorce or desertion have been found to have a high rate of later suicide attempts, especially during adolescence. This correlation is especially pronounced if the loss occurred very early in a young person's life (Stanley and Barter 1970; Greer 1964). It is important to note that threatened, but not actual, parental loss experienced by young children has also been related to suicide attempts during teenage years (Barter, Swaback and Todd 1968; Margolin and Teicher 1968; Schrut 1968; Jacobs 1971).

Other family problems, especially conflicts in the relationship between adolescents and their parents, have also been associated with adolescent suicide attempts. This is not surprising in light of the fact that many teenagers today say they have longstanding and extreme problems with their parents (Teicher 1970) and they report how very upsetting and damaging a bad parent/teenager relationship can be (Barter et al. 1968). Many adolescents view their families as more maladjusted than others (Topol and Reznikoff 1982), report that communication with their parents is poor and say they have difficulty establishing meaningful relationships with them (Barter et al. 1968; Margolin et al. 1968). Adolescents often see their parents as passive and uninvolved (Marks and Haller 1977) and many report that their parents are frequently not at home (Garfinkle, Froese and Hood 1982). In general, adolescents say they feel parentally deprived and believe that their parents have an unconscious wish to be rid of them (Marks and Haller 1977). Parental discipline is often viewed by adolescents as unfair and rejecting, and they describe their parents as nagging (Jacobs 1971; Teicher 1970). Parents' attempts to discourage what they regard as unwanted behavior are often perceived by adolescents as rejection (Teicher 1970). In all, difficulty in the parent/adolescent relationship often results in teenagers' loss of love for and approval of their parents (Margolin and Teicher 1968; Schrut 1964). This loss of love and respect causes teenagers to reject their parents and it contributes to their isolation and alienation. Also, a lot of quarreling among the parents (Schrut 1968; Jacobs 1971) and stressful competition among other family members (Barter, Swaback and Todd 1968) has been found in suicidal adolescents. A significant percentage of paternal unemployment has also been seen in the families of suicidal adolescents (Garfinkle et al. 1982).

Illness, both medical and psychological, has also been found to be more common in the families of adolescent suicide attempters (Jacobs 1971; Teicher 1970; Garfinkle, Froese and Hood 1982). Also, substance abuse (Garfinkle et al. 1982), especially alcoholism (Jacobs 1971; Stanley et al. 1970; Marks et al. 1977), is significant in the families of suicidal adolescents as is a higher incidence of suicidal behavior among parents and other family members (Margolin et al. 1968; Jacobs 1971). The disrupting effects of illness of parents or other family members often force the teenagers to take on a parental role, which has been found to be a risk factor for later suicide attempts (Margolin et al. 1968; Teicher 1970).

This chapter assesses the impact of disruptive family relations on adolescent suicide attempts. When conducting this study, we were particularly interested in whether the loss of love that occurs in dysfunctional families can be identified as a precipitating factor for adolescent suicide attempts.

METHOD

Over a period of 2½ years, 50 cases of suicide attempts, sufficiently serious to warrant admission to a hospital pediatrics ward, were evaluated by the authors. The psychiatric diagnosis, the severity of the suicide attempt and the stated precipitant of the attempt were compared for adolescents who were from stable families versus those who were from disruptive families.

To simplify data analysis, certain groupings were used. The psychiatric diagnoses were made according to DSM III and were then divided into two categories: (1) milder reactive problems consisting of adjustment disorders and conduct disorders; and (2) serious psychiatric disturbances consisting of dysthymic disorder, major depression (both unipolar and bipolar depression), borderline personality disorder and schizophrenia.

The severity of the suicide attempt was rated using the SADS medical lethality scale:

1. No danger/threat only—had pills in pocket
2. Minimal—scratched wrists
3. Mild—took 10 aspirins
4. Moderate—brief unconsciousness
5. Severe—cut throat
6. Extreme—respiratory arrest

The severity was further divided into Group A, Mild to Moderate (i.e., ratings of 2, 3 and 4 as we did not have any ratings of 1); and Group B, Severe/Extreme (ratings of 5 and 6).

The precipitant of the suicide attempt was obtained from the patient during the evaluation and categorized as related to family problems, girlfriend/boyfriend problems, school problems, or internal pressure. This last category included feelings of worthlessness or the belief that life is not worthwhile and, in one case, voices telling the person to commit suicide. In each case in this last category the precipitant was not related to external problems. The families were classified into four types:

1. Intact. This type of family may have had some problems; however, there were no major upheavals or disruptions in the family's ability to function as a unit.
2. Divorced, but stable. This family could be a reconstituted family or a single-parent family, but again, there were no major disruptions.
3. Enmeshed. In this family, generation boundaries were not well delineated, leading to disturbed functioning of the family as a unit.
4. Chaotic. In this family there were either multiple separations and reconciliations, abuse or multiple serial partners. (In the most seriously disturbed and chaotic families in the study, family violence had led to one parent killing the other.)

The two samples compared were *dysfunctional families* (chaotic plus enmeshed families) versus *functional families* (intact plus divorced but stable families). The variables considered were the precipitant of the attempt, the psychiatric diagnosis and the severity of the suicide attempt itself. The data analysis was done by using the chi-square test to determine if differences between samples were statistically significant.

Description of Sample

All 50 patients were admitted to the pediatrics ward following a suicide attempt. Some of the patients were initially admitted to the Intensive Care Unit, but in all cases a psychiatric evaluation was done as soon as the patient was responsive. In the vast majority of cases, the parents were also interviewed. In a few cases the parents were unavailable. The patients consisted of teenagers, ages 13 to 18. There were 37 females and 13 males. Of the sample, 35 were white, 9 were black and 6 were Asian, Hispanic or East Indian. The most frequent method they used to commit suicide was overdose of a variety of medications. In a few cases, attempts were made by cutting (usually wrist cutting; however, one patient attempted to cut his throat). Asphyxia by carbon monoxide poisoning was used in two cases and self-immolation in one case. We had no attempts made by gunshot or by multiple vehicle crash or by jumping. All of our suicide attempters survived; one had residual brain damage. Of the 50 attempters, 21 were repeaters (i.e., had a previous history of making a suicide attempt), while 29 represented first attempters. Three attempters had a history of making three or more previous suicide attempts.

RESULTS

Of the 50 suicide attempters, 30 came from dysfunctional families (21 chaotic families and nine enmeshed families). The remaining 20 were considered to be from functional families (15 intact families and five divorced but stable families). In comparing these two family groupings according to the precipitant, the trigger for suicide attempt, we found family arguments and family problems were far more frequent in the dysfunctional group. For 19 adolescents from the dysfunctional group, family arguments or problems were the precipitant. In the functional or normal family, only five adolescents attributed the attempt to family pressures. When the dysfunctional family group was compared with the functional family group for other precipitants, there was no significant difference between the two groups. Girlfriend/boyfriend problems were the precipitant in six attempts in the dysfunctional family and in eight attempts in the functional family group. Internal pressures accounted for five attempts in the dysfunctional and five attempts in the functional family group. School problems were rare in both. None reported school as a precipitant in the dysfunctional family group and only two in the functional family group.

Seriousness of psychiatric disturbance was measured by the psychiatric diagnosis and, as described previously, was divided into less serious problems (adjustment disorders and conduct disorders) and serious problems (dysthymic disorder, unipolar and bipolar depression, borderline personality disorder and schizophrenia). In the dysfunctional family group, 17 were classified as having less serious disturbances and 13 as having more serious psychiatric disturbances. In the functional family group, 13 were classified as having less serious psychiatric disturbances and seven as having more serious psychiatric disturbances. These differences were statistically not significant.

The seriousness of the suicide attempt likewise showed no significant difference between the two family groups. The severe, extreme classification of lethality of attempt occurred seven times in both groups. The remainder, i.e., 13 in the functional family and 23 in the dysfunctional family, were mild to moderately lethal attempts.

In summary, from the above data analysis, we found the only significant variable that distinguishes the suicide attempters who were from dysfunctional families from the suicide attempters from functional families was the precipitant of family arguments or family problems. All the other precipitants, as well as the seriousness of the psychiatric disturbance and the medical lethality of the suicide attempt, showed no significant difference in the two family groups.

After completing this portion of our analysis, we were curious if our data would tell us more about suicide attempts in general. Further analysis indicated that the medical lethality of the attempts was randomly distributed throughout our sample, as was the seriousness of psychiatric disturbance. The only statistically significant finding was that the precipitant of internal pressure was related to severity of psychiatric disturbance. Of the total sample of 50, 10 suicide attempts were triggered by internal pressures. Eight were diagnosed as having a serious psychiatric disturbance and only two had a less serious psychiatric disturbance.

DISCUSSION

Contemporary authors on psychopathology have viewed suicide from three perspectives: (1) as an aggression against the self (especially the self as it represents the introject of the parents); (2) as an aggressive, manipulative or attention-seeking behavior; and (3) as expression of severe underlying psychopathology. We did not evaluate our data from the perspective of manipulative or attention-seeking behavior. However, the other two explanations of suicidal behavior can be seen from our findings on the precipitants.

It is easy to see the connection between severity of psychiatric disturbance and the precipitant of internal pressure. Severely disturbed adolescents show a withdrawal from external investments, they focus their energies on resolving abstract struggles or preoccupations. Even without the presence of an external stressor, internal pressures or the feeling of despondency and hopelessness can lead to a suicide attempt. One of our patients, a girl who had no external precipitant for attempting suicide and who described an internal pressure as the reason, said, "I just felt bored and tired. There was nothing to look forward to; I was just going to school and coming home." This girl came from an intact, upper-middle-class family. She was an excellent student and was involved in extracurricular activities. Prior to the attempt she began sleeping more, going out less and generally appeared depressed. She was diagnosed as having a major depressive episode. Her family history indicated that there was probably a strong biological predisposition toward depression, as several family members previously had been diagnosed as having either a unipolar or bipolar depression.

The precipitant of family problems being more frequent in a dysfunctional family warrants more explanation. Superficially, one could argue that in a dysfunctional family, the loss of love has already occurred, the adolescent has already withdrawn from family members and, therefore, a precipitant of family problems is unlikely to cause conflicts. Actually, the opposite is true. To aid in this explanation, the following case example will be used.

CASE STUDY

Meg, a 14-year-old girl, was admitted to the Intensive Care Unit of a hospital following an overdose of Tylenol. She attributed the overdose to anger at her mother, who she felt was always critical and "did not trust me." The night of her attempt, Meg was to visit some teenage friends. When she did not return home on time, her mother and stepfather went looking for her. When they went to the first friend's house, they were told that Meg was not there. After visiting several friends' homes, her parents found out that Meg was at the first friend's home after all. Meg, however, gave vague explanations as to what had actually happened. An argument ensued and the suicide attempt occurred later that evening. At the time of the evaluation, following the attempt, Meg expressed much anger at her mother and was particularly angry that her mother did not trust her. Usually, however, it appeared that the stepfather was the focus of Meg's anger. The mother disclosed that Meg was often angry at her stepfather and that she often urged her mother to leave him and to reconcile with the natural father. In the past, prior to the divorce, the parents had several separations and reconciliations. However, at this time, both of them had remarried. In addition, sometime in the past, the mother and stepfather had also separated. During this separation the mother lived with another man. When angry, Meg often urged her mother to return to this former live-in partner.

After the suicide attempt, Meg again began complaining about her stepfather, viewing him as inadequate. At that time she appeared to reconcile with her mother. It was our feeling at that time that Meg showed a splitting of the parental image. She saw her stepfather as inadequate and blamed him for most problems. She rarely appeared angry with her mother and even tolerated the mother's frequent withdrawals. On the occasion of the suicide attempt, Meg's anger was not only directed at her mother herself, but also at the early introject of the mother, i.e., at Meg.

In his writings on adolescence, Blos (1976) describes how, in the normal adolescent stage of development, the early splitting of the "good" and "bad" parent is relived. This reliving is usually done through the peer group. The adolescent appears to select peer groups with attributes that can be associated with her parents as well as attributes that are a reflection of herself. These attributes have both positive and negative aspects. By reliving them through peer relationships, the adolescent is able to integrate and unify negative and positive aspects, not only in external object relationships, but also in the split self-image. This appears to be an important aspect in the adolescent's development of self-esteem. If, however, the adolescent's family is so dysfunctional that the adolescent is unable to disengage sufficiently from her family to resolve the split through her peer group or, if the adolescent was never able to adequately internalize the parental image earlier in childhood, problems in resolving the split can occur. In such cases, the adolescent is more likely to regress to earlier developmental stages in attempting to resolve parental conflicts, as well as self-esteem issues. The good and bad split may persist or the adolescent may wish to regress and find the child's ideal love, which was lost as he grew. Erlich (1978) describes how frequently in the analysis of adolescents there appears to be a regressive pull, which he describes as "a longing to merge with a maternal object, a return to the oceanic feeling of blissful symbiosis with the mother" (p. 264). He goes on to hypothesize that this wish as well as the adolescent's unusual abstract thinking are two important factors associated with adolescent suicide attempts.

Our findings of the adolescents from dysfunctional families, showing a highly significant incidence of family problems as the precipitant for the attempt, support this hypothesis. In other words, the adolescent from a dysfunctional family is still struggling to resolve preadolescent object relations within the family. An additional stress with these objects can precipitate anger at the still-ambivalent internalized parental image and at the self, which is a concomitant; thus, a suicide attempt may be the outcome. This theme of love, loss of love and hope for reunification with a mother figure is the theme of the poem quoted at the beginning of this chapter. The basic concept of adolescents making a suicide attempt in order to fulfill these longings has been described by Erlich (1978). Our data suggest these dynamics are more likely to occur when unresolved family conflicts are present. In such dysfunctional families, a stress related to the family is more likely to produce regression and to precipitate a suicide attempt.

REFERENCES

Barter, J.T., D.O. Swaback and D. Todd. Adolescent suicide attempts: a follow-up study of hospitalized patients. *Archives of General Psychiatry* 19:523-527, 1968.

Blos, P. The split parental image in adolescent social relations: an inquiry into group psychology. *The Psychoanalytic Study of the Child* 31:72-73, 1976.

Dorpat, T.L., J.K. Jackson and H.S. Ripley. Broken homes and attempted and completed suicide. *Archives of General Psychiatry* 12:213-216, 1965.

Erlich, H.S. Adolescent suicide: maternal longing and cognitive development. *The Psychoanalytic Study of the Child* 33:261-277, 1978.

Garfinkle, B.D., A. Froese and J. Hood. Suicide attempts in children and adolescents. *American Journal of Psychiatry* 139:1257-1261, 1982.

Greer, S. The relationship between parental loss and attempted suicide: a control study. *British Journal of Psychiatry* 110:698-705, 1964.

Hawton, K. *Suicide and Attempted Suicide Among Children and Adolescents.* Beverly Hills, CA: Sage Publications, 1986.

Jacobs, J. *Adolescent Suicide.* New York: Wiley Interscience, 1971.

Margolin, N. and J. Teicher. Thirteen adolescent male suicide attempts: dynamic considerations. *Journal of the American Academy of Child Psychiatry* 7:296-315, 1968.

Marks, P.A. and D.L. Haller. Now I lay me down for keeps: a study of adolescent suicide attempts. *Journal of Clinical Psychology* 33:390-400, 1977.

Petzel, S.V. and M. Riddle. Adolescent suicide: psychosocial and cognitive aspects. *Adolescent Psychiatry* 9:343-398, 1981.

Schrut, A. Some typical patterns in the behavior and background of adolescent girls who attempted suicide. *American Journal of Psychiatry* 125:107-112, 1968.

Schrut, A. Suicidal adolescents and children. *Journal of the American Medical Association* 188:1103-1107, 1964.

Stanley, E.J. and J.T. Barter. Adolescent suicidal behavior. *American Journal of Orthopsychiatry* 40:87-95, 1970.

Teicher, J.D. Children and adolescents who attempt suicide. *Pediatric Clinics of North America* 17:687-696, 1970.

Topol, P. and M. Reznikoff. Perceived peer and family relationships, hopelessness and locus of control as factors in adolescent suicide attempts. *Suicide and Life-Threatening Behavior* 12:141-150, 1982.

Wenz, F.V. Sociological correlates of alienation among adolescent suicide attempts. *Adolescence* 14:19-30, 1979.

19

Helping Students Cope with Death: Guidelines for Educators

Robert G. Stevenson, EdD and Harry L. Powers, EdD

The day promised to be one of those that a school principal really enjoys. The previous evening consisted of meetings with active, positive and involved parents who were willing to contribute to the improvement of the curriculum and who were going to help assemble a great post-prom celebration. Today's schedule included a faculty meeting to be followed that night with an impressive foreign language induction for French and Spanish honor students, as well as the annual football boosters' banquet to honor the undefeated state champion team.

Suddenly, however, all happy thoughts of anticipation were dashed when a faculty member reported to the principal that the physical education class was in shock. Apparently, the class had just found out that Bill, a senior student and member of the football team, had died in his sleep early that morning. Some students were becoming hysterical and there was a lot of chaos. Teachers wanted to know if Bill had really died?

The principal contacted a student who seemed to know what had happened and asked him to come to his office to verify the source of his information. At the same time, a teacher who knew Bill and had heard the rumor volunteered to visit Bill's house to see if he could be of any assistance and agreed to call the school once he got there to confirm or deny the rumor. The student who first imparted the information about Bill's death did indeed have personal knowledge of the situation and the teacher's eventual call also confirmed the sad truth of the senior's death.

A year earlier, in the aftermath of the space shuttle Challenger tragedy, the principal had designed a system for schools to use when informing students of death. The faculty had been introduced to the steps of that plan at faculty meetings during the previous school year. Now, that plan would be tested by the need to notify faculty, staff and students of the death of a young person who was a member of this school community. The following section is a first-person account from the principal who was in that position.

PUTTING THEORY INTO PRACTICE

I met with the counselors, administrators and a cadre of teachers who had previously indicated that they would be willing to assist if, or rather when, this type of situation occurred. I shared with the group all of the facts I knew and answered their questions. It was stressed that we had no information to suggest that Bill's death had been caused by suicide or substance abuse. Because no information concerning funeral arrangements was yet available, I told everyone that it would be provided through the main office as soon as possible.

Following this meeting I used the public address system to announce that we had experienced a tragedy and that students and teachers should remain in their classrooms so that a faculty member could visit each room to share specific information with them. Bells were discontinued as staff members and I visited assigned rooms to explain the tragedy to the students. After each classroom had been visited, I again used the public address system to review the situation and asked for a moment of silence in remembrance of Bill.

Counselors and qualified teachers were encouraged to make themselves available to counsel and support students who were experiencing severe grief reactions. Later in the day I met with the advisors and members of the student government organization. They outlined plans for a memorial fund to be started in Bill's name. The officers of the football boosters' club conferred with school officials, and as Bill had been a member of the team, they decided to begin the dinner already planned for that evening with a memorial to Bill. Eulogies were to be delivered by coaches and team members.

The students were dismissed one hour early the next day and a memorial service was held for any students or staff who wished to attend. The auditorium was overflowing with hundreds of students and staff and the members of Bill's family. The grief over our common loss was shared and for most there was a feeling of unity, and perhaps support, that was to provide each of us with a starting point as we moved on from this tragic loss.

VARIED REACTIONS

The overall reaction to the way in which the staff and students responded to their loss was very positive. Teachers, students, parents and board of education members commented with pride, if not relief, on the way in which all elements of the school community had worked together at a most difficult time.

By speaking openly of the loss, and by bringing the school together, those people who were suffering and needed assistance with problems concerning the death, felt that they could go to any of several sources for support. Counselors, teachers, administrators and peer listeners all played a part in providing this follow-up support.

By acknowledging how the loss of one classmate caused a change in the school as a community, individuals were provided with a feeling that they mattered, that each had a unique role to play and a contribution to make, that together, as a unit, they comprised a strong mutual support.

By seeing Bill's football photos and awards displayed with the team's championship trophy for several weeks, people were reminded that he was still in our thoughts and that feelings don't just stop because a physical body is gone and because an active relationship has ended.

By sharing feelings (or the lack of them) about Bill's death, students were helped to realize that they were not alone in their reactions, whatever their reaction happened to be. They also found that some of the things that frightened them were actually normal ways in which some people experience grief.

By observing the way in which those who had been seen as "outside" the mainstream of academic life conducted themselves during the memorial for their friend, many students and staff discovered a new and positive perspective on individuals that they had viewed in a negative way before. Bill had been a friend to students from many areas of school life, including some who were very involved in school activities and others who did not seem to have much of an interest in school. One teacher explained her tears after the memorial service by saying that she now saw that she had underestimated certain young people. She was crying because she was wondering how many other young people she might have underestimated in the same way. She said that thinking of this day might help her to avoid making the same mistake again.

By having the school accept the responsibility of a central role in working through this loss, students saw the school as a positive force in helping them to deal with their problems. While it is hard to measure, this may foster a more positive attitude in students toward all areas of school life.

There were two negative reactions to the response of the school community. The first was expressed by an administrator who feared that the open expression of sorrow by so many students might cause self-destructive behavior by some. Time has proved this concern to be unfounded. However, it was a possibility that was kept in mind as concerned adults and peer listeners sought out students who might have experienced such a negative reaction. The second concern was voiced by teachers who thought that too much was being made of the entire incident and that some students might have taken it as an opportunity to skip class by going to speak to a counselor or attending Bill's funeral. It is true that in any large group there might indeed be a few students who would seek to use such a tragedy for their own ends. However, this behavior was a constant for these students and it was felt that it would be a second tragedy if the needs of hundreds of students remained unmet because of the possible misconduct of a few.

The reaction of the teachers who had negative reactions highlights the fact that in times of stress, some of us fall back on coping behaviors that we are familiar with and have used in the past. When one part of our lives seems out of control (as it could after a death), we sometimes seek to restore a feeling of balance by asserting greater control in those areas where we can. Concerns about attendance on the part of some teachers represented just such an attempt at reestablishing control. Most teachers dropped their objections when they were reassured that the students concerned really did need to talk and that grief reactions might still be present days or weeks later.

WHY GIVE SCHOOLS ANOTHER JOB?

As educational leaders, we believe we should be prepared for every possible problem situation in our schools. We attend seminars and workshops and read professional journals to learn how to deal with teacher strikes, budget crises, legal actions, media invasions, standardized tests, declining enrollments, AIDS, loss of teacher motivation and dozens of other possibilities. We may need to use this preparation or we may be very fortunate and have a situation pass us by. However, we may have to deal with the effects of a situation on a student or a colleague. Our choice is to ignore the odds and be surprised or to establish a plan of action and handle the situation in an orderly and professional manner.

When a death occurs, administrators must have definite procedures that allow them to provide clear, decisive and meaningful direction to the rest of the school—both staff and students. It is not enough to be a passive participant by attending a funeral or memorial service. When a death occurs, the actions of individual educators and the leadership role of the school will be evaluated by the entire community. The morale and motivation of teachers and staff are clearly affected by the manner in which administrators show that they care and by the direction they provide. Isn't it logical to believe that students are affected in the same way by the caring and direction demonstrated by their teachers and staff?

It is difficult to remain objective and unemotional during tragic situations. However, in such cases, the school community has an opportunity to demonstrate through example that the loss is tragic and will be acknowledged and also that life can and will go on.

If we as educators wait until a tragedy occurs, we will be forced to decide what to do and how to do it under the pressure of too little time and highly charged emotions. But as most would agree, an ounce of prevention can curtail a pound of negative consequences. In the case discussed above, the ounce of prevention manifested itself as a set of guidelines we had already put in place in our system (Stevenson and Powers 1986). We developed these guidelines by drawing on our backgrounds as administrators, teachers, counselors and death educators. These guidelines can readily be adapted to suit the needs of other educators in other situations.

GUIDELINES FOR INFORMING AN INDIVIDUAL STUDENT OF A DEATH

When informing an individual student of a death, the following guidelines should be kept in mind:

1. The student should be informed of a death by someone who is trusted and seen as an authority figure. The principal is often the logical choice.

2. Someone who is close to the student (teacher, nurse, counselor or fellow student) should be asked to remain with the student after the news is received.

3. The student should be taken to a place where there is privacy and where the student can remain and rest after receiving the news. The student should be able to sit or lie down if necessary. In most schools, the nurse's office meets both of these requirements.

4. In a quiet, simple and direct manner, the student should be told what has happened. Platitudes and religious symbolism should be avoided. All questions should be answered simply and honestly, but unnecessary details need not be offered. One should not be afraid to speak openly of feelings and emotions. This can help the student to sort out confusing reactions and to see the school as assuming a supportive role, even if this feeling only occurs at a later date.

5. Remember, there is no one "correct" response to news of a death. After a student has been told the news, any number of reactions are possible and each is valid.

6. Offering physical contact to the student may have a calming effect, but not all students will want this. If the student wishes to merely sit, this choice should be respected. However, the student should not be left alone.

7. If the student remains silent, inform her that it is all right to say how she feels.
8. All of the student's teachers should be informed as soon as possible.

Most of the points listed above are intended for interaction with an individual and would be of little value if the entire school community is affected. The sheer numbers of affected students would make it impossible for everyone's individual needs to be addressed by a single person. Such a traumatic situation requires the cooperation of all school personnel.

GUIDELINES FOR DEALING WITH "COMMUNITY" GRIEF

When dealing with larger groups, these guidelines concerning the announcement of a death are practical:

1. The chief school administrator makes an announcement to the entire student body. The students are instructed to remain in their classes and are told that they will receive more information shortly. Teachers and aides should be aware that this directive requires full cooperation on everyone's part and may require that staff and students stay in their classrooms beyond what would normally be the end of the class period.
2. One or more persons will then go to each class and convey the news of the event. All available information should be given in a calm, direct manner. The person conveying the information can then answer questions or allow time to discuss feelings and reactions. After the departure of the contact person, the classroom teacher may discuss the meaning and effects of the loss, answer questions about funeral etiquette, or help the class decide if they wish to have some observance as a group. This observance might consist of helping to meet some of the immediate needs of the deceased's family.
3. When all classes have been informed, a followup schoolwide announcement can be made. It may be appropriate to observe a moment of silence at this time in memory of the deceased.
4. If a memorial is planned in the school, students should be allowed and encouraged to take part in the planning.

Since faculty members play such a vital part in all of this, staff workshops should be scheduled *before* a tragedy occurs so that teachers can determine what feelings and experiences of their own might help or complicate such a situation. Working with staff and students after a tragedy is not impossible, but the process of "psychic annulment" makes helping them far more difficult if a groundwork has not been laid beforehand.

Because dealing with death is never pleasant or easy, a school must be prepared in advance. This preparation can reduce the intensity of the situation, eliminate the possibility of tactless or embarrassing mistakes and affirm the leadership role of the school in the community.

REFERENCES

Bordewich, F.M. Mortal fears: courses in death education get mixed reviews. *Atlantic Monthly* 261(2):30-34, 1988.

McHugh, M. *Young People Talk About Death*. New York: Franklin Watts, 1980.

Schowalter, J.E., et al., eds., *Children and Death: Perspectives from Birth through Adolescence*. New York: Praeger, 1987.

Stevenson, R.G. The child and suffering: the role of the school. In R. DeBellis et al., eds., *Suffering: Psychological and Social Aspects in Loss, Grief and Care*. Binghamton, NY: Haworth, 1987.

Stevenson, R.G. Measuring the effects of death education in the classroom. In *Children and Death: Proceedings of the 1985 King's College Conference*. London, Ontario: King's College, 1985.

Stevenson, R.G. How to handle death in the school. *Education Digest* 52(9):42-43, 1987.

Stevenson, R.G. and Powers, H.L. How to handle death in the school. *Tips for Principals*, December 1986.

20

Death Themes in Literature: Uses in the High School Classroom

Joyce Garvin, MS

Whatever else education accomplishes in the way of transmitting data, polishing skills, enlarging critical and creative capacities and making the physical and psychological worlds more understandable, certainly our schools should also introduce young people to what we resignedly but somehow affectionately call the "human condition." And to do this—to teach about life—means we must also provide information about death. Many years ago, when the River Dell Board of Education was first considering the adoption of our "Perspectives on Death" course, one horrified antagonist complained, "Why should we teach them about death when they don't even know where Africa is?" The answer is clear: students today are more likely to encounter death than they are to need to know where Africa is. Also, each area of the curriculum has something unique to offer in terms of the subject of death. The antagonist might as well have asked, why teach students how to read when they can't play the piano?

Death education courses can be offered separately, but most disciplines already make reference to death and could easily be expanded to use those references to include information about death. For example: health and family living classes can examine retirement provisions; history classes can discuss the lives lost to war and famine; psychology and sociology can directly teach about death rituals, fears and conventions. Arithmetic word problems could incorporate the subject of death by the measurement of cemetery plots and the evaluation of life insurance benefits. Even if these examples seem somewhat far-fetched, the idea is clear; death should not be a subject that is always shunned. Such a matter-of-fact approach to death education would surely weaken that ubiquitous reflex shiver, "Oh, I don't want to talk about death; it is too depressing and frightening."

The study of English offers the broadest opportunity to legitimize death, to allow students to think and write and speak naturally, without the constraints that now silence the subject. In writing, fears about death are pointedly expressed through folk idioms: dead silence; sudden death overtime; deadbeat; dead tired; dead end; I could have died laughing; you'll be the death of me; sick to death; dead to the world; I'm dying to go; over my dead body; and, it's a dead issue!

Fulfilling an open-ended writing assignment that asks students to describe a moving experience, someone will invariably mention death. At such times a sensitive teacher can lead a class into the kind of discussion that genuinely connects young people. But the occasion doesn't have to be infrequent. One of our aims is to make the subject of dying more accessible, less taboo. Directing open discussions about death doesn't mean that we lose the respect, awe, or sadness that keeps death mysterious. If we can talk about love without tarnishing it and continue to esteem *that* emotion from the pulpit, on the street, in bars and classrooms, why not death?

The teaching of grammar, spelling, syntax and punctuation does not proceed through abstraction. Language use demands frequent examples. In order to learn parallelism, we concoct parallel sentences: "The last time I attended a funeral I cried, I fidgeted, then I felt bored"; "Whenever I visit my aunt, who is dying of cancer, I tell her stories and read her articles, but inside my feelings are angry and frightened and confused"; "To be young is to pursue experience; to be old is to approach death." Since death is our shared fate, it should not be exiled from classroom exercise (nor, of course, should it be bludgeoned [to death!] through forced application).

Art, especially literature, has always richly conveyed our apprehensions and our convictions about ourselves as human beings. We cannot honestly survey the worlds within and without unless we attend to death. Such an omission would be like teaching about the "good" without reference to the "bad"; like teaching about "teaching" without consideration of "learning."

At some point, during every serious high school literature course, students will wistfully—but not belligerently—complain that the stories and plays they read are so sad; why can't they study happy stuff? They've got a point. Great art is inspired by those painful acts of existence that scar us all. We seem to need to air our wounds through the indirection of art. Storytelling is communal. Perhaps the recognition that we're all in this mess together is the best way of treating those existential throbbings. Although literature also celebrates joy, we don't really need the help of art to feel good. We can revel in joy and pleasure sufficiently on our own, person-to-person. But we are haunted by memories of bad times and sometimes we feel lonely. Yes, I answer my students, literature scratches the wounds that itch, literature addresses our discomforts. I remind them that we socialize children in order to make life more understandable. To protect them, we warn about some of the problems and obstacles that lie ahead. Learning to give up animal freedom and to conform to social necessity is hard and painful; these are lessons accompanied by resentment, frustration, impatience and disappointment. But we have an obligation to the young. "Hey, that's life," we say. In similar fashion, as teachers of fiction, drama and poetry, we are not just presenting an art form; we are also socializing and sensitizing our students through that art form; and we would be remiss if our literature did not reflect the heartbreak of humankind. "Hey, that's life; hey, that's death." A fuzzy mirror is dishonest.

Literature is concrete. Literary death happens to a particular character or group of characters, and it is observed and responded to by other characters (and also by the reader). Authors have their own reasons for writing about death. Having dramatized the fact that life is finite and we all must die, a writer may lead us to question how we should pass our time during this one earthly fling: how can we best avoid final regrets and self-recriminations? Sometimes death is only a secondary theme. In the following anti-war poem, for example, e.e. cummings is satirically concerned with the self-indulgence and insensitivity of home-front patriots:

> My sweet old etcetera
> aunt Lucy during the recent
> war could and what
> is more did tell you just
> what everybody was fighting
> for,
> my sister
>
> Isabel created hundreds
> (and
> hundreds) of socks, not to
> mention shirts fleaproof earwarmers
> etcetera wristers etcetera, my
> mother hoped that
> I would die etcetera
> bravely of course my father used
> to become hoarse talking about how it was
> a privilege and if only he
> could meanwhile my
> self etcetera lay quietly
> in the deep mud et
> cetera
> (dreaming,

et
cetera, of
your smile
eyes knees and of your Etcetera-

I have never distinguished the following works as "death literature."
Moved by what they portray, and admiring the language and imagery that
express their meaning (perhaps even *create* their meaning), I have taught
each piece because I love and respect it. Any addicted English teacher (as
babies we crawled from the womb to the library, beguiled by the magic of
"once upon a time") can give you just as meaningful a list. There are stories
for kindergartners and for graduating seniors; poems that feed the dull or
nourish the gifted; novels that provoke the indifferent or soothe the embat-
tled.

In John Millington Synge's "Riders to the Sea," old Maurya says wearily,
"They're all gone now and there isn't anything more the sea can do to me...
No man at all can be living forever and we must be satisfied." Centuries
ago, as a student in sophomore English, I read those lines. And I remember
how my high school classmates and I were silenced by the awesome
thought that we were all "riders to the sea" (that powerful, shifting symbol
of both life and death). We murmured a few condolences, cried a little
inside, and for a very short time—but I still recall it!—we felt close to each
other.

Another very touching play (accessible to practically everybody) is
Thornton Wilder's "Our Town": you hear the dead commenting from their
graveyard, but the dialogue is never morbid. The play celebrates ordinary
life and the need to seize it. Tom Stoppard's "Rosencrantz and Guildenstern
Are Dead," by contrast, is a wry, existentially detached appraisal that I
study only with Advanced Placement seniors. They nod when Rosencrantz
quietly admits, "Immortality is all I seek," and even perk up a bit when one
of the Players assures them that every exit may be looked on as an entrance
to somewhere else. Although Stoppard's play is wittily self-reflexive, with
elegant word-play that promotes intellectual, rather than emotional, response, there are many sobering thoughts. Rosencrantz reflects:

It could go on forever. Well, not for *ever*, I suppose. Do you ever think of
yourself as actually *dead*, lying in a box with a lid on it?... It's silly to be
depressed by the thought of it. I mean one thinks of it like being alive in a box,
one keeps forgetting to take into account the fact that one is *dead*...which
should make all the difference...shouldn't it? I mean, you'd never know you
were in a box, would you? It would be just like being asleep in a box. Not that
I'd like to sleep in a box, mind you, not without any air—you'd wake dead,
for a start, and then where would you be? Stuffed in a box like that, I mean
you'd be in there forever. Even taking into account the fact that you're dead,
it isn't a pleasant thought. *Especially* if you're dead, really... ask yourself, if I

asked you straight off—I'm going to stuff you in this box now, would you rather be alive or dead? Naturally you'd prefer to be alive. Life in a box is better than no life at all, I expect. You'd have a chance at least. You could lie there thinking—well, at least I'm not dead!

Stoppard has a way of beating a dead horse that is tragicomic: painful but funny at the same time. On the other hand, his desperation can be quite direct:

Whatever became of the moment when one first knew about death? There must have been one, a moment, in childhood, when it first occurred to you that you don't go on forever. It must be born with an intuition of mortality. Before we know the words for it, before we know there are words, out we come, bloodied and squalling with the knowledge that for all the compasses in the world, there's only one direction and time is its only measure.

Oddly, these grim little sallies seem to relieve, not upset, my students, probably by virtue of Stoppard's crazy logic ("after all, you won't know that you're dead") and verbal pyrotechnics, or maybe Aristotle was right: whenever drama arouses pity and terror, it serves as catharsis. The act of recognizing and confronting our fears drains the emotions. Isn't that one of the professed aims of psychological therapy? Being left to acknowledge an experience so paralyzing that the patient had repressed it or dealt with it poorly? Narrating experience (during therapy or in the confessional; telling stories or writing poems) brings spiritual renewal, release from tension. Putting us through the wringer, the creators of high-voltage literature often reduce our anxiety.

Take Michael Cristofer's 1976 Tony Award-winning drama, "The Shadow Box." Three terminally ill patients are facing imminent death. With their families, they live in separate cottages on the grounds of a hospital. We who have not yet shared the lingering weeks and days and hours of a loved one's death wonder how we will manage in such extremity. Will we shatter? Cristofer does not indulge in wishy-washy sentimentality, but neither is he unnecessarily brutal. Joe, the first patient, wants his wife and son with him, but Maggie lacks courage. She can scarcely enter the cottage, much less tell their boy the truth. The second patient, Brian, a gifted and philosophic bisexual, needs the company of both his affectionate ex-wife and his male lover. Brian tries to live in the present: to smooth the edges of unfinished business, to undertake new skills. But behind this brave energy Brian is terrified: "They think it's supposed to last forever... The trouble is that most of us spend our entire lives trying to forget that we're going to die, and some of us succeed. It's like pulling the cart without the horse." In the last cottage a suffering, querulous, bitter old woman keeps herself alive, unbearably exploiting one daughter, while she fantasizes the return of her favored daughter, long dead.

This is the drama of life poised one heartbeat away from death; this is the naked edge. Before the curtain closes we have a deep and certain sense of these three and the people closest to them. Their past human history is implicit in the way they now approach death, the moment of truth. There is no sheltering metaphor. Are teenagers too frail for such trauma? Well, one of the patients gives a partial answer: "They should have told us when we were kids!"

Do artistic rehearsals like "The Shadow Box" build up emotional strength, so that we play our human role with greater composure when the time comes? Are we somehow better prepared for the real thing? Let me try to answer: I took several classes to see this play and they were disturbed, excited, moved and voluble, all at the same time. What grew increasingly clear was that my *own* reaction was not so intense as theirs. This difference in the level of our emotional response intrigued me. True, they were especially sensitive young adults, but I'm sensitive, too. The explanation lay in the fact that I had already experienced and assimilated monuments and volumes of great art with strong death overtones. I had already internalized much of the wisdom of this wonderful play. My students were undergoing powerful insights to which literature—not life itself—had already exposed me. It was not just the gap in our ages, nor was it the related probability that I had lived through a greater number of actual deaths. (I had *not*: we discussed this question at length in class.)

Art causes significant change in us; it is an emotional event, a genuine happening to the mind and soul. We are spiritually altered. Because of my greater exposure to literature, I had learned to bear the presence of death more comprehensively than my students. Although just as moved as they, I could tolerate the hurt better. So yes, I believe in education for life, which, by extension, implies education for death.

And what a mammoth reservoir of material to draw from! In Somerset Maugham's play "Sheppy," Death, as a character, recounts the following vignette:

> There was a merchant in Baghdad who sent his servant to market to buy provisions, and in a little while the servant came back, white and trembling, and said, Master, just now when I was in the marketplace I was jostled by a woman in the crowd and when I turned it was Death that jostled me. She looked at me and made a threatening gesture; now, lend me your horse, and I will ride away from this city and avoid fate. I will go to Samarra and there Death will not find me.' The merchant lent him his horse, and the servant mounted it, and he dug his spurs in its flanks and as fast as the horse could gallop he went. Then the merchant went down to the market place and he saw Death standing in the crowd and he came to Death and said, 'Why did you make a threatening gesture to my servant when you saw him this morning?' 'That was not a threatening gesture,' Death said. 'It was only a start of surprise. I was astonished to see him in Baghdad, for I had an appointment with him tonight in Samarra.'

This little story invariably provokes argument, even philosophic and religious comment (without the heavy and deadening jargon more learned scholars bring to discourse). Because the matter-of-factness of its tone is edged by the fabulous and exotic, it appeals to both ingenuous fourth graders and sophisticated seniors.

For a brief arouser, read G.B. Shaw's essay occasioned by his mother's death and cremation. Students groan when I pass this out. They anticipate wracking sorrow; they experience unexpected delight. Everyone can profit from Shaw's loving and whimsical tribute. One student spoke for the whole class when he realized that we can keep our beloved dead with us in happy memory. Being human means living in the mind, in the imagination and fantasy, just as much as it means living in the body. And, like good old G.B., we can dip into our memory banks and replay scenes that keep the dead memorably, not morbidly, intact. We can even play healthy "make believe," speculating how they might have advised us on certain present problems, or reacted to current experiences with us. Obviously we must never blur the clean line between the real and the imagined. But research has disclosed that good fantasy does wonders for the immune system.

The British writer Elizabeth Taylor penned a stunning four-page story called "The Sad Garden"; it's a tale both poignant and funny. A rather acerbic lady, whose husband and son tragically died some time back, finally falls to pieces, actually goes mad for a bit, while she's swinging her young niece. The reader, who has already learned that Sybil was "a tired woman who was lonely," and that "there was nothing against her except that she had once been brave when she should have been overcome," understands that this lady has never allowed herself to grieve and mourn as she should have, as bereavement demands. The emotions bottled inside her like a poison suddenly expand and burst into hysteria. And yet, shaded by the deft hand of a brilliant storyteller, the incident is not at all oppressive. The contrast between Sybil's dead son Adam and her demurely obedient little robot of a niece is sharply comic. So, too, is Sybil's deadly and disparaging wit (which she always keeps to herself, but which we, as privileged intruders into her thoughts, can share).

How about an American classic? Edgar Allan Poe's "The Masque of the Red Death" has fascinated readers for a century and a half. Whether you travel into the collective unconscious with Jung, or peer at symbols through some other critical lens, this is one of the most imaginative examinations of Death (with a blood-red capital D) in all of literature.

I much prefer Donald Barthelme's incredible little piece, "School." I couldn't suggest a more enchanting literary treat. The narrator, a thoroughly lovable teacher of the young, obviously wants to imbue her children with a robust reverence for life. But during one terrible term there's a long, sad parade of disastrous deaths: from the lesser trauma of dying trees and snakes through the demise of her gardens, salamanders, gerbils, white mice, tropical fish and pet puppy. The story then explores genuine terrors of the heart: the deaths of a Korean orphan, her grandparents and parents, and goes on to heart attacks, suicides, a car accident, a drowning, the collapse of a negligently built federal office building, and a fatal knifing. Barthelme's "School" is, of course, a revelation of existence. And yet the story is painless to teach (the touch is so caressing and the tone so plaintively off-beat though undeniably tragic). The last lines are wonderful: "I said that they shouldn't be frightened (although I am often frightened) and that there was value everywhere. Helen came and embraced me. I kissed her a few times on the brow. We held each other. The children were excited. Then there was a knock on the door, I opened the door, and the new gerbil walked in. The children cheered wildly." (My students, too, cheer wildly after this ending.) What else need one say about the uplift of hope and the dependable continuity of life?

I must make an obligatory reference to Tolstoy's "The Death of Ivan Ilych," since it is probably the most famous examination of our theme: the story even opens with an obituary notice. Tolstoy punishes Ivan with an excruciating death, capped by three final days of uninterrupted screaming. What has Ivan *done* to warrant such authorial crucifixion? Ivan is a kind of Everyman, a John Smith whose ambitions, achievements, values and diversions rather disquietingly parallel our own. Is that so terrible? Tolstoy, that stern saint, evidently felt great contempt for a society that lived for pleasure and material advancement, refusing to acknowledge death because it's such a shivering idea. Ivan's family and friends will not admit—or let Ivan admit—that he is dying. Instead they practice an ugly pretense and force Ivan to comply. In not allowing him the refuge of honest feeling and expression, they rob him of death with humanity. Like a child, Ivan yearns for simple comforting, a sharing of sorrow. Only his little boy, not yet corrupted into a socialized refusal of death, and his pleasant servant Gerasim, similarly innocent of the conventions that armor Ivan's society against emotion—only these two can ease his anguish a little.

In "Pale Horse, Pale Rider," Katherine Anne Porter's title comes from the Bible, Revelations 6:8, "And I looked and behold a pale horse: and his name that sat on him was Death." This novella, undeniably depressing, carries us back to the influenza epidemic that decimated our population just after World War I, also seen as a disease, had killed millions. We view wartime hype through Miranda's eyes as she succumbs to high fever. What she sees, interrupted by ongoing funeral processions, is vanity and manipulation, ugly and brutal power plays. Only Adam, beautiful and patriotic, the personification of both the American Dream and the sacrificial lamb, is exempt from the charade. Porter builds layer on layer of metaphoric exchange: life as a journey toward death, despite the noble intervention of medicine; life as a battleground, as warfare, as a terminal illness; social posturing as an ironic death-in-life. When Miranda lies on her hospital bed, given up for dead, she has an exquisite out-of-body vision of heaven (this was Katherine Anne Porter's actual experience which, she said, was essentially impossible to reproduce and which left her with a melancholy yearning for the rest of her years). Indeed, Miranda wants to die. She knows that Adam will not survive the war and she cannot tolerate the idea of living without him. But operating independently, that singular, obstinate center of desire, the sheer will to remain alive, defeats her conscious wish for death. She returns to life knowing that, in time, she will rejoin the courageous conspiracy that affirms and pursues life, even though membership is only temporary. In her story, Porter tears away the veil of euphemisms that keep out the existential chill; in its place she gives us the urgency of the life force itself: "Trust me; I stay." (One of my students taped the words to his bedroom mirror.)

Turning to novels, we jump immediately to James Agee's *A Death in the Family* and recall the child's nighttime encounter with Nothingness, with Death, with the disappearance of the self. My students are always drawn to that poetic evocation of their own surprisingly well-remembered bedtime fears. They almost touch hands as they hear from their peers reassuring echoes of childhood apprehensions far more common than they had dreamed. Eventually, too, we talk about the adult hypocrisy increasingly revealed in the story. (After all, shouldn't literature about death also reveal wisdom about life?)

By the carloads, high school English teachers still assign Aldous Huxley's *Brave New World*, that classic illustration that a clever blend of psychological and drug treatment can produce human beings who do not waste themselves through hate and fear. Prenatally conditioned, they appreciate each other and are content with whatever life circumstances they have been designed for. (Today such theory is old hat: if we could start from scratch, fortified by what we now know about pills and behavior, DNA and biogenetic engineering, we could replicate Huxley's fantasy world where nobody fears death, where people are trained to welcome it.) Children are ritually brought to hospitals to see the dying, who, drugged and euphoric, are enjoying their last hours. These occasions are celebrated as holidays. Public education stresses that the dead, scientifically recycled, continue to enrich the community through the post-mortem generosity of their chemical elements. Everybody belongs to everybody else; lingering commitments are frowned upon, if not downright punishable. Babies are test-tube commodities, government controlled, so family love never develops. Since all relationships are therefore temporary and one-dimensional, nobody is much upset by the death of another person. And there you have it—a cheerful and productive life (eminently cost-efficient!), a happy death, the prevention of that jagged suffering that familiarly accompanies our mortal festering. Students draw uneasy (and appropriate) comparisons: church services that coax them to be happy for the blessed dead who can now live eternally with God; wakes and funerals that socialize the act of dying; pain-killers that turn the dying into zombies. They cut through flabby moralizing and seriously consider the trade-offs. Many resent their own death fears. One 16-year-old complained flat out: "I'd do anything to change it; I just know that worrying about death is going to ruin life for me." They realize very well that in order to extirpate their dread of dying, they must relinquish a certain way of being human, the only way they've known so far—a way that prizes passion and values the permanency of love. They bemoan this double-bind: caring about others makes us vulnerable. Displaying sensitivity rare in today's classrooms, they begin to assess just what it means to be human. They end up quietly aware that our deepest sense of humanity derives from that shared recognition of death. "Hey, we're all in this together!" Unwilling to take up residence in Huxley's world, but equally loath to continue fearing death, they begin to speculate about new systems for belief and behavior that might lighten their anxieties without destroying their humanity. The discussion becomes critical and creative, an interdisciplinary prism dispersing light from psychology, philosophy, art, religion, history, sociology, even physical fitness! These high school students have no notion that the ideas they are groping for and tentatively formulating are long-acknowledged concepts already taught at college. (In addition to dealing with death, they are learning to think for themselves.)

The last sentence of a most remarkable novel says, "In the world according to Garp we are all terminal cases." Analyzing this book clarifies the basic issue of death education in the schools. Our academic opponents maintain that we have no right to integrate death studies because kids don't like to admit they're going to die. "Besides," they add, "it's a family matter." In rebuttal, let me ask why *The World According to Garp*, the John Irving novel that dramatizes every mode of dying from the bizarre to the serene, was a modern phenomenon translated into more languages than one can track down. If people really wanted to hide from death, they wouldn't read *Garp*, where death is the first premise, the given. Its central metaphor, the Under Toad, lurks everywhere and pounces without due notice. ("Tod" is the German word for death.) The truth, of course, is that most of us feel a deep need to bring death out of the closet into the open air of discussion. Young people today are learning neither a sufficient reverence for life nor a sufficient respect for death. (These principles are fellow travelers; they go hand in hand.) The two establishments we used to depend on, religion and family, for various reasons are no longer adequately humanizing the young. So, if the task is essential, public education must again extend itself into an area of learning that was not its original province. Inevitably life forces confusion, even disaster, upon all of us. Children who have been misled into believing that only good things happen have no defenses to call upon when the Under Toad claims them, and they tumble out of the Garden of Eden into the world outside (the world according to Garp). They cannot cope; they have not "tried on" any of the appropriate models for experiencing death. (Children are no longer widely raised on those wise and edifying fairy tales that spoke to and answered early emotional needs.)

Most behaviors are learned through experience and imitation. Children sense evasion. If parents and other significant adults shrink from the subject or dodge behind platitudes, children soon learn that death is unthinkable; too scary to be accosted by words; a black creature of the night. Kids want to talk: thoughts so frightening that a child does not have the courage to look at them alone can be discussed in a group, in class, provided that the teacher has fitting sensitivity and skill. There is such relief in hearing that other kids are similarly plagued and haunted. I keep returning to this central point and reemphasizing our trepidation before the unknown. We comfort each other during the mutual admission of fears and the exchange of private ways of coping.

Of all the literature I have ever taught (from elementary to graduate school level), *Garp* is the work most passionately loved by students. Although it carries the strongest overt insistence on death and pain, it is *not* despairing. John Irving's people face the terrible truth and still manage to live purposefully. They do not settle for frightened survival.

I always begin my classes on *Garp* by studying Randall Jarrell's brief poem, "The Death of the Ball Turret Gunner." Irving would want me to: his book alludes to, exploits and then deliberately denies Jarrell's terrifying vision of nonlife. T.S. Garp's father was also a ball turret gunner—no accident!—lodged in that womblike metal sphere suspended from the belly of a fighter plane. But as *he* died, he created new life with his "last good shot"; he did not *cause* death with a barrage of anti-aircraft fire. He felt pleasure at the end ("good," he breathed) and, reversing Jarrell's imagery, he returned happily to the womb. In Jarrell's lines, the ball turret gunner drops from the womb into savagery and an unspeakable animal death. I take the opening of this often-baroque novel, Garp's conception, as an extraordinary manifestation that the rest of the book amply supports: true, life will batter us through death and disillusion, through accident and betrayal, through the abuse of children, through aging and weakening, through every horrific ill this flesh is heir to. But (oh, what a determining "but"!) with Garp and his family we practice the few real means of comfort available to us: we love, we talk and listen to each other, we cry together, we rant and rave and finally accept what we have to. We do not abdicate either energy or heart. All over the world more people read and reread *Garp* than any other book in recent publishing history, probably because it lays unadorned death before the reader but unequivocally validates life at the same time. I know how my students receive *Garp*. Again this past term my seniors affirmed that although the story kept them constantly alert to the dangers and fragility of life, they felt within themselves the growth of a new kind of courage. Haven't we come here to help all students find ways to bear up better when death intrudes?

All art deals somehow with death. But if a teacher quite specifically chooses to guide students into this kind of reflection, poetry may be the smoothest vehicle. Through the imagery of sense impressions, through specially chosen diction, through metaphor and rhythm, poetry expresses certain feelings we cannot articulate any other way. It transports shadows from the unconscious and gives them daylight shape. A good poem generates fresh perspectives in the listener because it avoids stock comparison and shabby platitude. Impact is immediate. Like a powerful microscope, a poem can focus brilliantly on just those few observations the poet has deliberately fused and wishes to display in a new light. Thus it is a most economical medium that allows a teacher to fashion and control a particular lesson with finesse. She can isolate and achieve whatever effects are sought, within whatever length of discussion is expedient. She can assign the poem for independent speculation at home, encouraging a private experience, or can read it aloud in class, fostering a spontaneous group reaction. Insights and feelings that arise are especially strong and enduring because of the way the poetic process works. Anything learned under heightened emotion tends to stay with us, and the rhythms of poetry arouse emotional intensity.

Poems should not be read silently; like music, they must be heard to be properly suggestive. Human beings who are emitting deep grief or rage or some other passion utter sounds that fall into natural rhythmic patterns. Their language surges, swells, subsides; they favor repetition. ("We want a hit! We want a hit!") There is probably some intrinsic connection with the heartbeat, the flow of blood. One of literature's most rending expressions of the loneliness of aging and death was a poem. Shakespeare wrote "King Lear," as he did all his major work, in iambic pentameter, turning to prose only when he dealt with the trivial. Poetic rhythms are distinctive, varying biological, sensory and artistic means to raise or lower emotional pitch. Poets have always tackled our most intimate themes.

The Romantic Shelley maintained (and certainly no English teacher of my acquaintance has ever disagreed) that poets are our "unacknowledged legislators." No, they don't sit in parliaments and hammer out laws, but they do somehow tell us how to live—and die—as human beings. "Poetry makes nothing happen," W.H. Auden lamented ironically. True, poetry is not a lever for public action—if only because there are so few confirmed poetry lovers around! We would lack the number to form a respectable political lobby. Poetry was never intended to promote that kind of broad change. At its most meaningful, it's the medium of language through which one single, sensitive soul communicates with another about the kind of personal experience most human beings go through. As Auden really knew, something *does* "happen" within the reader of poetry, and she feels important human kinship with the poet. This evidence of shared emotion somehow persuades us that life has meaning. It gives us faith to believe what we cannot empirically prove.

We cannot accept death well until we are convinced that daily (dare I say "ordinary"?) human life has significance. I am not speaking in religious terms now. Emily Brontë's famous poem "No Coward Soul Is Mine" did not inspire my students. Hers was a rather orthodox statement of faith. She saw "heaven's glories shine" because of "God within [her] breast," and this steadfast belief armed her against all fear of dying. Unfortunately, Emily's faith left my kids cold because they had not been moved to empathy. Even those who were themselves traditionally religious were not in synch with the poet's private authority. (They found her smug and complained that she had made no effort to invite them.) But Shelley's shattering lines, "Death is here, death is there/Death is round us everywhere," produced the kind of classroom tumult that makes a teacher rejoice. My students loved the deliberately sing-song Hallmark card rhythm: light, empty, a bauble, it forced ironic contrast with the words, as though to mitigate the awful truth through a cheerful jingle. "Maybe that's how you have to handle terror," they said. "Just blow it away." (It only hurts me when I laugh?) Death *is* "round us everywhere," as ubiquitous as a Hallmark card, so we must close our eyes a little to soften the glare. We have to keep a sensible distance from the fire, even though it's always crackling somewhere.

Nobody can ever enter the consciousness of another person. Each of us is a prototype as differently etched as our fingerprints, and we all apprehend death with original antennae. But through the magic of poetry I get an achingly keen sense of how the poet feels about death (and other commonplaces!) and this awareness spurs me to clarify my own sentiments. As Ellen Greenfield suggests in her chapter, it can do the same for students as well.

21

Coping with Death and Loss Through Writing

Ellen S. Greenfield

In a world that increasingly seems like a vast sea filled with tumult and confusion, it is easy for people to be pulled away from the shore by the current. At the same time, the rest of us are so caught up in trying to keep our own selves afloat, we don't even realize the tide has been tugging at others until we happen to look up to find them gone.

That is the reason for this chapter. There is a need in today's society for people to sit up and take notice of themselves and each other. Far too many people are floundering in the water, almost drowning, feeling there is no hope, wishing that someone, anyone, would throw them a lifeline. Creative self-expression, whether through writing or another form of art, can be just such a lifeline.

It is imperative, then, that as educators, we recognize the necessity of allowing and encouraging this self-expression to exist. It can permit our students to own what is rightfully theirs: a bit of dignity and hope.

For as long as I can remember, people have been asking me why I write. For the most part, I could never come up with a particularly good answer. After many attempts, two reasons finally came to mind. One is that I write because I have to. Many times I am overcome by an intense urge to put pen to paper, even though I may not know what it is that I've set out to write. The other is that, put simply, it makes me feel better.

I enjoy writing. Sometimes I sit down and consciously say to myself, "Let's write something," but that kind of writing is different, that's a form of intellectual exercise. But the writing that comes from my soul, that stirs my feelings and threatens to drive me crazy if ignored, is the writing I'm speaking of here. This is the type of writing that "makes me feel better."

To a lesser extent, there is a third reason I write. I write to ask questions.

These are questions that plague my mind, body and soul—questions to which I have not yet found acceptable answers. Perhaps I never will find the answers, but writing guides me in my search for these elusive answers and gives me an outlet when I find myself in emotional distress. Be it an emotion of pain or pleasure, writing provides me with a world far away from everyone else's reality. Writing allows me to create a reality all my own. This creative reality is uniquely mine—a reality that may, when reread somewhere down the road, suggest an answer to a question or two. Possibly, just possibly, I can shape a reality that can be shared with others.

Until 1975 my questions about death addressed familiar philosophical issues. What happens when you die? Is there life after death? Perhaps death is the beginning of life…and life of death? These were the scenarios my mind played out. Until I took a closer look.

My first memory was that of my grandmother. Her death was really a blessing in disguise. She had suffered enough. Her mind and body had deteriorated to the point of no return. It was time to let her truly rest. That was easy compared to what still lay ahead. Death reappeared to take a 7-year-old boy, the nephew of my closest friend, in a tragic accident. Now my stomach started to churn. This was unfathomable. I was in shock. I just could not comprehend something like this happening. This was something you only heard about on the news, and you know those people are not real anyway. And so more pressing questions began.

Then, in December 1981, the 20-year-old brother of another friend was killed in a car accident. Again, death claimed an innocent victim undeserving of such a fate. It was then that push came to shove and I could not ignore this gnawing need to find answers to my questions. It was then that I wrote "Shadow of Death."

Three years later, a man to whom I'll be forever grateful for twice saving my dog's life died mysteriously. Death again appeared as an event over which no one had any control, least of all me. Once again my frustrations were put down on paper. Once again I asked questions, demanding answers. Those questions became "Immortal Games."

In August 1986 my uncle died suddenly. He was a second father to me, someone with whom I shared a silent, secret bond. For him I sat myself down to write; to write because I wanted to —but something happened. I could not write. For one year I tried to write for him but the words just would not come. Sometimes you can't force these things, but it upset me greatly that I could not do this for him.

Then, almost one year later to the day, a very dear friend of mine died from a horrifying disease that has thus far been a death sentence to those who contract it. As of this writing, I'm still not sure I've accepted the finality of his death. But this time I had no control over my pen and "Stalemate" was the result.

Each of these three poems was written independently of the others, with no prior intention to combine them. After writing "Stalemate" I recalled the others, and something from within urged me to put them together as a trilogy. When I wrote the Foreword to that trilogy, I knew why. It was my uncle to whom I would dedicate *Demon Dance*.

When I was asked to write a chapter for this book, the guidelines were broad. The editor believed that writing could help students to express and understand emotions related to loss and grief. I was asked to expand upon my poems, provide background information to explain what had inspired me to write them and to determine what, if anything, I had resolved through this writing. In other words, I was to attempt to answer yet another question: What is the point of expressing oneself through creative writing?

The answer to this last question is that writing offers a way of coping when life seems overwhelming. It is a lifeline when you feel you are drowning. Whether you write poetry, fiction or simply keep a narrative journal, writing provides a release for all the emotions your otherwise pragmatic self won't allow you to consciously acknowledge. Writing provides a safe haven for you to let yourself feel without threat of painful ramifications.

If, after reading this, a closed door opens somewhere for a teacher or student, if a light of insight seeps into a previously darkened room, then this chapter has achieved its goal. Its purpose will have been fulfilled. If by chance it touches a nerve, I encourage you to let yourself feel the emotions that surface. And if it elicits even the remotest desire to try your hand at writing, I implore you to follow that desire. Write...no one else need ever know.

DEMON DANCE

This trilogy of death was written over a seven-year period when Death introduced itself to me. Until then Death and I were relative strangers, although I had felt its hand brush past from time to time.

"Shadow of Death" was written in memory of Gary, the brother of a friend whose young life was taken by the recklessness of others.

"Immortal Games" was written for Dr. Purse, who devoted his life to the care of animals and the humans who cherish them.

"Stalemate" was for my special friend Michael who spent every waking moment spreading sunshine over all he touched.

Finally, I dedicate *Demon Dance* to my dear Uncle Irving, who always supported and encouraged me in anything I tried, especially in my writing, and at whose passing I could not find words.

Shadow of Death

Sometimes there is no rhyme or reason.
How does he choose which one is next?
What are his criteria—his prerequisites?
There is no justice in Life, so there can be none in Death—
    as for after Death, well, who knows?
Death himself walks down a well trodden path.
You'd think even he would tire of this game.
Reaching out for the helpless, the ones who can't run.
And if one should try, no matter how hard, with all his might,
Death still reaches 'round and pulls him down.
It's as though Death stands upon a pinnacle, far above us all
Looking out over the crowded seas of people
Pointing his finger and shaking his head, while that smirk of
    a smile forms on his lips.
He picks and he chooses,
This one or that.
But why?
How does he make his decision?

Sometimes he gives you a chance to cry out.
Others he may quickly stifle.
In any event, all he need do
Is call out your name and you must obey.

Yet there are those who stay and fight—
And maybe some can even win.
But struggling is of no avail
Because he always wins out in the end.
For no matter how hard you try to survive,
Death won't let you stay alive.

So live every moment fully, my Friend—
Appreciate every sound, every sight, in the World.
Enjoy it all now—every minute, every day,
Because you never know where Death is waiting to play.

For Gary, December 23, 1981

Immortal Games

The shadow of Death returns to haunt
Those he enjoys most to taunt.
As into their midst this spirit drifts;
Hungrily through their souls he sifts.
Seeking to torch his failing lamp;
He claws and tears through the cold and damp.
Until at last he halts by one
Unsuspecting soul whose work is done,
And then he rears his ugly head
To fill all the world with fear and dread.

I don't know why he does not rest;
Is Life some kind of Godly test
To use as proof of strong or weak,
Or those who never strove to seek
The building of foundations form
So Death can find no fuel to burn?
I wonder why Life often throws
Such godforsaken, fatal blows.
And then in pure frustration scream—
But no one hears my waking dream.

No one hears, or so I thought.
But deep within, my feelings fought
To find a willing ear to bend—
An ear belonging to a friend.
It's then I realized what these had tried
So hard to teach—so hard that now I cried.
For what I learned is merely this,
Although those now gone I'll surely miss,
Their spirits which have touched me deep
Will outlive Death's eternal sleep.

These people I call friends were such,
That taught me Faith and, oh, so much.
People on whom I learned to depend—
People who gave till the very end.
These are the Friends of whom I speak;
These are the Spirits I'll forever seek.
When times get tough and moods swing low,
I'll think of them and then I'll know
That Death never really won the game,
Only one mere, mortal frame.

For Dr. Purse, March 29, 1985

Stalemate

For the third time Death has played his hand
And still I'm taken by surprise.
I questioned then—I question now,
Will I never stop believing Faith's vicious lies?

I just don't understand what good befalls
When one so loving, young and kind
Is taken from this world so quick—
What should he expect to find?

Some say that it is not God's will—
Others just believe
That there is some deeper reason
Why those on Earth must grieve.

As for me, I know not why—
Merely that it Is.
And play the Game called Life I must,
Following rules that are unjust.

Rules that usually remain submerged
Until the very end—
When at last they surface
Far too late to defend.

No time to ward off Evil,
No time to think and plan
A strategy to counter
The Coming of Death's Clan.

So one becomes a pawn
In a cosmic game of chess,
Leaving one without control
And little time to rest.

But who is this Games Master,
Where does he dwell?
I find it hard to disbelieve
He lives within our Hell.

A private Hell that each must enter,
Taking Peril by the hand
So that we may trudge safely
Into a fairer land.

For Michael, August 18, 1987

WRITING ABOUT DEATH: A STUDENT'S EXAMPLE

The following selection by Brian Thornton illustrates the type of writing we have discussed in this chapter. Brian wrote these selections when he was a student at River Dell High School, in his junior and senior years.

In death we find a wide variety of causes, interpretations and effects. There are thousands of ways in which it has an impact on us. People's beliefs extend from death as being the end of everything, to a hopeful anticipation of an afterlife.

Death affects each of us differently, yet similarities do exist. This is illustrated through the five stages of death: Denial, Anger, Bargaining, Depression and Acceptance. These five stages do have an impact on all of us. However, the time that each stage lasts can be extremely different depending on the individual.

Through the art of poetry, one can express one's true feelings and convictions on a chosen topic. Death has been this topic for centuries. Famous poets, such as Arthur Rimbaud, have given us a vivid and shocking outlook on death.

In my own poetry, I express my inner moods and opinions. Written words sometimes seem to have a stronger impact than those that are spoken:

> Thoughts at night seldom heard
> Thoughts that spite
> The written word...

True poetry exists in the minds and hearts of those who believe in their writing or the writing of others. My poetry is an extension of my conscious and subconscious self, combining to allow me to express my opinions and convictions. I feel that poetry unites real-life feelings and experience with self-examination, to form a truly unique and important art.

Rose Offering

> In the wind a voice cried out
> In the wind there came a shout
> Wailing and crying endlessly trying
> Find me please...
> Help me I'm dying
>
> Wide-eyed man filled with fear
> All alone and no one near
> Watch him run, see him stagger
> Blood flowing, wound from a dagger
>
> Emptiness inside, he's growing weary
> There will be no recovery
> Only painful screeching
> Gasping and reaching
>
> Step over into the night
> Now you've found peace...serenity
> You've finished your plight
> Here you exist in perpetual tranquility
> Come...see the light
>
> Now she enters
> A rich delight
> Enticingly free
> But it is uninvited beauty

She speaks to you softly
Offering a lustful Red Rose
Reaching out, you rise slowly
Come, she says, you will see

Grasping the Rose your sight is cleared
Her smile and beauty have disappeared
Rigid and cold, again you are alone
Death has found you
Eternally sown...

Memoriam

Adorned by flowers
A once live man lay sleeping
Perpetual silence
Amidst never-ending weeping

Time has passed
And so has he
How very precious
Is the memory

Once a leader now an admired soul
His glory remains
Innocence has stayed
No one can fill the role

Gifted with talent and uniting our grace
Keeping us all together in our place
Constantly winning the love and attention
With all the world's appreciation

Desperation

Wandering about
Leading me away
Running...Soaring...
Going astray

On the edge
Over the top
It'll be better
The pain will stop

Leaving your mind with the ferocity of a lion
Twisting and writhing opening the door
Waiting and hoping...
Searching for more

We're almost there
Just about through
It's time to leave
And pay my due...

(Untitled)

Die old friend
Die as you will
Die old friend
Fall down the hill

For life, it may seem
is only a dream
With a promise of pleasure
Sown in the scheme

Sleep for now old friend
And rest between the lines
We must create while we can
and always remember these times

22

The Theme of Death in Student Art and Writing

Robert G. Stevenson, EdD, Joyce Garvin, MS
and Christine VanDerVelde, MA

The subject of death has been one that has motivated some of the world's greatest artists and writers. Many people have used their talents to reveal their thoughts and feelings about this powerful topic. Poetry, prose and the visual arts have long provided important insights into the different ways that individuals and whole societies understand mortality. Writing about death is just as important today. For students, it can be a valuable way to know more about their own personalities and for parents and educators, it can be a means of reaching students.

A national conference dealing with issues in death education ("Teaching About Death: Death Education in the School [Pre-K through 12], Theory and Practice") was held at the Columbia Presbyterian Medical Center in New York City in November 1987. An important part of this conference was a collection of student works of art and writings on the theme of death.

Selected schools from the New Jersey and New York area were invited to gather and submit original work from students in grades 4 through 12. One person from each school was responsible for coordinating the submission of student work.

The purpose of this project was to gather a sample of student work on the subject of death for professionals to view and also to allow students to contribute their views of death in forms of their own choice. Each student was allowed to prepare a contribution in writing, music or art.

Student writings included poems, essays and short stories. No dramatic scripts were submitted. Music was required to be presented in written form, but an accompanying recording was encouraged. The submitted works of art included oil paintings, charcoal drawings, pencil sketches, pen and ink drawings, watercolors, mixed media and photography. Because of space limitations and lack of separate display facilities, works of sculpture were discouraged.

To help ensure as accurate a comparison of student works as possible (and to minimize the impact of the differences in each teacher's presentation of the assignment), it was strongly suggested to participating educators that they use one of three following scripts when they presented this assignment to their students. Teachers were told that they were free to modify the script to accommodate the age and language skills of their students. Teachers were also requested to submit a good cross section of student work, and especially those that stood out for any reason. The conference art committee knew in advance that it would not be possible to display every work produced by students, but tried to represent as many points of view as possible.

The seminar co-chairpersons and the symposium fine arts/writing coordinator were available to assist teachers who desired consultation. However, few teachers had additional questions or needed to depart from the prepared texts.

All assignments were entitled, "An Invitation to Student Contributors." Script 1 drew on classic works, Script 2 on popular references, and Script 3 was intended for use with elementary school students.

AN INVITATION TO STUDENT CONTRIBUTORS

Script 1

Through the centuries, the idea of our mortality—of death—has been an inspiration to many great writers and artists. King David used one of his psalms to try to allay fears of death by drawing on his belief in the Almighty:

> "Yea, though I walk through the valley of the shadow of death I shall fear no evil for Thou art with me."

English poet John Donne tried to reach the same end by making death, his enemy, look foolish:

> "Death be not proud though some have called thee mighty, thou art not so." With his own fears comforted, he claimed victory with the line: "Death, thou shalt die."

When much of the world found it difficult to confront the horrors of war and the effects of a massive aerial bombing in Spain, Pablo Picasso painted the disturbing and powerful "Guernica." Death was also the theme of the sublime "Pieta," in which Michelangelo portrayed in marble the grief of the Virgin Mary holding the body of Jesus after He was taken down from the cross.

Of course, one need not be famous to have feelings, thoughts or images related to the word death. The people who are conducting an upcoming conference on ways of dealing with grief and loss would like to see the ways in which you choose to express your feelings, thoughts or images of death. You are now invited to create a work of your choice (using the guidelines cited above) to be included at the conference.

Script 2

Everything that lives will one day die, and thinking about death always causes people to react strongly. People often want to find a way to show other people how they feel. Some people use words to show their feelings through poetry, prose or songs. Most of you can remember a movie or a television show that expressed feelings that you may have also felt. Some of these films and shows started as a story. The songs that you hear year after year often began as poems. The music was added to make the feelings even clearer. ("Abraham, Martin and John" was a popular song that expressed some of the strong feelings people had after the deaths of John and Robert Kennedy and Martin Luther King.)

For other people music alone is the best way to show how they feel. (Bill Cosby composed "Martin's Funeral" to express his feelings after the death of Dr. King, and he played piano as "Badfoot Brown" in a group known as "Badfoot Brown and the Bunions Bradford Funeral and Marching Band." It was his way to show strong feelings of sadness, anger, depression and hurt.)

Other people use paintings, drawings or photos to show people how they feel or even to make their own feelings clearer to themselves. Whatever way is right for you, art (whether written, sung, painted, etc.) allows people not only to express their feelings, but also to preserve those feelings for other people to share and perhaps to learn from.

One need not be famous to have feelings, thoughts or images related to the word death. The people who will be conducting a conference on ways of dealing with grief and loss would like to see the ways in which you choose to express your feelings, thoughts or images of death. You are now invited to create a work of your choice (using the guidelines cited above) to be included at the conference.

Script 3

Everyone has feelings. These feelings can be exciting, happy, scary or confusing. Sometimes we can't tell other people what these feelings are. We may not even be sure ourselves. One way to show these feelings to other people or to ourselves is to put them on paper. A drawing, painting, story or poem can make these feelings clearer.

The word death causes people to have many different feelings. There is going to be a conference on ways of dealing with the feelings that can be caused by death. The people who will be there would like to see the way you choose to show your feelings about death. They are inviting you to submit a picture or story (using the guidelines cited above) to be shown at that meeting.

(Students were given a deadline and were also told that the art submitted had to be personally made.)

STUDENT WRITING

One school, River Dell Regional High School in Oradell, New Jersey, responded to this invitation in a unique way. They developed a comprehensive program that includes: an elective death education course for juniors and seniors in the social studies department; a suicide/depression prevention program required of all sophomores as part of the health/physical education program; selections about death in the English curriculum and assignments relating to death for students in the "gifted and talented" program; and an art course.

Gifted and Talented

Students in the "gifted and talented" program submitted work based on Script 1. The artwork focused on emotion, cause and type of death, a fatal event and life after death. Writing dealt with emotions, the concept of death with descriptions of personal views and illustrations of personal attempts at coping with a death or the grief that followed.

Students exhibited so many varied feelings about death with such a diversity of forms of language that it is difficult to provide general statements to describe them. Many young people (grades 7 through 12) were eager to speculate, to make concrete through words the grief they felt that had been caused by the loss of someone dear, or even to distance themselves from the concept of death through light fiction and comedy.

Dark and morbid issues were confronted. A few students fantasized— through stories—about the state of mind of people who commit suicide or about characters who go through life experiencing anguish and despair (the feeling of death-in-life). Other students presented honest and touching responses to the death of people they had loved, perhaps in an attempt to find strength. These were not bitter revelations; for the most part they were very moving outpourings of sorrow for the loss of a grandparent, a father taken by cancer, a child, a mother, a friend. Other comments revealed a sentiment of kinship with animals and anger that some people are indifferent to the killing of whales or seals or deer.

Curiosity (and accompanying anxiety) about death were manifested through a wide range of techniques, stories, poems, and essays. They explored the following ideas: out-of-body experiences; the belief that a mother's love can pull a mortally ill child back into life; wayward behavior at wakes and funerals; "waking up" in "heaven" and missing one's family; rage at ugly, obscene and unnecessary death (war, crime, indifference); many metaphoric exchanges, often through parallels with nature, that were honest intellectual attempts to understand the whole baffling concept of death; recognition that physical death finally breaks down all the social barriers that separate people in life; and exhilarating statements about the importance of the felt moment, the direct experience of being alive.

Students even rationalized about the *need* for death. They offered realizations about the cycles of the physical and biological worlds and observations about societal necessities. Some student fiction exhibited humor, untainted by black or mournful comedy: computerized heavens (buying and selling fate through an electronic network); decked-out corpses and financial affectations that can attend death; even the philosophic reflections of a "dying" computer. The last class of student response is creative satire in the form of attempts to evaluate the social scene and slyly illustrate human frailties.

STUDENT ART

Contemporary Issues of Life and Death

This is a one-semester, 18-week death education elective offered by the social studies department to sophomore, junior and senior students. The students who choose to take this class have a regular art assignment which involves an introduction different from those listed above. After the class has spent time discussing definitions of death, and just prior to examining the ways in which the abstract concept of death has been "personified" in the art and literature of the past, the students are presented with the assignment described below.

A View of Death

It is late on a winter afternoon. You have returned to this room following an after-school activity to get a book you left in the classroom. As you are about to leave you notice it is very still outside. There is no noise in the halls or in the parking lot. You start down the hallway toward the stairs and as you reach an adjoining hall, you feel as if someone is watching you. You look down the hall and there at the end you see "Death." Draw a picture of what you see.

The drawings produced as part of this assignment serve as the basis for a student discussion of their views of death. It has been found through such assignments that abstract representations of death are produced by those who view death as an abstract concept. More concrete representations indicate concern about a specific death or type of death (sometimes based on past losses). In these discussions, some students tell of initially wanting to create a totally abstract work (such as an all-black or all-white sheet of paper), but then change their mind to draw death in a specific way. This is the most common reaction among students and can be used to illustrate the difference between our thoughts about a topic (the intellectual response being represented by the abstract view) and our feelings produced by that same topic (the emotional response represented by the specific illustration that is finally submitted).

The most common illustrations of a concrete "Death" followed themes that have traditionally been used by Western artists: the dark, hooded form of the "grim reaper" (often complete with scythe), a "grinning" skull, or a human form (in the classic "kneeling-running" position of one about to die, in repose in a casket, or as a seductive, beckoning figure).

It is important to remember that the classroom is not the place for "therapy." Projective tests are used by therapists, but in a school setting, fostering communication and increasing student knowledge are the goals. These exercises allow students to express thoughts and feelings that may be difficult to put into words and to give them insight into themselves and they help educators to better know the young people with whom they are working.

Art Classes

The projects described above were supplemented by a new variation on a traditional art project. For years at River Dell, students have been required to complete a self-portrait for their portfolio for art class. In 1987 this assignment was altered to provide each student with a personal look at the aging process and old age. Students were given the following instructions: You are going to create a self-portrait to place in your art portfolio. Divide your work in half to look at yourself in the present and the future. On one side of the canvas show yourself as you appear now. On the other side, show yourself as you will look when you are 80 years old.

Students studied the faces of older relatives, descriptions of the aging process and their own physical appearance to prepare this assignment. Two students, however, showed themselves as skeletons. They said they would be "long dead" before they turned 80. This was quite an insight into the way these young people viewed old age and their own futures. The students who participated in this project allowed their work to be exhibited at the November 1987 symposium for educators and death education students.

AN INTERDISCIPLINARY APPROACH

The creative themes of "aging" and "death" were used in English classes, "gifted and talented," social studies and art classes. The instructors of these courses worked together to create an interdisciplinary approach to address student concerns about death and aging. Along with units in the health and physical education program dealing with life-and-death issues (such as drugs, disease and bioethics) and guidance programs (such as programs to combat adolescent suicide, depression and drug abuse), these units use the arts and writing skills to work toward the main goal of public education: to address the needs of, and to educate, the "whole person."

REFERENCES

Bach, S.R. *Spontaneous Pictures of Leukemic Children as an Expression of the Total Personality, Mind and Body*. New York: Schwabe & Co, 1975.

Bettelheim, B. *The Uses of Enchantment: The Meaning and Importance of Fairy Tales*. New York: Vintage Books, 1976.

Burns, R.C. and S.H. Kaufman. *Actions and Styles and Symbols in Kinetic Family Drawings*. New York: Brunner/Mazel, 1972.

Burns, R.C. and S.H. Kaufman. *Kinetic Family Drawings*. New York: Brunner/Mazel, 1970.

Dennis, W. *Group Values Through Children's Drawings*. New York: John Wiley & Sons, 1966.

DiLeo, J.H. *Young Children and Their Drawings*. New York: Brunner/Mazel, 1970.

Edwards, B. *Drawing on the Right Side of the Brain*. New York: J.P. Tarcher, 1979.

Favat, F.A. *Child and Tale: The Origins of Interest*. Urbana, IL: National Council of Teachers of English, 1977.

Furth, G. The use of drawings made at significant times in one's life. In Elisabeth Kübler-Ross (ed.), *Living with Death and Dying*. New York: Macmillan, 1981.

Kellogg, R. *The Psychology of Children's Art*. Chicago: CRM Inc, 1967.

Schildkrout, M.S., I.R. Shenker and M. Sonnenblick. *Human Figure Drawings in Adolescence*. New York: Brunner/Mazel, 1970.

Von Franz, M.L. *Interpretation of Fairy Tales*. Zurich: Spring Publications, 1975.

23

Children's Literature on Death, Grief and Loss: An Annotated Bibliography

Richard R. Ellis, PhD and Laura S. Ellis, PhD

Editor's Note: This chapter presents an annotated list of publications that are suitable for various purposes of death education. It is importyant for readers to recognize that newer books are not necessarily better books and, as such, this chapter presents a listing of classic works. All of these books can easily be found at most libraries. Note that *About Dying* (Stein 1974), *Tell Me, Papa* (Johnson and Johnson 1978) and *I Had a Friend Named Peter* (Cohn 1987) are excellent for parents and children to share together.

BOOKS FOR YOUNG CHILDREN ABOUT DEATH

Aliki (1979). *The Two of Them*. New York: Greenwillow Books. (Ages 4-8)

Written in verse, this is the story of a loving relationship between grandfather and granddaughter. The lovely text and charming illustrations will touch both young and old. A beautiful book.

Bartoli, J. (1975). *Nonna*. New York: Harvey House. (Ages 4-7)

A young boy tells of the events and his feelings following the death of his beloved grandmother. He describes the behavior and feelings of his parents, his younger sister and his older brother. The story follows the family through the funeral, the burial and the resumption of life afterward. The story portrays how young children respond to the death of a loved one.

Breebaart, J. and P. Breebaart (1993). *When I Die, Will I Get Better?* New York: Peter Bedrick Books. (Ages 4-10)

The story tells of two brothers, Fred and Joe Rabbit. Joe becomes ill. Dr. Owl tries to help him, but he cannot and Joe dies. The story shows how Fred works through the funeral (putting Joe's favorite toys in the casket) and then through his grief. Fred's anger is understandable and will be something important for grieving children to see. The end provides a nice resolution as Fred and his friends play in the field where Joe is buried.

Brown, C. and D. Paterson (1985). *Bouncy Bunny's Bravery*. Burlington, VT: Creative Expressions. (Ages 4-8)

This book is a family story about a bunny family, designed to help children who are themselves chronically ill or who know others who are ill. The story concerns a young bunny who finds out that he has a kidney ailment. We follow Bouncy Bunny through his treatment, his hospital experiences, the new friends he meets who are also chronically ill, his operation, his recovery, and his return home. It can help children with their own struggle with confusing emotions. Its use by adults can provide caring, supportive encouragement.

Brown, M. (1965). *The Dead Bird*. Reading, MA: Addison-Wesley. (Ages 4-8)

The story is about a group of children who find a dead bird in the park. They decide to have a funeral and burial. Every day they return to the grave with flowers. They continue this until one day they forget. The story is tender but straightforward and matter-of-fact.

Buscaglia, L. (1982). *The Fall of Freddie the Leaf*. Thorofare, NJ: Charles B. Slack. (Ages 4-8)

This is a warm, simple story about a leaf named Freddie. The story tells how Freddie and his friends, the other leaves, change with the seasons, finally falling to the ground with the winter's snow. Both children and adults will be touched by this sensitive treatment of the delicate balance between life and death. The photographs are beautiful and capture the beauty of the changes in nature. The use of the word "sleep" rather than "death" at the story's close may cause a problem if it is not addressed with the child.

Carrick, C. (1976). *The Accident*. New York: Seabury Press. (Ages 4-8)

Christopher and his dog, Badger, were walking down to the lake to meet his parents. Christopher heard the pickup truck coming. He called to Badger, but the dog came too late. The accident was no one's fault, but Christopher was angry at the driver. He was also angry with himself, feeling guilty and blaming himself. Christopher and his father look for a stone for Badger's grave. Then Christopher remembers how Badger loved the cold water of the lake. Finally, he is able to cry and feels much better. A sensitive story.

Clardy, A. (1984). *Dusty was My Friend*. New York: Human Sciences Press. (Ages 5-10)

This book presents a child's experience of bereavement in simple, straightforward, but touching terms. It is the story of the accidental death of a child as seen by an 8-year-old, who goes through the gradual process of mourning and acceptance. It is suitable for children who have suffered a loss, but also for introducing the topic of grief and mourning to those who have not yet had direct experience with these realities.

Coerr, E. (1977). *Sadako and the Thousand Cranes*. New York: G.P. Putnam's Sons. (Ages 12-14)

This story is based on the life of a real little girl who lived in Japan from 1943 to 1955. She died from leukemia as a result of the atomic bombing of Hiroshima in 1945. The story is derived from Sadako's letters which were collected by her classmates. The author read these letters and tells of the last year of her life. In Japan there is a legend that God will give health to the sick person who makes 1,000 paper cranes. Sadako folded 644 paper cranes before her death. Today Sadako is a heroine to the children of Japan who visit her memorial in Hiroshima Peace Park to leave their paper cranes in her honor.

Cohn, J. (1987). *I Had a Friend Named Peter*. Illustrated by G. Owens. New York: William Morris. (Ages 5-9)

The introductory section of this book addresses adults. It raises important questions about talking with young people about death, and it supplies useful guidelines for dealing with those questions. The story is about Betsy, a little girl who goes to school and has a friend named Peter. One night Betsy's parents tell her that Peter was struck by a car and killed. The story provides a warm, loving introduction. This is an excellent book for both children and adults, especially when they can share it together.

Coutant, H. (1974). *First Snow*. New York: Knopf. (Ages 5-8)

This story is about a Vietnamese family during their first year in New England. It might be thought of as a story about death, but it is also a story about life. Lien's grandmother is weak, becomes ill, and is going to die. Of all the family members, Lien's grandmother helps her to understand dying. A touching story.

DePaola, T. (1973). *Nana Upstairs and Nana Downstairs*. New York: G.P. Putnam's Sons. (Ages 4-7)

This describes the loving relationship between Tommy, his great grand-mother (Nana Upstairs) who is confined to her bed and his grandmother (Nana Downstairs). Nana Upstairs dies. Tommy's mother explains death in a direct and honest way. Later his grandmother becomes ill and moves upstairs. She, too, dies. The story describes a little boy's loving relationship with his grandmothers and his feelings at their loss.

Ehrlich, A. (1994). *Maggie & Silky & Joe.* New York: Viking Children's Books. (Ages 4-10)

This story of a boy and his two dogs shows the strong bond between a child and his pets. The older dog, Maggie, had been home since before the boy was born. The author describes the grief that follows for the boy and his family when the older dog is found to have died during a rainstorm. The illustrations of Robert Blake add to the impact of the story.

Farley, C. (1975). *The Garden is Doing Fine.* New York: Atheneum. (Ages 6-18)

Connie's father is dying of cancer. It is very difficult for her to understand and accept what is happening. Gradually Connie comes to see what death means and what it does not mean. She finally understands what her dad has been trying to tell her.

Graebner, C. (1982). *Mustard.* New York: Macmillan. (Ages 6-9)

Alex thinks Mustard is the most wonderful cat in the world. Mustard had been a part of the family since he was born, even before Alex was born. Everyone says Mustard is getting old. Then the vet diagnoses a heart ailment and Alex must come to terms with Mustard's illness and eventual death. A warm, moving story about love and loss.

Greenlee, S. (1992). *When Someone Dies.* Atlanta: Peachtree Publications. (Ages 4-10)

The author presents information about death and grief and seeks to address the questions and concerns of bereaved children. The comments, presented in the second person, are often gentle and comforting, and the matter-of-fact style works well. This simple, straightforward approach to the grief of children could reach a wider range of young people than the age bracket cited above. The only drawback is the attempt by the author to copy a child's speech, which can be distracting at times, even to children. This book, however, is one of the few that successfully provides grief therapy in the style of a nonfiction children's book.

Holland, I. (1975). *Of Love and Death and Other Journeys.* Philadelphia: J.B. Lippincott. (Ages 12 and up)

This is a serious, insightful, but often humorous story of a young girl's experiences of the joy and grief of life. Meg was traveling about Europe with her mother and a young painter named Coton. Why, after 15 years, did her mother want her to meet her father, whom she had never seen? This was an omen of things to come, but she never dreamed how complete the change would be.

Johnson, J. and M. Johnson (1978). *Tell Me, Papa*. Omaha, NE: The Centering Corp. (Ages 5-12)

This is a book to be shared by families and their children. Through the words of a grandfather, Papa, the book answers children's questions about death, funerals and burial. The feelings that accompany the death of a loved one are explained and shared. The child learns that these feelings are normal, that "feelings shared are feelings diminished."

Johnson, J., M. Johnson, R. Goldstein and J. Goldstein (1982). *Where's Jess?* Omaha, NE: The Centering Corp. (Ages 5-8)

A beautiful, simple story of a little boy whose younger brother died. His parents answer his many questions and respond to his feelings with honesty, directness, and love.

Kontrowitz, M. (1973). *When Violet Died*. New York: Parents Magazine Press. (Ages 4-8)

Amy and Eva conduct a funeral for Violet, their pet bird who died. They read a poem and sing a song. After the refreshments are served, the guests drift away. The children's cat is going to have kittens. Suddenly Eva knew how life can go on for a long, long time. It is a story full of warmth and love, written with understanding of children's feelings.

Lancaster, M. (1983). *Hang Tough*. Mahwah, NJ: Paulist Press. (Ages 10-15)

This book was written by a 10-year-old boy who had a cancer that finally took his life. It is a stirring expression of a child's fight to live and his reactions to his experiences while he did so. His drawings and his words are powerful reminders of his courage and determination.

Levy, E. (1982). *Children are Not Paper Dolls*. Cary, IL: Erin Linn Levy. (Ages 7 and up)

The book is a collection of drawings made by children together with their spontaneous verbal expressions of feelings concerning the death of a sibling. Through these pages we can come closer to understanding and meeting children's emotional needs as they mourn and try to work through the grief process. It is a book that can be shared with a bereaved child.

Lichtman, W. (1975). *Blew and the Death of the Mag*. Albion, CA: Freestone. (Ages 10 and up)

A sensitive story told by a young girl about the death of her mother. The story explores her feelings of love, fear, anger and finally understanding.

London, J. (1994). *Liplap and the Snowbunny.* San Francisco: Chronicle Books. (Ages 3-8)

Liplap is a young rabbit. When he is building a snowbunny, it reminds him of his grandma and how she used to help him. She hadn't lived to see the snow this year. His mother speaks to him of loss and death and shows him how he can still feel Grandma's presence.

McFarlane, S. (1993). *Waiting for the Whales.* New York: G.P. Putnam's Sons. (Ages 4-8)

This story describes the life of an old man whose home looks out on the sea. He watches the whales swim past, tends his garden and enjoys walks in the woods. His daughter comes to live with him and he helps to raise his granddaughter. When he dies, his daughter and granddaughter carry on the things he loved. The story deals with death as part of the life cycle and is told in a gentle manner that should please both parents and children alike.

Mellonie, B. and R. Ingpen (1983). *Lifetimes.* New York: Bantam Books. (Ages 5-9)

This book explains life and death in a sensitive, caring and beautiful way. It tells about beginnings and endings. It tells about plants, animals and people. It can help children to understand that dying is a part of living.

Miles, A. (1971). *Annie and the Old One.* Boston: Little, Brown. (Ages 5-10)

Annie, a Navajo girl, tries to stop her grandmother from finishing a rug she is working on, for she connects its completion with her grandmother's death. Her grandmother gently explains how everything is part of the life cycle. In the end she accepts death as a part of life. A beautiful story.

Moody, A. (1975). *Mr. Death: Four Stories.* New York: Harper & Row. (Ages 12 and up)

These four eerie stories are set in Mississippi. Suicide, murder and accidents bring fear and terror as death intrudes on the lives of ordinary people. Then it leaves as quietly as it came, a part of life itself. The book goes beyond the surface from terrors of death to the love that only the experience of death can reveal.

O'Neal, Z. (1982). *A Formal Feeling.* New York: Viking Press. (Ages 12 and up)

Sixteen-year-old Anne is home from boarding school for winter vacation. The death of her mother a year ago and the presence of her stepmother make being home very difficult. The title of the book is taken from one of Emily Dickinson's poems, which conveys the stages of Anne's mourning and acceptance. It is a perceptive and affecting story.

Porter, W. (O. Henry) (1980). *The Last Leaf*. Mankato, MN: Creative Education. (Ages 12 and up)

A sick artist with no will to live feels she will die when the last leaf falls from the tree outside her window. Yet, for some reason, the leaf hangs on. A touching story.

Rushton, L. (1993). *Death Customs*. Boston: Thomson Learning. (Ages 7-10)

This short book attempts a monumental task. It compares the teachings of the world's major religions on death-related topics, such as rituals for the dying, burial, afterlife beliefs and mourning. It is a companion to the book *Birth Customs*. This treatment is clearly not definitive, but it is a good starting point in helping a child to see that there are different ways in which people relate to death and grief.

Smith, B.A. (1993). *Somewhere Just Beyond*. New York: Macmillan. (Ages 8-12)

A young girl, Callie, goes to spend her summer visiting her Aunt Lil and she has to find a way to cope with the progressive decline of her grandmother who has become seriously ill. The story shows the important role played by family and religion as Callie learns to find a way to "say goodbye" to her grandmother.

Smith, D. (1973). *A Taste of Blackberries*. New York: Crowell. (Ages 5-9)

A little boy feels lonely and guilty when his friend Jamie is stung by a bee and dies of an allergic reaction. Jamie had a way of fooling around and his friend didn't understand what was happening. After the funeral he offers to be a substitute son to Jamie's mother. It is a sensitive and touching story.

Stein, S. (1974). *About Dying*. New York: Walker. (Ages 4-9)

This book presents an excellent shared experience for children and parents. The book has separate texts for the adult and the child. The photographs are excellent, showing the death of the pet bird. Later on the children's grandfather dies. The children participate in both funerals. The mother supportively deals with the children's questions and needs. The story explains that remembering helps us to deal with our feelings. An excellent resource.

Stevens, C. (1980). *Stories from a Snowy Meadow*. New York: G.P. Putnam's Sons. (Ages 5-8)

Here are four stories about four small animals living in a meadow. The stories treat the themes of friendship, love and loss in a way that appeals to children. Mole, Shrew and Mouse loved to visit Vole, who was very old, to listen to the stories she told. One day at the end of the winter, Vole died. At the burial her three friends share their sorrow and Mouse creates a poem in Vole's memory.

Stevens, M. (1979). *When Grandpa Died*. Chicago: Children's Press. (Ages 4-8)

When Grandpa dies, the little girl feels hurt and angry. With her parents' help she learns to accept his death. Later, she shares her memories with her younger sister.

Stull, E. (1964). *My Turtle Died Today*. New York: Holt, Rinehart & Winston. (Ages 4-8)

A little boy's turtle dies. The boy and his friends have a funeral. The story tells about the boy's sadness and how he tries to understand the difference between life and death.

Tobias, T. (1978). *Petey*. New York: G.P. Putnam's Sons. (Ages 6-9)

Emily tells about her gerbil and how he gets sick and dies in spite of all her efforts. She expresses her anger, love and sadness. She mourns her loss, but eventually accepts it. A touching story.

Toensend, M. and R. Stern (1980). *Pop's Secret*. Reading, MA: Addison-Wesley. (Ages 5-10)

Mark tells his story of his grandfather's life through photographs of his "Pop" during his lifetime. Mark learns how to live with this loss. Remembering helps. It is a book of love, but also of grief.

Tresselt, A. (1972). *The Dead Tree*. New York: Parents Magazine Press. (Ages 4-7)

This book tells the story of the life cycle of an oak tree. Death is shown as a part of life. It is both informative and hopeful.

Viorst, T. (1971). *The Tenth Good Thing about Barney*. New York: Atheneum. (Ages 5-9)

Barney, a pet cat, dies. His master, a little boy, decides to have a funeral for him. He tries to think of ten good things to say about Barney, but can think of only nine. Finally his father helps him with the tenth. The book is gentle and hopeful.

White, E.B. (1952). *Charlotte's Web*. New York: Harper & Row. (Ages 8-12)

Charlotte the spider and Wilbur the pig become loving friends. When Charlotte dies, Wilbur holds her memory close and takes care of her children, grandchildren and great grandchildren. The story describes the sadness and sorrow experienced by loving friends and how memories are kept alive. A wonderful story and a true classic.

Zolotow, C. (1974). *My Grandson, Lew.* New York: Harper & Row. (Ages 4-8)

Lewis, who is six, tells his mother of how he misses his grandfather. They share loving memories of his dead grandfather. The mother helps the boy cope with his sadness and grief. Sharing memories makes the sadness easier to bear.

BOOKS FOR ADULTS ABOUT CHILDREN AND DEATH

Arnold, J. and P. Gemma (1994). *A Child Dies: A Portrait of Family Grief, 2nd Ed.* Philadelphia: The Charles Press.

Arnstein, H. (1960). *What to Tell Your Child about Birth and Death.* Indianapolis: Bobbs-Merrill.

Bertman, S. (1984). Children's and others' thoughts and expressions about death. In H. Wass and C. Corr (eds.), *Helping Children Cope with Death, 2nd Ed.* Bristol, PA: Hemisphere.

Bernstein, J. (1983). *Books to Help Children Cope with Separation and Loss.* New York: Bowker.

Corr, C. (1984). Books for adults. In H. Wass and C. Corr (eds.), *Childhood and Death.* Bristol, PA: Hemisphere.

Corr, C. (1984). Books for adults: An annotated bibliography. In H. Wass and C. Corr (eds.), *Helping Children Cope with Death, 2nd Ed.* Bristol, PA: Hemisphere.

Corr, C. (1984). Helping with death education. In H. Wass and C. Corr (eds.), *Helping Children Cope with Death, 2nd Ed.* Bristol, PA: Hemisphere.

DeSpelder, L. and A. Strickland (1987). *The Last Dance: Encountering Death and Dying, 3rd Ed.* (Chapter 3, Socialization: How we learn about death as children; Chapter 8, Death in children's lives). Palo Alto, CA: Mayfield.

Fassler, J. (1978). *Helping Children Cope.* New York: Free Press.

Grollman, E. (1967). *Explaining Death to Children.* Boston: Beacon Press.

Grollman, E. (1990). *Talking about Death: A Dialogue Between Parent and Child, 3rd Ed.* Boston: Beacon Press.

Gullo, S., et al. (eds.) (1985). *Death and Children: A Guide for Educators, Parents and Caregivers.* Dobbs Ferry, NY: Tappan Press.

Jackson, E. (1965). *Telling a Child about Death.* New York: Hawthorne Press.

Jewett, C. (1982). *Helping Children Cope with Separation and Loss.* Cambridge, MA: Harvard University Press.

Morgan, J.D. (ed.) (1990). *The Dying and the Bereaved Teenager.* Philadelphia: The Charles Press.

Pacholski, R. (1985). Thanatological topics in literature. In H. Wass, C. Corr, R. Pacholski and C. Forfar (eds.), *Death Education II: An Annotated Resource Guide*. Bristol, PA: Hemisphere.

Rudman, M. (1984). *Children's Literature: An Issues Approach, 2nd Ed. New York: Longman, Chapter 8*.

Sahler, O. (ed.) (1978). *The Child and Death*. St. Louis: C.V. Mosby.

Schaefer, D. and C. Lyons (1986). *How Do We Tell the Children? When Someone Dies*. New York: Newmarket.

Schowalter, J., et al. (eds.) (1983). *The Child and Death*. New York: Columbia University Press.

Stevenson, R.G. (ed.) (1995). *What Will We Do? Preparing a School Community to Cope with Crises*. Amityville, NY: Baywood.

Wass, H. (1984). Books for children. In H. Wass and C. Corr (eds.), *Childhood and Death*. Bristol, PA: Hemisphere.

Wass, H. (1984). Books for children: An annotated bibliography. In H. Wass and C. Corr (eds.), *Helping Children Cope with Death, 2nd Ed*. Bristol, PA: Hemisphere.

Wass, H. (1984). Parents, teachers, and health professionals as helpers. In H. Wass and C. Corr (eds.), *Helping Children Cope with Death, 2nd Ed*. Bristol, PA: Hemisphere.

Wass, H. (1984). Books for children. In H. Wass, C. Corr, R. Pacholski and C. Forfar (eds.), *Death in Education II: An Annotated Resource Guide*. Bristol, PA: Hemisphere.

Wolf, A. (1973). *Helping Your Child to Understand Death, Rev. Ed*. New York: Child Study Press.

24

Teaching Peers How to Help Each Other Cope with Loss

Claire Marino, MA and Joseph Cafaro, MA

When students need help facing a loss, they do not necessarily turn to adult authority figures. For this reason, peer counseling has been developed as a program to make students available to other students as a source of help with loss and other issues. An example of such a program exists at River Dell High School in Oradell, New Jersey. Approximately 60 juniors and seniors (about 10 percent of the school's enrollment) are members of Peer Listener Assistants Network (PLAN). This network is a safety net of students trained to reach out to those in need and to respond with a caring attitude and good referral skills.

PLAN provides an atmosphere of understanding in which students can accept each other as they are, validate each other's experiences and feelings, and offer support through troubled periods. It also provides young people to assist each other in times of stress, both expected (such as new students arriving in the senior high school each year) and unexpected (such as the emotional aftermath of the sudden death of a student in gym class).

One of the central lessons of the Adolescent Suicide Awareness Program (ASAP) at River Dell, another program for students, is that each individual can be a powerful aide in helping another by listening, by being aware of the warning signs of suicide and knowing when to refer a troubled peer to a professional. PLAN expands this concept. Through its members, PLAN infuses the student body with a positive attitude.

The staff at River Dell noted several cases where a caring student has referred a troubled youngster who then was seen and helped by a professional. PLAN provides peer support for students facing all the issues of growing up including the many different losses and stresses teenagers often encounter.

GOALS

PLAN is a part of a program of services offered to students at River Dell. The overall objective of student services is to link together the existing services of academic counseling, crisis counseling and awareness counseling. PLAN is ongoing and, as such, not only complements existing services, but increases the school's opportunity to provide an atmosphere of concern for its students. It is the goal of the school to have someone available for any student who needs help. There are various different times when a student may be called on to fulfill that role and PLAN seeks to prepare members for the task.

SELECTION PROCESS

The building of trust within a school community takes time. It is, therefore, desirable to have PLAN representatives from many social groups. A cross section of students breaks down stereotypes and enhances the potential success of a reach-out program such as this.

At River Dell, juniors and seniors interested in becoming PLAN members simply identify themselves. Also, teachers and counselors are asked to point out natural leaders—students who seem to be respected by students (regardless of academic standing or extracurricular participation). Students are also invited to join PLAN at an orientation meeting held at the beginning of the school year.

All interested students submit a personal statement about their strengths and possible weaknesses as a potential peer listener. Then, each student is interviewed by professional staff and previously installed PLAN members. During the interview, students are asked to describe how they would handle potential situations, such as a boy/girl conflict. Their responses help the group to determine their abilities to be nonjudgmental and resourceful, as well as trustworthy and confidential. In addition, all PLAN members must go through an initial training session.

TRAINING

The training of PLAN members involves a basic 5-hour workshop to improve students' listening skills. Activities are designed to build a sharing environment and a sense of bonding among PLAN members. Specific listening skills that are stressed include:

1. involvement
2. exploration
3. understanding

4. developing a plan of action.

During the initial training sessions, the students practice their listening skills by participating in role plays that involve typical situations they may encounter. Some of the "roles" deal with peer pressure to use drugs, broken relationships and parent discord. The PLAN members are critiqued on their use of the above-mentioned four stages of listening and are given suggestions by group members on how to improve. Another key element stressed to the students is that they are listeners, not therapists. Thus, specific information on when and where to refer troubled peers is included in the first training session.

Training Session Agenda and Timeline

4:00 p.m.
Overview of Day (goals, activities, timelines)
Review of Goals

1. To build a sense of group identity
2. To learn about and practice effective learning skills
3. To know when and where to refer a troubled peer
4. To reinforce importance of confidentiality

4:30 p.m.
Group Activities (to form group identity)

- Ice breakers (nonverbal activity)
- Safe, brief self-disclosure to experience acceptance and trust together

5:00 p.m.
Effective Listening Skills—Large Group

- Lecturette (involvement, exploration, understanding, action)
- Role play of four stages by trainers

5:30 p.m.
Effective Listening Skills—Small Group

- Students role-play and practice listening skills
- Students provide feedback on effectiveness

6:30 p.m.
Dinner Break

- Community building activity: students prepare, serve and share a meal

7:30 p.m
Referral Skills

- Brainstorming of list of issues on problems that should be referred by PLAN members to a professional
- Specific names and telephone numbers of school and community sources of help

8:00 p.m.
Group Activity

- Possible artwork (logo)
- Poem

8:20 p.m.
Wrap-up and Evaluation of Workshop

- Students grade the content and presentation of the evening's events

8:30 p.m.
Conclusion

The evening scheduling of training has been a topic of much debate. Should training be done during school hours, to show the emphasis placed on this work by the school, or on weekends, to show a commitment by the students? It was decided to keep the evening training sessions. School time is needed for PLAN students to meet with junior high school students and for other PLAN programs. Weekends are used to attend regional PLAN training sessions.

Training of PLAN students is continued during bi-monthly meetings. New skills are introduced and existing skills are reviewed and practiced by the students. In addition, professionals in other mental health areas are asked to speak to the PLAN members on specific topics, such as AIDS, pregnancy and substance abuse.

Judging from comments made by PLAN members, they were highly satisfied with the training sessions. They felt that the emphasis on effective listening skills was most beneficial not only in one-to-one peer counseling, but also in their everyday interaction with classmates at school.

When PLAN was being considered for the school, a school-wide survey was conducted by Robert Stevenson, a social studies instructor, and Claire Marino, a guidance counselor. In that poll, the students expressed a fear that violations of confidentiality would undermine the possible success of any such student group. The double-bind of confidentiality has been a major focus of the training program. Students are told that confidentiality is absolute *unless a student or someone else might be hurt by that silence.*

SERVICES AND PROGRAMS

Members of PLAN are aware of the full range of losses experienced by their peers. In addition to the death of parents, siblings and grandparents and friends, PLAN members understand that there are other losses students frequently encounter. They include: divorce, not making a sports team, the death of a pet, not being accepted to a certain college, a sibling going off to college, a friend moving away and breaking up with a boyfriend or girlfriend.

It is not surprising that PLAN members are most frequently sought by peers facing the breakup of a romance. But whether they are sought for this loss or any other, PLAN members know that ways of helping include: listening and validating feelings, allowing the person to grieve and express hurt, and reaching out with support and concern while the person begins to rebuild.

Other PLAN activities involve group discussions with seventh graders on peer pressure, seventh- and tenth-grade orientation, the program for new and transfer students, involvement with the tenth-grade Adolescent Suicide Awareness Program and lunchtime discussion groups for seniors.

CONCLUSION

PLAN is based on a simple concept. Kids trust kids in their everyday sharing, and "natural leaders" can fill the communication gap that may occur between adolescents and adults. Approximately 10 percent of the students are "trained listeners" and help weave a fabric of caring throughout the school. Everyday problems, as well as major traumas, have the potential of being handled in a more positive way through this cooperative effort.

25

Organ and Tissue Donation and Transplantation: An Integral Part of Death Education

John M. Kiernan

If schools are to provide students with a complete, holistic education, we must teach not only about life, but about death as well. Perhaps to some people, the idea of offering information on organ donation to high school students may seem peculiar, but it makes perfect sense. Organ donation and transplantation is an especially useful topic in a death education program because by the virtue of its nature—providing life with death—it brings the often hard-to-talk-about subject of death into the realm of easy discussion. The subject is truly multidisciplinary, lending itself generously to many areas of discussion that are integral to all education: ethics, philosophy, theology, psychology and biology, just to name a few. No death education program would be complete without an examination of the many issues and problems related to organ and tissue donation and transplantation.

GENERAL BACKGROUND

Transplantation is a medical and social phenomenon of the post-World War II era. Kidney transplantation began in earnest in 1954 in Boston. The '60s saw the first limited successes in liver, heart and pancreas transplantation. Heart-lung and single lung transplantation met with some modest success in the '80s. The clinical history of solid organ transplantation, spanning over 35 years, has been marked by dramatic improvements in techniques for organ removal and preservation, growing reliance on postmortem donors, increasingly effective therapies to suppress the immune response and reverse organ rejection and ever-increasing lists of candidates. Almost

11,000 individuals were on the waiting lists for various transplantation procedures as of August 1987. One year later, the number increased to 15,000 and it has increased steadily since that time.

Transplantation is a multi-dimensional social phenomenon that includes among its many interrelated facets ethics, health policy and economics, psychology, sociology, religion and thanatology. Legal developments in the area span almost 20 years beginning with the Uniform Anatomical Gift Act (UAGA) of the late 1960s. UAGA was established by the National Conference of Commissioners on Uniform State Law to serve as a model statute for enactment by the 50 states. Its purpose was to eliminate contradictory and confusing practices resulting from variations in, or absence of, state laws and to codify the rights of individuals and their survivors with respect to organ and tissue donation. The act was adopted by all 50 states in the late '60s and early '70s and served to validate the use of uniform donor cards and driver's licenses as indicators of a person's wishes about donation in case of death. A second round of legal initiatives occurred in the mid-1980s as a result of growing public and governmental concern about the efficacy of the nation's voluntary approach to organ and tissue donation and the widely perceived lack of a system to fairly allocate organs on the basis of medical need. The National Organ Transplant Act of 1984 (PL 98-507) required the creation of a nationwide network to ensure efficient, effective retrieval of organs and tissues and their equitable distribution on the basis of medical need. At the same time concern was mounting about the persistent shortage of organs and tissues in spite of perceived public support for organ transplantation. Oregon, New York and California were among the first states to enact routine-inquiry or required-request laws to stimulate donation and provide more organs and tissues for transplantation and research. New York's statute, Article 43-A of the Public Health Law, took effect on January 1, 1986 and has resulted in notable increases in tissue donation. Improvements in the area of solid organ donation have not been as marked for a variety or reasons. The Omnibus Budget Reconciliation Act of 1986 (PL 99-509) required that as of October 1987, any hospital in the United States receiving Medicare and Medicaid reimbursement had to implement policies and procedures to offer the option of organ and tissue donation to the families of deceased patients, as permitted by medical circumstances. These laws do not require that a request be made if the individual gave prior notice of objection or if it would violate the religious or moral beliefs of the decedent.

PUBLIC OPINION

Public opinion surveys yield interesting results about attitudes toward donation and transplantation. A Gallup Poll conducted for the National

Kidney Foundation in January 1983 revealed significant discrepancies between the public's awareness of the benefits of transplantation and the existence of donor cards and its taking concrete steps in the form of reaching personal decisions about donating, obtaining and signing donor cards and informing next of kin (The Gallup Organization 1983). Awareness does not necessarily lead to action. Twenty percent of those polled had never given the matter any thought and another 20 percent did not like the idea of having organs surgically removed from their bodies after death. Religion did not seem to be a major barrier to donation. The public appears reticent about discussing organ donation. Few of those very or somewhat likely to want their kidneys donated had obtained a donor card and fewer still informed their families, friends or physicians of their wishes. It is highly probable that organ and tissue donation serves as a reminder of dying and death in a society that actively denies dying and death, preferring to avoid these subjects and their many manifestations. Findings from a 1985 survey by researchers at the Battelle Human Affairs Research Centers suggest the need for greater public education about organ and tissue donation. The goal of such an effort would be to foster more favorable attitudes toward donation, informing the public about the existing, highly favorable attitudes toward transplantation (Manninen and Evans 1985). High school students in death education classes can be asked if they have signed the organ donation space on their driver's license. They can be asked if they were even aware of its existence. A driver's license, focal point of life itself for many adolescents, becomes a teaching aid and prompts discussion both in the classroom and at home.

DONATION AND TRANSPLANTATION TODAY

Organ and tissue transplantation procedures are increasingly common and successful. Many people who would otherwise be dead are alive today because they were able to get a donated organ and/or tissue. Routine inquiry or required-request initiatives ensure that many individuals and families will be confronted with the option to donate organs and tissues following the deaths of immediate family members in hospital settings. It is generally felt by health professionals working in organ and tissue retrieval that families can make decisions more readily and with less stress when they know the decedent's wishes. This entails prior discussion of the matter, a discussion that is not likely to occur in most families given the commonplace avoidance of the taboo subject of death.

IMPLICATIONS FOR DEATH EDUCATION

Organ and tissue donation for transplantation can serve as an important topic in death education programs at the secondary level and beyond. It can be used as a teaching device to integrate a wide variety of subjects and issues, stimulate discussion and promote communication with peers, teachers and family members. Organ donation and transplantation are matters of life and death. Adolescents who are developing into young adults endure tremendous changes, pressures, conflict and confusion during this crucial stage in their lives. They may think themselves immortal and indestructible, yet they increasingly run significant risks of premature death due to accidental causes, drug abuse, suicide and violence. Many organ donors are quite young. One study has indicated that 78 percent of potential and 92 percent of actual postmortem kidney donors in the sample were under age 39. The largest number of potential and actual donors fell in the age range of 5 to 14 years. The mean age of donors at The Presbyterian Hospital in New York and its affiliated donor hospitals between 1979 and 1987 was 32 years with a range of 4 to 60 years. Many of the individuals on transplantation waiting lists are also youngsters. The issue is therefore of relevance to young people and should be a component of death education at the secondary school level.

Two Approaches to the Topic

Two approaches can be taken to teaching high school students about organ donation and transplantation. The first would be a discrete learning module taught over a predefined number of periods or classroom hours. The other, and perhaps more interesting, approach would be to incorporate the topic into related courses in the biological sciences, health and physical education, social studies and the humanities, as well as inclusion in any specific death education curriculum.

It should be immediately obvious that many aspects of human biology, anatomy and physiology can be demonstrated by an examination of the process of organ donation and transplantation. Solid organs that may be transplanted include the kidneys, heart, heart and lungs together, single lungs, liver, pancreas and, potentially, the small intestine. Transplantable tissues include the corneas and sclera of the eye, bone, bone marrow, joints, ligaments, tendons, certain valves of the heart and skin. There are many questions that can provide a focus for class discussion and give practical meaning to abstract theory:

- What are the anatomical and functional relationships of the various organs and tissues? What roles do they play in a healthy individual?
- What happens when they become diseased or fail completely?
- How do lifestyle and health habits contribute to good health and disease prevention?

- Which diseases and behaviors lead most often to end-stage organ failure?
- Why is organ transplantation considered a therapy and not a cure for end-stage organ failure?
- What is the immune system and how does it work?
- How does it recognize and reject organs?
- What is life like with a transplanted organ?
- Would students be willing to give or accept a kidney or bone marrow transplant in the event of their own need or the need of an immediate family member?
- What is life like for a kidney dialysis patient?
- Would students be interested in a career in health care?

Organ retrieval and transplantation are multidisciplinary, labor-intensive activities involving the full range of health professions: medicine, nursing, transplantation coordination, social work, laboratory technology, physical, respiratory and occupational therapy, pastoral care, administration, computer science, education, dentistry, nutrition, pharmacy, and research among others. The task of vocational counseling can take place in the context of organ retrieval and transplantation can actually allow a student to look at and probe further into any of almost 200 occupations.

The determination of death plays a crucial role in solid organ donation. Organs are recovered from donors who are pronounced dead on the basis of neurological criteria. The heart beats independently of the brain as high school students demonstrate in biology labs by pithing a frog's brain, removing its heart and watching it beat for a period of time in a nutrient solution in a petri dish. The organ donor's heartbeat is artificially maintained. Hence an examination of the medical and legal aspects of the definition of death is necessary, with emphasis on the concept of brain death. This leads to further questions:

- What is brain death? Is it the medical and legal equivalent of the death of the individual?
- Are there different cultural, religious and philosophical views about brain death? What ethical issues arise from the concept of brain death?
- Why is the use of anencephalic newborns as organ donors so controversial?
- What is the Uniform Determination of Death Act and why is it felt to be necessary?

One common cause of death among organ donors is head trauma and such an injury can occur in many ways. This topic allows reinforcement of the reasons for using seat belts, wearing bicycle helmets and driving safely and soberly. A drug overdose can lead to respiratory and cardiac arrest and fatally injure the brain. High blood pressure, if undetected, untreated or poorly controlled, can eventually cause an artery to rupture in the brain. Some organ donors are suicides. The theme of good health habits, disease prevention and common-sense, safety practices at work and play recurs here and can be positively reinforced. Students come to see that the deaths of many donors are both premature and preventable.

Additional questions may be pursued:

- What happens to the body during the process of dying and after death? To whom does the body "belong" now? Who assumes the rights and responsibilities in matters such as burial?
- Can students visualize the situation or do they have firsthand experience through the death of a relative or friend?
- Should there be, or must there be, an autopsy? What is the purpose of an autopsy?
- Should the body be buried intact or should its useful parts be shared to help others live or function normally? What attitudes prevail toward specific body parts, such as the heart or the eyes?
- Is it appropriate to use organs and tissues for research, transplantation and education?
- What impact, if any, will donation have on the funeral of the donor?

Organ and tissue removal doesn't disfigure the body and causes no expense to the donor's family or estate. Donation should not cause any delay of the funeral service or burial, both of which remain the financial responsibility of the family or state.

Also worthy of discussion are the rights of potential donors. The Uniform Anatomical Gift Act grants rights to individuals, their survivors and the physicians, hospitals and agencies that serve as donees of anatomical gifts. The donor card was intended to have the strength of a will, yet it may be overridden by next of kin. How is that justifiable? Those under age 18 may sign donor cards, but a parent must be one of the witnesses. The gift of organs and tissues may be restricted or unrestricted according to the wishes of the individual or be restricted to the donor's survivors. An individual has a right not to be a donor and may give notice of objection. Donor cards can be destroyed if their holders have a change of mind. Families too have a right to grant or withhold consent to donation and are often left to make decisions for those who have died without knowing what the decedents wanted. The importance of a thorough family discussion about organ and tissue donation is again underscored. Whether or not one will be a donor at death is a function of the medical circumstances of the death and consent by surviving next of kin. Laws governing organ and tissue donation and determination of death are reserved to the states. Our nation's reliance on voluntary organ donation and antipathy toward presumed consent reflect broadly held beliefs about due process, individual freedoms, personal autonomy and the right to privacy as embodied in the Constitution and American way of life. An examination of the legislative and regulatory processes that come to bear on organ and tissue donation demonstrates the workings of the federal and state governments, reservation of powers to each and the use of laws and regulations to meet societal needs. The rights of the donor and his survivors under the UAGA may also be considered in light of any correlative responsibilities to those in need, for example, of organ and tissue transplants. These needs will go unmet if usable organs and tissues are sent to the grave or cremated. A classroom debate about the pros and cons of our voluntary system of donation and the system of presumed consent employed in some foreign countries could be interesting and instructive.

THE SCHOOL-HOME PARTNERSHIP

Dying, death and organ donation are sensitive issues prompting a wide range of cultural, religious and philosophical responses. These dimensions should be explored as part of classroom discussion about donation. They must also be discussed at home. Students should assess their own attitudes as well as those of the family members who are likely to make decisions for them. Students should be encouraged to find out what their religious denomination has to say about organ and tissue donation. The following are good questions for parents to discuss with their children:

- Does brain death pose any problems for the adherents of a particular religion?
- Do the burial laws and rites of the particular religion accommodate organ and tissue removal?
- Does organ and tissue donation pose any problems for those who believe in the resurrection of the body?

Organ and tissue donation is held to be consistent with the major religious and ethical traditions of the West but can be discussed in terms of world religions and their views on dying, death and the fates of body and soul. Organ donation and transplantation also raise many ethical issues such as informed consent, fairness and equity in the health care system, the limitations of medical technology, distributive justice, allocation of scarce resources and conflict between individual and societal good. The subject serves as the basis for a discussion of real ethical dilemmas which students may encounter on television, in newspapers or in their own lives.

It is often stressed that there are no universal right or wrong answers when it comes to organ and tissue donation. The issues are further complicated by the clear benefits of successful transplantation procedures and the consequences of not obtaining a needed transplant. The student should know why a given decision about donation is reached and what its consequences are. The myriad of fascinating issues in organ donation and transplantation can stimulate student thinking about the precious nature of life and good health and the meaning of death.

CURRICULUM DEVELOPMENT

Curriculum development can be facilitated by the many organizations active in the field of organ and tissue donation and transplantation. These include: the American Council on Transplantation, the American Association of Tissue Banks, the American Liver Foundation, the Children's Liver Foundation, Eye Bank Association of America, Juvenile Diabetes Association, the National Kidney Foundation, North American Transplant Coordinators Organization and the United Network for Organ Sharing. There are approximately 110 independent and hospital-based organ retrieval agencies serving more than two hundred transplantation centers around the country. There are also many tissue banks that can serve as resources for students, teachers, schools and school districts. The organizations above can provide brochures, donor cards, posters, fact sheets, statistics, guest speakers, audiovisual materials, public education specialists and programs for minority groups. There is a wide variety of materials that can be distributed in the classroom or be made available through a school library. Newspaper and magazine articles about donation and transplantation are common and can be collected in a clipping file. Students should play an *active* role in bringing this together in the form of a class or school project and as a meaningful learning experience. There is much that teachers can learn as well.

CONCLUSION

The inclusion of donation and transplantation in the death education curriculum or the general curriculum at the secondary level can serve many useful and important purposes. The progress of medical research and the constant developments in biotechnology will require many of today's students to face some difficult decisions in their lives. These students need a knowledge base in order to make informed and intelligent decisions. They need to know the facts. Students need to know that in some cases there is no right or wrong answer. The study and discussion of issues in organ donation and transplantation provide the student with an opportunity to confront life-and-death issues in a concrete and personal way.

Life is a precious gift. Its complexities also defy easy answers. Including the topics of organ donation and transplantation in the high school curriculum can open the door to better and deeper communication between students and their peers, families and teachers about dying and death. It can assist each of these parties to determine their own desires regarding donation—a most critical ingredient to the lives of many.

REFERENCES

Bart, K.J., et al. Increasing the Supply of Cadaveric Kidneys for Transplantation. *Transplantation* 31(5):383-387, 1981.

The Gallup Organization. *Attitudes and Opinions of the American Public Toward Kidney Donation: Executive Summary.* Princeton, NJ: Gallup Publications, 1983.

Manninen, D.L. and R.W. Evans. Public Attitudes and Behavior Regarding Organ Donation. *Journal of the American Medical Association* 253(21):3111-3115, 1985.

ADDITIONAL RESOURCES

American Council on Transplantation (ACT), 700 N. Fairfax Street, Suite 505, Alexandria, VA 22314-2046.

National Health Council, Inc., 622 Third Avenue, New York, NY 10017.

North American Transplant Coordinators Organization (NATCO), P.O. Box 15384, Lexena, KS 66215.

United Network for Organ Sharing (UNOS), 3001 Hungary Spring Road, P.O. Box 28010, Richmond, VA 23228.

26

High School Athletes and Injuries: An Application of Death Studies

Robert G. Stevenson, EdD

One of the concerns voiced by some members of the educational establishment is that thanatology—the study of death—has only limited applicability to other areas in life and in school and, for that reason, there may be little reason to teach death education to young people in school. This chapter provides the example of high school athletes who have suffered an injury. It examines the different ways in which different students react and deal with this situation and the different ways in which the coach can help them recover. This chapter shows just one way in which the study of death and means of coping with it can be applied to other areas of education.

Knowledge of individual coping styles and the effects of the different meanings that each person gives to illness (and potential death) are main subjects of research in thanatology. This chapter illustrates how this method of looking at behavior can be applicable elsewhere and, in this case, in the coaching of high school athletes. The two areas seem to have little in common, but this discussion shows how the means of coping with illness can be similar to coping with a sports injury. The study of death can be useful on a secondary school level in unexpected ways.

INJURIES AND THE DECISION TO PLAY

One of the most difficult decisions for a coach is making the decision about whether to return an injured athlete to the game. The athlete's own decision regarding his ability to compete plays a major role in this decision. A doctor's opinion as to whether the player is fit to compete means little if the athlete himself does not believe he is able to perform. Take the case of an athlete who has not had a previous injury and for the first time suffers a minor hurt. The coach may feel that the player can return to play, but the player states that he is too injured to compete—and he really believes this. This is a difficult situation for the coach and the athlete and it is not made easier when other teammates who suffer similar injuries decide they want to get right back into the game. The coach is now faced with a difficult decision. Twenty years of coaching have provided me with countless examples of this exact same situation.

Consider these cases: Two sprinters suffer similar muscle pulls during cold, early-season workouts. One returns after a week without a problem, while the other makes several half-hearted attempts to run, but is lost for the rest of the season. Two distance runners complain of leg pain and are both found by a physician to have strained leg muscles. A two-week rest is indicated and after that time the doctor certifies that each is able to run. One runs as if there had been no interruption in his training routine, while the other postpones workouts, saying that he has become too weak and can no longer compete. How should the coach proceed in such a situation?

Season-ending injuries are a sad reality in athletic competition and some athletes lose the desire to compete when they are faced with repeated or unexpected obstacles. However, each of the individuals described above firmly stated that he wished to resume competition and in each case the athlete's doctor said that there was no physical injury that would prevent him from doing so.

The success or failure of any attempt to help these athletes rejoin their teammates may well rest on an understanding of three factors: the "coping style" of the athlete, the "coping behaviors" demonstrated by the athlete and the "meaning" that the athlete gives to the injury.

COPING STYLES OF ATHLETES

A serious injury forces an athlete to make adjustments in current behavior (training) and future goals (standards on which to judge the success of the current season or a career). Based on their individual personalities, injured athletes may employ any of several coping styles. Each style has its own set of behaviors and each requires an individual response on the part of a coach. These coping styles can be combined into six major groups: accepting, altruistic, defiant, facilitating, optimistic or submissive.

Accepting

The accepting athlete is like a personification of the serenity prayer. That prayer asks for "the serenity to accept what cannot be changed, the courage to change what can be changed and the wisdom to know the difference." This athlete wants to know how he should direct his energies most productively to overcome this injury. He may ask a seemingly endless stream of questions about his condition and the reasons for rest or treatment. These questions are designed to give the athlete the "wisdom to know the difference." The questions can become tiring or downright annoying but to refuse to answer will produce anger and can even cause the athlete to separate permanently from both coach and team. The coach must take the time to answer the questions of the acceptor. This can give the athlete a feeling of being "in control," and create a positive attitude about recovery.

Altruistic

This athlete looks past the effects this injury will have on him personally and instead looks to its effect on the team as a whole. He tries to find ways to still help the team. The negative effects of this may include attempting to compete despite the injury or quitting the team due to feelings of guilt caused by his inability to compete. The coach must listen to the athlete's teammates who often know better than the coach if the athlete is trying to conceal an injury. The altruistic athlete can be helped by being reminded that everyone on a team has to work together if the team is to succeed. His job at this time is to rest (or follow prescribed therapy) and recover and that is the best way he can help his teammates.

Defiant

The defiant athlete is angry. This anger comes from the "unfairness" of the injury and the way it seems to have upset everything in the athlete's life. This anger can spill out onto teammates and coaches, or be held in by the athlete who then turns it against himself. The coach must help the athlete see that the injury is no one's fault, acknowledge the anger and show the athlete how the energy of that emotion can eventually be used in the recovery process. For example, one runner's long-term recovery after being struck by a car involved sessions of physical therapy which he described as ranging from uncomfortable to painful. He said he was able to stand the discomfort by thinking of his injury as the enemy and the therapy as a fight to get better. One year later he was again running in competition.

Facilitating

The athlete who facilitates his injury consciously or unconsciously does things that make his condition worse. He is reacting to the feeling of uncertainty that accompanies an injury. The tension he feels about not knowing when he will be able to compete (or how he will do when he does) is broken, bringing about the very thing he fears: an end to competition.

The coach must avoid putting pressure on the facilitator and can help this athlete deal with pressure by showing how he has placed much of it on himself. This can be done by helping the athlete realize that he is not being controlled by others or by circumstances; instead he is really "in control." Realistic goals, both long- and short-range (even daily), and the best means of reaching them should be established by the athlete with guidance from the coach.

Optimistic

After an injury and being told that the odds of reaching his former level of performance are only 1 in 100, the optimistic athlete will respond, "What a relief! I was afraid you'd say there was no hope." This athlete believes he is in control of the situation and that no goal is ever out of reach if he just works hard enough. The negative effect of this coping style comes when goals are not reached by a deadline (the end of a season, for example). If the goal was attainable but was not reached, the athlete may feel it was his own fault. The coach must be careful to keep this athlete in touch with reality while not crushing the enthusiasm that he uses to attack new challenges.

Submissive

The injured athlete who copes by being submissive believes that he is helpless. Control of his life resides "outside" in the persons or circumstances that surround him. He will be no "trouble" to anyone and will follow all instructions, but he believes that returning to competition is up to others or things beyond his control (the coach, doctor or physical therapist, his diet or the environment). The coach must be careful to show to this athlete that each bit of recovery is due to something he himself did and he should encourage the athlete to take as active a role in his own recovery as possible. This coping style is formed early in childhood and has implications that can affect the athlete in every area of life.

COPING BEHAVIORS

Whichever coping style the injured athlete uses, his behavior will generally fall into one of three behavior patterns: avoiding, surrendering to or attacking the injury.

Avoiding

The athlete acts as though he is not injured. He refuses to change his behavior and tries to avoid having to deal with the reality of being injured by refusing to acknowledge the injury. He believes that if there is no problem, then there is no need to find a solution. The injured athlete who avoids the reality of an injury will in most cases not help the team or himself and may cause further injury before finally seeking treatment.

Surrendering

The athlete adopts a worst-case outlook and sees only the worst possible result of each decision or action. In effect, he capitulates to his injury. The injury wins and he loses. A sore leg becomes a severe limp and each abrasion requires a large, prominent bandage. He admits to the reality of the injury but does not try to overcome it and may refuse to take treatment because in his opinion the injury cannot be overcome.

Attacking

The athlete admits to being injured, but refuses to surrender to the injury and does everything in his power to regain his health and ability to compete effectively. He is willing to listen to the opinions of others (parent, doctor, coach, trainer) but believes that his efforts alone will make the difference in the final analysis.

THE MEANING OF THE INJURY

By understanding different coping styles and behaviors, the coach can relate and respond to the needs of each individual athlete. In order to help the athlete return to full competition, it is also important for the coach to understand the meaning the athlete has given to an injury because this meaning often dictates the athlete's coping style and behavior. There are five basic meanings that athletes attribute to their injuries: challenge, loss, gain, punishment and reality.

Injury as a Challenge

Injury is seen as an enemy to be overcome. The injury becomes the focus of the athlete's attention and its defeat his final goal. An athlete who chooses this meaning may make remarkable progress in recovery, but upon returning to the team finds that he has less energy to devote to competition. His main goal was "defeating" the injury, and after this has been done, the athlete is no longer "challenged" by a mere game or meet.

Injury as a Loss

The injury is seen as a loss of one or more valued things. Possible losses are the ability to compete, possible all-star honors and self-confidence. Athletes must learn to accept these losses. As long as the athlete focuses on what he has lost, he will be not be able to make a full recovery. Because he focuses only on what he has lost, he cannot draw upon any of the strengths he may have or the goals he may still achieve.

Injury as a Gain

The athlete sees the injury as a gain or as relief from an unpleasant or stressful situation, such as extreme pressure from competition (whether self-imposed or from others). The injury is seen as a gain to be enjoyed. While injured, the pressure is off and because he sees recovery as a loss, actual recovery is unlikely.

This case clearly shows why it is important for a coach to look at what type of "meaning" an athlete gives to an injury and recovery. If a coach believes that this is the case, it is not the injury that must be addressed, but the way the athlete looks at himself and at the entire area of sports competition. One athlete who had been a high school track star for three years could not face the possibility of losing to a younger, stronger teammate in his senior year. Just before the first meet, he pulled a muscle and by not having to compete, had found the relief he sought. This injury solved his problem and he welcomed the relief. Athletes who give this type of meaning to an injury need to be shown what is really happening and encouraged to look at their injuries in a different way. Otherwise, physical therapy alone is doomed to failure.

Injury as a Punishment

A sense of guilt over some event, whether real or imaginary, causes the athlete to see his injury as a punishment that has to be endured. The missed free throw, dropped pass or lost race must be atoned for. The athlete wants to return to competition, but endures this injury to do penance for past failures (which may lie outside of sports in the athlete's personal life). As is the case with those who see injury as a gain, athletes who see injury as a punishment will not return to competition until the debt caused by their guilt has been fully repaid.

Injury as a Reality

Athletes who adopt this meaning to injury are able to see recovery as a team effort. The injury is a reality to be assessed and treated. The coach must help the athlete understand that the injury is real as are the steps that are necessary for recovery. Rest, medical treatment, physical therapy, determination and patience all play a role in recovery. So too do all of the parties involved including the athlete, parents, coaches, doctors and trainers. Each person must recognize the role of the others and do all that is possible to help the process of recovery. When this occurs, the open communication that results can help almost any situation be dealt with more effectively, even the possibility that this injury may be serious enough to bar the athlete from further competition.

SUMMARY

Athletes give a meaning to each injury and that meaning may be more important than rest or treatment in determining when, or if, the athlete will return to competition. A coach must identify the meaning chosen by the athlete and help the athlete realize just how much control he has over the recovery process. The coach must work with the injured athlete as well as all other team members, to foster a view of sports injuries as reality. This reality need not be faced alone, but faced with the support of all those who care about the athlete as person: parents, doctors, trainers, and coaches.

Anyone who works with individuals facing a life-threatening illness will see many similarities between them and the athletes discussed in this chapter. Both types of people are faced with losses and both need to make some sort of decision regarding how they are going to deal with the situation. Even though it would seem as if there is little comparison between possibly losing life and possibly losing the ability to be on the track team, there are, in fact, many similarities between the way in which these two groups cope with their respective losses. There are also many similarities in the way in which both of these groups can be assisted by others.

Transfer of knowledge through insight to new applications is an important component of higher thinking. Death education provides information that can be applied to many areas of life. The only limit to its broader application is the human imagination.

Index